THE KINGDOM OF MAN

Evangelicalism and the Distortion of Christianity

ERIC SCOT ENGLISH

First Edition

Cover Design by Matthew J. Distefano
Cover Image by Keith Giles
Interior Layout by Matthew J. Distefano

PRINT ISBN 978-1-964252-31-5
ELECTRONIC ISBN 978-1-964252-32-2
Printed in the United States of America

Published by Quoir
Chico, California
www.quoir.com

For Emma, Olivia, and Elias,
I hope to leave you a better Church than I found.

CONTENTS

FOREWORD

I HAVE BEEN A pastor for nearly all of my adult life. I have spent the majority of that in the Evangelical tradition. This tradition welcomed me into the faith as a teenager in the early 1980s in the suburbs of Minneapolis. In those years I have seen significant dangers and debates in the Christian world. I have been at the forefront of seeking to make Christianity and Evangelicalism more open and inclusive. I have worked to train leaders in church starting and church management in ways that would build on the human spirit and strive for human flourishing.

Eight years ago I did not believe Christian Nationalism in the United States was something most of us needed to be concerned with. I knew it existed. I knew it was growing in influence among the most fringe conservatives in the US. But for ordinary people, I believed it would stay out of sight, and out of mind.

That has all changed. And this book is the ideal guide to show how and why.

In recent years, we have witnessed the rise of a troubling phenomenon that threatens both our faith and our democracy: Christian nationalism. This ideology, which conflates religious belief with national identity, has gained significant traction in the United States, manifesting in alarming ways that challenge the very foundations of our society. Christian nationalism is not merely a political stance; it is a theological error that distorts the gospel and endangers the witness of the church.

As a pastor, I have seen firsthand how political and religious identities can become dangerously intertwined, leading to a distortion of the Gospel and a betrayal of the values we hold dear.

Christian nationalism is not merely a partisan issue; it is a profound spiritual crisis that calls us to reevaluate our understanding of faith and its role in the public sphere. On January 6, 2021, the world watched in horror as symbols of Christianity were co-opted in a violent attempt to overturn a democratic election. Flags bearing the name of Jesus were flown alongside calls for insurrection, revealing a disturbing fusion of faith and nationalism that undermines the core message of Christ.

This book delves into the historical and ideological roots of this phenomenon, tracing its development from the early days of fundamentalism to its current entanglement with political conservatism. English's analysis is both rigorous and deeply personal, drawing on his own experiences within the evangelical church to highlight the dangers of placing political allegiance above spiritual integrity.

One of the central themes of *The Kingdom of Man* is the concept of theological "boxes"—rigid frameworks that limit our understanding of God and the world. These boxes often lead to an exclusionary and insular worldview, resistant to change and hostile to those who differ. By challenging these constructs, English invites us to embrace a more expansive and inclusive vision of faith, one that is grounded in love, justice, and compassion.

The rise of Christian nationalism in the United States is part of a broader trend of religious nationalism worldwide. From the imposition of "biblical citizenship training" to the rejection of the separation of church and state, we see a growing movement that seeks to align civil law with a narrow interpretation of religious doctrine. This conflation of religion and politics not only threatens democratic principles but also distorts the essence of our faith.

The Kingdom of Man by Eric Scot English addresses this critical issue with both urgency and depth. English's work is a clarion call to recognize and resist the encroachment of Christian nationalism within the fabric of American Evangelicalism. This book is not just an academic exploration but a heartfelt plea for a return to the core tenets of Christianity—love, justice, and humility.

Christian nationalism asserts that America has a special covenant with God, akin to that of ancient Israel, and that it is uniquely favored and chosen by God. This belief fosters a sense of divine entitlement and a justification for exclusionary practices. It entwines patriotism with piety, often leading to the idolatry of the nation-state. This conflation of faith and flag distorts the message of the gospel and undermines the church's mission to be a beacon of hope and reconciliation.

The dangers of Christian nationalism are manifold. It promotes a revisionist history that glorifies America's past while ignoring its injustices. It encourages an us-versus-them mentality, where non-Christians and even Christians who dissent from the nationalist agenda are viewed with suspicion or outright hostility. This ideology often results in policies that marginalize vulnerable populations, contradicting the biblical mandate to care for the least of these.

Globally, we see similar patterns of religious nationalism emerging. From India to Russia to parts of Europe, religious nationalism is used to consolidate power, suppress dissent, and justify persecution. These movements reveal a troubling trend where religious identity is wielded as a tool of division rather than a source of universal love and solidarity. English's examination of these issues places American Christian nationalism within a broader context, highlighting its potential to contribute to a global crisis of faith and democracy.

As the executive director of Vote Common Good, we seek to help people adopt the common good as their voting criteria and identity.

Politics, for many, is about identity. The political parties know it, and many people feel it. As we travel the country, our work includes running training sessions for leaders and laypeople alike on the threat of Christian Nationalism in the United States. I have learned that many people feel deeply opposed to Christian Nationalism, but when asked if they can give a definition, they are satisfied with explaining what it is;

most people keep their hands lowered. This book is a rare gift to help with that frustration many people feel—I oppose it, but I'm not sure what it is and how it shows itself in my community.

Eric Scot English meticulously dissects the theological and cultural underpinnings of Christian nationalism. He challenges the notion that to be a good Christian is to be a good American, exposing the fallacy of equating national loyalty with spiritual fidelity. By doing so, he calls us back to a purer, more inclusive expression of faith that transcends national boundaries and political ideologies.

The incredible value of *The Kingdom of Man*, is in its articulation of Christian Nationalism's inherent distortion of the true nature of the Kingdom of God. Jesus proclaimed a kingdom not of this world, a realm where the last are first and the peacemakers are blessed. This kingdom is not defined by borders or political power but by radical love and justice. English urges us to realign our priorities, to seek first the Kingdom of God and its righteousness, rather than the fleeting power and glory of earthly nations.

The book's strength lies in its blend of scholarly analysis and personal narrative. Eric's own journey through the evangelical landscape lends authenticity to his critique and is very compelling. He speaks not as an outsider but as one deeply embedded within the tradition, offering a perspective that is both critical and compassionate. His call to action is rooted in a deep love for the church and a desire to see it fulfill its true calling.

Christian nationalism's impact on public policy is particularly concerning. Policies driven by this ideology often prioritize a narrow interpretation of religious freedom that privileges Christians over others. This has led to efforts to undermine the separation of church and state, erode civil liberties, and impose religious beliefs on public institutions. English warns that such policies not only threaten democracy but also compromise the church's integrity.

Furthermore, Christian nationalism's entanglement with partisan politics has led to a significant erosion of the church's prophetic voice.

When the church aligns itself too closely with political power, it risks losing its ability to speak truth to that power. English calls for a renewed commitment to the prophetic tradition of the Bible, where the church stands as a moral witness against injustice, regardless of political affiliations.

The book also addresses the racial dimensions of Christian nationalism. English highlights how this ideology often intersects with white supremacy, creating a toxic mix that perpetuates racial divisions and inequalities. He challenges white evangelicals to confront their complicity in these systems of oppression and to work toward a more just and equitable society. This call is particularly urgent in light of the racial reckoning that the United States is currently undergoing.

As you read *The Kingdom of Man*, I encourage you to reflect on the ways in which Christian nationalism may have subtly influenced your own beliefs and practices. This book is not just for those who explicitly identify with the nationalist agenda but for all of us who are seeking to understand the complex relationship between faith and politics in our time. English's insights will challenge you to think more deeply about what it means to be a follower of Christ in a politically charged world.

The Kingdom of Man is a vital and timely contribution to the ongoing conversation about faith, politics, and identity in this crucial time. Eric Scot English offers a compelling vision of a Christianity that is unbound by nationalism and rooted in the radical love and justice of Jesus. This book is a call to reclaim our faith from the clutches of political idolatry and live out the Gospel's true message in all its transformative power for the benefit and blessing of all.

I believe this book will inspire you to confront the forces of Christian nationalism with courage and conviction. Let us remember that our ultimate allegiance is not to any earthly kingdom but to the Kingdom of God—a kingdom of peace, justice, and unending love for all.

— **DOUG PAGITT**
Pastor, Activist, Speaker

ACKNOWLEDGEMENTS

A SPECIAL THANKS TO Anika Ojeda for her artistic ability to sculpt something special out of the lump of clay she was given. Her wordsmithing, mind, and our conversations truly made this book what it is. She is a wonderful editor but an even better friend.

I would like to thank Brian McLaren whose support over the years has remained a constant encouragement to continue writing; and whose constant humility has provided an example of how a follower of Jesus should be in the world.

I would also like to thank my wife, Cynthia who gave me space to research and work. She has remained a continuous source of encouragement throughout the years. She has believed in me even when I have not believed in myself.

Finally, I want to thank those evangelicals who have helped shape the person I am today. For those who still walk amongst us, I hope you find this book a way for me to give back to you for your investment in my life.

PREFACE

ANYTIME ONE WRITES ABOUT Evangelicalism they have to be careful to clearly define what they mean when they use the term. The term evangelical has often been used as a catch-all for conservatism. However, this would be a gross misrepresentation of the diverse intellectualism that exists within its history and modern iteration. In general, I use a modified version of historian David Bebbington's definition as is standard practice.

This definition is also approved by the National Association of Evangelicals. Moreover, in general, Evangelicalism can be identified by the following characteristics:

- **Conversionism**: The belief that lives need to be transformed through a "born-again" experience and a lifelong process of following Jesus.

- **Activism**: The expression and demonstration of the Gospel in missionary and social reform efforts.

- **Biblicism**: A high regard for and obedience to the Bible as the ultimate authority.

- **Crucicentrism**: A stress on the sacrifice of Jesus Christ on the cross as making possible the redemption of humanity.

Although these principles are accurate in defining aspects of the evangelical faith, they are largely unhelpful in distinguishing evangelicals from other Christian groups. Many non-evangelicals hold the same or similar beliefs. Therefore, I have recalibrated the aforementioned definition. I believe this definition more accurately and fairly represents what it means to be an evangelical in today's world and will be what I am referring to when referencing them.

- **Conversionism**: The belief that lives need to be transformed through a "born-again" experience and a lifelong process of following Jesus who is the only way to God.

- **Activism**: The expression and demonstration of the Gospel in missionary and conservative social reform efforts.

- **Biblicism**: The belief that the Bible is the inerrant Word of God and is, therefore, an authoritative basis for the truth of Christianity.

- **Crucicentrism**: The importance of the sacrifice of Jesus Christ on the cross as making possible the redemption of humanity. It is only through this atoning sacrifice that sins can be forgiven.

There are also many subgroups within Evangelicalism and not all of them will be addressed in this book. Important subgroups like Black, Latino, and Asian evangelicals exist throughout the country and even though they would likely adhere to the aforementioned definition, they are *not* the focus of this book. Rather, this book focuses on *white evangelicals* as a unique class of evangelical Christians who are distinct from minority subgroups. The following chapters will demonstrate the reason for the racial differentiation.

Evangelicals also span the political spectrum. Therefore, although I may not always qualify the term evangelical, I am always referring to evangelicals who are politically and theologically conservative.

I also use the term fundamentalist (and its derivatives) throughout. Although most Christian fundamentalists are evangelicals, not all evangelicals are fundamentalists. Therefore, I make that distinction as necessary throughout.

A Note to My Reader

Steps have been taken to ensure the quality of the research contained in this book. Sources have been thoroughly vetted to ensure legitimacy. Additionally, I have attempted to include as many sources as possible in order for the reader to verify the information that is presented.

The evangelicals represented in this analysis were carefully considered. One of the aims of this book was to avoid creating strawman arguments by only focusing on fringe evangelicals. The evangelicals represented were largely based on their overall influence and not caricatures. However, it is important to note that many of those fringe elements have become a part of mainstream Evangelicalism and therefore cannot be ignored.

A Note to My Reader

INTRODUCTION

I WAS "BORN AGAIN" in 1996 when I was 16 years old. I was "saved" by a local Baptist evangelist who would often visit school sporting events handing out tracts. I was a young, impressionable "street kid" who was fed up with life and deeply depressed. Being depressed and being introduced to Jesus are two things that went well together, at least for me at this time in my life. Needless to say, Christianity was not a difficult leap for me. Jesus brought to me the hope, love, and purpose I was desperately craving.

The Sunday following my conversion, I slipped into the back pew of our local fundamentalist Baptist church. There was a unique smell that seemed to permeate every nook of the church; a smell that would become familiar over the years. The smell was accompanied by an ugly green carpet, stained with various drinks that had been spilled throughout the years, and the groaning of the pipe organ provided the background music for the whole experience. It was everything stereotypical of a conservative evangelical church in the 1990s.

It was a formal atmosphere where the older men wore suits and the younger men wore ties. I certainly stood out with my tangly hair, baggy jeans, and polo shirt—the fanciest shirt I owned. As I entered, eyes fixed on me. The men were clearly judging my lack of formal clothes and the old ladies were smiling because another soul was saved. Despite being a 90s hippie, many befriended me and I slowly learned the implicit rules and social norms that everyone was expected to follow.

However, it was not long before I learned how dysfunctional the church was. Not just my church, but many churches like it across the nation. Within a few months, the church went through a large split because the pastor had allowed his daughter to attend prom. At this time, in most fundamentalist circles, attending a school dance was viewed as inviting the Devil's influence. After all, dancing leads to sex, right? If you are getting Footloose vibes, you wouldn't be far off.

This experience was far from the last time I would be confronted with issues like this. I quickly noticed how Christian fundamentalists seemed to care more about their storied traditions than they did people. Debates regarding the use of organs versus piano or guitar; or hymns versus choruses were commonplace and a significant number of people began leaving these churches over seemingly mundane issues. Breaching tradition was equated with slandering the Gospel. Whether I was attending or working in conservative evangelical churches these experiences were a common refrain.

A couple of years later, I attended a conservative Christian university in the Baptist tradition (General Baptists). There, I encountered a professor who, on the first day of our Introduction to Theology class, told a story about a brilliant student he once had. This student had the audacity to write a paper opposing the inerrancy of Scripture. The professor lauded the student's work and thought his arguments were both elegant and persuasive. The professor paused for a moment before letting us know that he gave this brilliant student an "F" on the paper. As though on cue, the professor paused for a brief moment so that we could all gasp. He reasoned that despite how well the paper was written the student did not write his paper following the doctrinal beliefs of the university. The professor's story was meant to be a warning and keenly illustrated the intolerance of the university toward students who dared to question the fundamental beliefs of Evangelicalism.

I had similar experiences throughout my time at other evangelical seminaries. At many seminaries and divinity schools across this nation, students are being taught *what* to believe but not *how* to believe. Their success lies in their ability to toe the line, rather than their ability to use logic and reason. Over the last 150 years, this practice has contributed to the inability of evangelicals to properly engage with culture.

As a result, pastors and other evangelical/political leaders are ill-equipped to handle today's cultural issues because those issues don't fit within their conception of the world. They have constructed a world for themselves that fits neatly within certain boundaries, which is also why they have thrived for so long. However, as we saw with the 2020 pandemic, the world is not static; and it is not black and white. The world and our lives are complex. In order to address these complexities, the world needs leaders who can problem-solve and improvise within this ever-evolving culture.

When the Church is in crisis, it naturally looks to its leaders for guidance and support. However, if its leaders are not properly equipped to handle these situations, then confusion and chaos ensue. When religious people feel threatened, they usually return to the safety of their dogmatic roots, as is being demonstrated in our present day and age. When this occurs it inevitably creates polarization and ostracization as people take sides and shut out opinions they find threatening or incongruent with their worldview.

Our current culture does not look kindly upon conservative or fundamentalist evangelicals. But why? Being evangelical used to be ubiquitous. If Evangelicalism was born out of the need for the Church to have cultural relevance, then why are evangelicals so out of touch? Much of the "why" question can be answered by looking deeper into the beliefs and practices of evangelicals; beliefs and practices that have created a worldview that undermines the purpose they were commissioned with.

An illustration might prove beneficial for understanding the intricacies of the problem.

The Box

Imagine a metaphorical box that each of us exists within. The box represents one's perspective and acts like the blinders that a horse might wear. That is, the individual sees and understands only that which exists within the confines of the box. The box is the individual's worldview.

Many pastors spend years in college and seminary fashioning their boxes. They tape it together, decorate it, and do all sorts of things to get it just right. By the time they graduate and start their first ministry position, their box is complete and their job becomes teaching others how to construct their own box. The pastor teaches people to take box construction seriously because it will guide them through life. Their box will protect them from the influences of the world and allow them to follow Jesus.

However, one day something catastrophic happens. Everyone looks around and they notice their boxes are beginning to disappear. Some may come to realize that the box is an illusion, but the pastor who has spent much of their adult life constructing their box begins to panic. He or she now faces two options. Do they admit that the box was indeed an illusion and begin teaching their people anew, or do they double down and create narratives that will convince people that their boxes are real and important?

You might wonder why a well-intentioned pastor would ever choose the second option. The answer is simple. The first option will cause many to leave this pastor's church, causing a significant decrease in giving and less investment in ministries. If enough people leave, they reason, the church could go under. It is their survival instinct that causes them to make the second choice.

It is also true that not all pastors are even aware of their box. They are under the impression that everyone else must see the world as they do, and those who don't are simply blind to the truth. These pastors are worse off because they don't recognize that the world they live in is simply self-constructed.

Those who acknowledge their box and choose to reinforce its validity, despite all evidence to the contrary, are oftentimes considered conservative evangelicals. Those who fail to recognize their own box in the first place are oftentimes characterized as fundamentalists.

The box is the certainty that accompanies specific beliefs about the world and the God that those who live in the box serve. However, in reality, the box does not exist. Or at least, no one else is in the box except for other like-minded people. Perhaps one day an individual begins to question an idea they heard or a thought they had. They decide they want to "investigate" the claim. They begin to read their favorite authors, watch their favorite news programs, or listen to their favorite podcasts. In other words, to answer their question they consult those who share their box. An environment like this is called an echo chamber. In an echo chamber, people only seek to confirm what they already believe. Beliefs become recycled and are simply re-affirmed over and over again regardless of their veracity. There is nothing inherently wrong with someone reading their favorite author as long as they are also willing to consider the most significant voices on the other side of the argument. This is called critical thinking.

The reason why critical thinking is not taught in most denomination-based seminaries or churches is that doing so would result in potential disagreement with whatever claims the professor or pastor considers to be true. In a movement that is largely governed by denominations, there is little choice but to stay in a box (or a denomination). That is, unless someone dares to go out on their own and deconstruct and reconstruct their belief system. Sometimes taking the road less traveled is necessary when proper discipleship is unavailable.

The boxes many have created are the reason why our nation (America) is so polarized. They are the reason that there is such a steep decline in church attendance within Evangelicalism. When smart young people realize that the box doesn't exist, or at least it doesn't match their experience of God and the world around them, they ask questions church leaders can't answer because all these leaders know is how to function within their box. Instead of coming to terms with the box as an illusion, church leaders begin to cast blame on others or create justifications for why things are the way they are. This results in a snowball effect where the misinformation presented grows into something unrecognizable. It is not difficult, then, to see why young people are leaving the Church, or why certain people within Evangelicalism believe what many on the outside view as irrational. From fake news to new truths, in this day and age anything is fair game. Moreover, while some are well-intentioned, many do this not because they really don't care about the truth, but to preserve the box they have built and feel comfortable within.

Until evangelical leaders begin to think outside the box, I do not foresee anything changing. Evangelicalism will continue to spiral downhill until these leaders quit blaming others for the problems they have created. I will argue that one must not just think outside the box but get rid of it entirely. The pseudo-shelter it creates benefits no one except the institutions that want to maintain power and control over their people. Those institutions that truly care for people; truly care for ministry; and truly care for God, will get rid of the boxes that they have created, because God does not work within man-made coffins.

This book is about the box that Evangelicalism has created. It is a box that insulates evangelicals from the world around them—not for their protection, but for the uniformity of the institution; a box laden with fabricated truths and perspectives that stand in stark contrast to what reason and logic would have people believe.

The Kingdom of Man not only sheds light on the box itself but also identifies how people can escape their captivity and meet Jesus again for the first time. It argues that despite their best efforts, evangelicals are not ushering in the Kingdom of God as they had hoped, but a kingdom for man. Moreover, unless they become willing to surrender to the God they wish existed, for the one that does, then they will become lost in their idealism; never able to break open the boxes that hold them captive.

"But seek first the Kingdom of God..."

— Matthew 6:33

"What looks like politics, and imagines itself to be political,
will one day unmask itself as a religious movement."

— Søren Kierkegaard

PART ONE

Christendom & Politics In the Evangelical Imagination

1

FUNDAMENTALISM & CONSERVATIVE EVANGELICALISM

THROUGHOUT ITS HISTORY, EVANGELICALISM has exhibited a range of theological beliefs and political stances, but in recent years, it has gained a reputation for Conservatism and Fundamentalism. Evangelicalism has always used political involvement as a way to protect its people from the secular world's influence, and as a result, it has been a significant force in shaping the American political and social landscape.

Although the United States has always been a secular nation, the influence of Evangelicalism cannot be overstated. Regardless of what politicians may argue, evangelicals hold an enormous amount of sway over the decisions made in our country. Over the years, however, evangelicals have felt their influence diminish as America has made an intentional move toward the secularization of government. Because the secularization of government is often conflated with the secularization of culture, this move has created significant tension for evangelicals and resulted in the polarization we see today.

The decline in membership within Evangelicalism is a clear reflection of the increasing extremism within the movement. In response to political uncertainty, evangelicals have sought solace in dogma as a means to regain influence. This move is not a new one, but rather a continuation of an age-old pattern. When religious institutions feel threatened, they return to their dogmatic roots and flex their social capital to influence political decision-making. This trend highlights the complex dynamics at play within Evangelicalism and the challenges it faces in adapting to a changing cultural landscape.

Returning to a dogmatic past has consequences. When societal problems are rehashed for the sake of religious dogmatism, important social progress achieved through years of struggle can be undone. A return to dogmatism also creates an idealistic mindset that is disconnected from or at odds with reality. This idealism limits one's ability to understand diverse opinions and see beyond polarized perspectives.

There are also underlying problems within Evangelicalism that extend beyond surface-level observations. These issues involve deeper theological concerns and occasionally sinister motivations, which serve as the basis for the current state of affairs. To understand Evangelicalism's current situation, it is necessary to analyze the events and conditions that have shaped its trajectory.

The History of Christian Fundamentalism

Christian Fundamentalism began in the UK and the US concurrently, which means tracing its exact origin is difficult as it doesn't have a singular starting point. The term in its current usage can be found as early as 1875 at the Niagara Bible Conference.[1] The conference was an annual gathering where evangelicals would preach and teach their various dispensationalist views and participate in debate and discussion.

However, despite its linguistic formation being fairly modern, Fundamentalism has been a part of Christianity since the Reformation. Therefore, it is important to distinguish between modern American Fundamentalism as a focused movement and fundamentalism as a general posture or attitude of extreme conservatism.

Many would argue that American Fundamentalism began as a movement of substance between 1910-1915. Evangelist R.A. Torrey (1856-1928) published a collection of essays by various pastors and conservative scholars in "The Fundamentals: A Testimony To The Truth." This was a reaction to the liberal ideas that had infiltrated Bible-believing churches, namely Darwinism and the debate around evolution vs.

creation. Torrey's publication empowered Christians to return to and defend the "fundamentals" of the Christian faith.

The theory of evolution was seen as a direct assault on the biblical account of creation, and its acceptance within other Christian circles led fundamentalists to reject scientific findings and rely solely on the Bible as the ultimate authority. Thus, the doctrine of inerrancy was born. It served not only as a pushback against the loose biblical interpretations of liberal Christians but also as an authoritative catch-all term that lay people could use to end any debate.

Fundamentalists have held strong opposition to science ever since, particularly regarding Darwinism. The relationship between Fundamentalism and science can be compared to the Catholic Church's relationship with the Copernican Revolution. Fundamentalists argue that humans cannot have evolved since they were created in the image of God. One such argument was made by Charles Hodge (1797-1878), a Professor of Theology at Princeton Seminary and a forerunner to Fundamentalism. Hodge argued that Darwinism could not be proven and was built on the premise of atheism, which left no room for God as a possible explanation.[2] Hodge based his argument on the assertion that Darwin was an atheist, despite Darwin's claims to the contrary.

Ultimately, Fundamentalism emerged as a response to the perceived threats of liberal Christianity and science. By returning to the fundamentals of the Christian faith and emphasizing the inerrancy of Scripture, fundamentalists sought to preserve traditional Christian beliefs in the face of changing societal norms and scientific discoveries. Fundamentalism did not appear out of thin air, however. Its theological roots had been slowly developing for decades. The theology known as Dispensationalism had already been created 75 years prior and in the decades that followed it became a theological staple for both fundamentalists and evangelicals.

Dispensationalism & Militant Christianity

Although we will go into greater detail about Dispensationalism in chapter 7, a brief explanation now will provide sufficient context for what follows. Dispensationalism is a theological framework that serves as the foundation for Christian Fundamentalism (and much of Evangelicalism). This theological framework was developed by John Nelson Darby (1800-1882), an evangelist who is believed to have based some of his ideas (specifically, the rapture) on the dream of a young Scottish girl named Margaret MacDonald. Others claim that Darby believed the girl's vision to be demonic and would have never used it to create his ideas. Throughout the years, Dispensationalism has been a topic of much debate and discussion among scholars and theologians, and its influence on Christian Fundamentalism and Evangelicalism cannot be overstated.

Dispensationalism played a significant role in shaping the theological foundation of early fundamentalists. Its emphasis on *urgency* provided a sense of purpose and direction for the movement. Its militant view of Christianity added a combative dimension to the faith. The notion that Jesus would return on a white horse to defeat Satan and his followers evokes the image of a commander leading his army into battle against a sworn enemy. In Dispensationalism, the adversary is Satan and his minions, including demons and the people of the world. Ultimately, the victory of Jesus will avenge the Father by casting Satan and his followers into the eternal fire, thereby destroying them forever. This eschatological view of Dispensationalism provides a framework for understanding the ultimate triumph of good over evil.

The dispensational imagination easily translated into the idea that Christians were at war with the principalities of darkness and the people of the world who were the servants of evil. Christians waged this war by resisting the temptations of the world and getting as many people as possible to turn against the world through salvation. This approach would oftentimes manifest itself in big tent revivals where Jesus was preached with the vigor of blood, sweat, and tears. Those who were unaccustomed to this type of presentation were intrigued (or frightened) by the various methods that were used to convert people.

None of those presentations were more popular than the "hell, fire, and brimstone" approach. This approach would "put the fear of hell" in people so that they would all but beg to be under the protection of Jesus. Such revivals were often marked by emotional displays, including weeping, shouting, and fainting.

Overall, the dispensationalist approach to evangelism was characterized by a sense of urgency and a belief in the imminent return of Christ. This approach was not without controversy as some critics argued that it focused too much on fear and guilt rather than love and grace. Nonetheless, it remains an important part of American religious history and continues to shape the beliefs and practices of many Christians today.

When individuals converted to Christianity, their practices and beliefs became infused with militancy. The strict adherence to Scripture was reminiscent of a first-century Pharisee's adherence to the Law. Attendance at Church was compulsory and pastors held significant influence over their congregations. Utilizing dispensationalist theology, pastors often attempted to persuade individuals that the return of Christ was largely dependent upon the establishment of a God-fearing nation—America was called to become The Kingdom of God on earth. This heightened the urgency of the Christian mission. Overall, the incorporation of militancy into Christian practices and beliefs, alongside the strong influence of pastors, was a defining characteristic of the conversion experience during this period.

Modernist philosophy, specifically Hegelianism, also had a profound impact on theologians, leading to the replacement of confessional theology with a more systematic approach. While systematic theology was not a new concept, its newer iterations had become more sophisticated and scientific in nature. This shift is evident in the works of theologians who have adopted a more intentional approach to systematizing their theological beliefs and it can be traced back to the works of Thomas

Aquinas (1225-1274) and his *Summa Theologica*. Overall, the adoption of a more systematic approach to theology reflects the influence of modernist philosophy on theological discourse. We will unpack more of this in subsequent chapters.

There seems to be a contradiction with fundamentalists embracing modernism on the one hand while attacking it on the other. It is true that the individuals targeted by fundamentalists as "modernists' were indeed proponents of modernism. However, fundamentalists failed to recognize their own embrace of modernism through their use of contemporary methodological systems. Despite positioning themselves as counter-cultural and anti-science, fundamentalists were, in fact, creating modern theological systems using the same philosophical foundations as science. Moreover, while fundamentalist writings may refer to "modernists' as a group of contemporaries, they are not referring to the larger philosophical epoch of modernism. This incongruence highlights the complexities of navigating philosophical movements and the challenges of identifying oppositional stances within the context of a dynamically changing culture.

The militant Christian worldview served as a perfect catalyst for the subsequent culture wars that would ensue. The fundamentalists were waging war against the liberal elites whom they believed were influencing society and destroying the Christendom they were working hard to build.

It is no coincidence that the first culture war Fundamentalism fought came on the heels of WWI. The tangible realities of a geopolitical war finally lit the tinderbox that had long been prepared by apocalyptic and militaristic preaching. Unfortunately, as pointed out by Kristin Du Mez in her book, *Jesus and John Wayne,* militant Christianity is not a flash in the pan but has remained a significant aspect of Evangelicalism throughout the 20th and 21st centuries.

The First Culture War

Fundamentalists have been fighting culture wars since their origin. It could be argued that Fundamentalism is built on a foundation of hostility. The first culture war fundamentalists fought was not against Starbucks, nor against the mainstream media, nor against big business trying to take the "Christ" out of Christmas. Instead, the first culture war was fought on two fronts: one against feminism and one against academia.

The first front is all too familiar to modern Christians; namely, the battle for the "family." The idea that fundamentalists were trying to *save* Christian family ideals is a bit of a misnomer. This was simply a linguistic disguise to address the issue of the new "feminism" that had sprung up and was affecting traditional family dynamics. In other words, the issue was not the "family," but specifically *wives*. It's no coincidence that the main warriors on this front were largely men. Their real aim was to uphold the power dynamics established in the Victorian era. This battle was waged against the individuality of women and aimed to restrict the progress of their evolving womanhood within culture.

The battle for Victorian womanhood was referred to, at the time, as the "two spheres." There was the domestic sphere, where women needed to be homemakers and take care of the children, and there was the vocational sphere, where men alone were supposed to carry the burden of earning an income to support the family.

The below quote is from a publication of the Los Angeles Bible Institute (now Biola University) called "King's Business". It was well-known at the time.

> "WANTED—MORE MOTHERS," proclaimed King's Business in 1921.
>
> ...we are thinking of *mothers*; *real* mothers *old-fashioned* mothers; *womanly* mothers; the kind that make the home. We are short on homes; *real* homes. We are short on mothers; *real* mothers. There are lots of 'tots' growing up and "kids" innumerable, but they are so different from *real* children, the kind that has the imprint of a *mother* upon them, the tokens of a mother's care, a mother's holy kiss...
>
> God designed a woman as the *homemaker*, but somehow she seems to have been side-tracked. There are so many good women, well-meaning, even Christian women, who have been harkening to a strange world—called to a "new sphere," a "higher sphere," a "cultured sphere"...[3]

There is nothing in the article itself that defends the author's statement "God designed a woman as the homemaker..." Perhaps, the author did not think any defense was necessary; that such a statement was axiomatic. This may demonstrate how ubiquitous this type of rhetoric was during this time.

The level to which the "sphere" ideology was reflective of the fundamentalist mentality can be seen in the following quote:

> There is a full-fledged rebellion underway not only against the headship of man in government and church in the home. Statistics from Yale and Harvard show that women of the better homes are not having children, the average showing less than one child to a family... The cultiva-

> tion of the modern woman's idea of 'my individuality' is bound to be a destroyer of the home life...[4]

These new ideas of womanhood significantly affected sex within marriage too, the primary effect being the reduced frequency of sexual activity among religious couples. As women began to balk at the idea of full submission to their husbands, men began to feel less comfortable making sexual demands of their wives, which had been their prerogative prior to the feminist influence.

Fundamentalism, as a movement, aimed to dismantle a woman's individuality. This was achieved through the use of language that appealed to women's emotions. For instance, the emphasis on "motherhood" was used to make women feel good about staying home. Additionally, words like "godly" or "biblical" were used to lend credibility to fundamentalist teachings. All of this was wrapped up in language that made women believe their role was just as important as their husbands. Phrases like "you are the queen of the castle" or "you are a divinely appointed guardian of the home" were commonly used. The reality, however, was that this language was designed to give men control over their wives and children. Ultimately, Fundamentalism used language to disguise its true intentions and covertly strip women of their individuality and their religious significance.

Women also became liable for the actions of their husbands. They were presumed to exercise quiet control over their family because they were responsible for the moral aggregation of the family unit. Moreover, women were the recipients of blame when their husbands misbehaved. Billy Sunday once wrote:

> A man is no better than a wife will let him be. The devil and women can damn this world, and Jesus and women can save this old world. It remains with womanhood to-

> day to lift our social life to a higher plane… women have kept themselves purer than men.[5]

Much of this serves as an important historical context for why certain religious teachings have encouraged women to "restrain their sinful urges" in order to preserve the family unit. This approach to feminism was based on the belief that Satan was tempting women to destroy the family unit - part of a classical ascetic formula that demanded the self-denial of worldly pleasure in order to suffer for the kingdom of God.[6] Women were taught to resist not only for the sake of their families and their divine purpose, but also for the glory of God.

It is important to note that this approach to feminism was not unique to one particular religion or denomination, but rather a common theme throughout many religious traditions. To fully comprehend their impact on women's lives, it is crucial to understand the historical context in which these teachings arose.

The second battle front was fought between academics. Specifically pastors and theologians against liberal scholars and scientists. The Scopes Monkey Trial, which took place in 1925, became one well-known battle on the academic front. Even though the trial was a sham meant to bring publicity to a small town, it nevertheless illustrated the type and intensity of debate that was taking place during this time.

The trial took place in Dayton, Tennessee, and involved John Scopes, a high school teacher accused of teaching evolution in violation of Tennessee's Butler Act. The Butler Act prohibited evolution from being taught in public schools. The act even prohibited the denunciation of traditional biblical orthodoxy. Ultimately the Butler Act was meant to create epistemic control over the general population and to legislate biblical authority and morality within the state.

Moreover, the Scopes trial was not just about Tennessee but seemed to represent a larger cultural posture that was playing out in states all throughout the country where fundamentalists had been sounding the alarm that evolution was being written into science textbooks. Parents were urged to look at their children's books to ensure that biblically sound teaching was present.[7]

By and large, the trial was a win for fundamentalists. They were now able to control what was taught to children through the public school system. In fact, you would be hard-pressed to find any mention of Darwin in a textbook anywhere in the United States for the next 30 years.[8]

Fundamentalism 2.0 & 3.0

Since the early revivalist days, fundamentalist leaders have used ascetics to safeguard the hearts and minds of their people. The practice includes prohibitions on smoking, drinking, dancing, watching movies, and other activities considered "worldly." By using the argument that these activities give Satan a foothold in a good Christian's life, fundamentalist leaders preach abstinence from them for the sake of spiritual growth and purity. This practice has been effective in creating a community of individuals who are committed to their faith and the principles of their religion, but it has also become a powerful tool of manipulation in the hands of fundamentalist leaders.

After the Scopes trial, support for Fundamentalism began to wane. This resulted in the redevelopment of Christian Fundamentalism. Christian Fundamentalism 2.0 was led by Princeton theologian J. Gresham Machen (1881-1937) who wrangled denominations like the Christian and Missionary Alliance, the Plymouth Brethren, and the Evangelical Free Church into an alliance for a rebirth.

One of the strategies of this new version of Fundamentalism was to establish or reestablish seminaries that could teach their most important doctrines. These doctrines included Dispensationalism, Penal Substitutionary Atonement, and Biblical Inerrancy. To achieve this, several schools were founded, including Moody Bible Institute, Los Angeles Bible Institute (later Biola University), Dallas Theological Seminary, Bob Jones College (later University), and Wheaton College (once one of the fastest-growing liberal arts colleges in the country). These institutions were considered "evolution-free" zones of education, to which fundamentalist parents could send their children for higher education.

It was also during this time that a new evangelist was emerging. His name was Billy Graham and he became responsible for giving Evangelicalism a face-lift—a type of "rebranding" into what was later called neo-Evangelicalism. Although Bob Jones had given Graham an honorary degree in 1948, by 1957 the evangelist had all but cut ties with the college and Fundamentalism as a whole. Although there may have been religious reasons for the split, the primary reason was that Graham wanted a wider ecumenical audience, which Fundamentalism prevented him from attracting.

This short period was quiet for fundamentalists as neo-Evangelicalism was beginning to take hold. Despite being quiet in the larger cultural milieu, they were still hard at work educating a new generation of leaders. The foresight of investing in the nation's top Christian Universities was about to pay off, and in a big way.

In the 1970s Fundamentalism reemerged with new vigor, when a large number of graduates from fundamentalist institutions entered the workforce and became key influencers in the larger religious and political landscape. This new wave of Fundamentalism was unprecedented in its scope and impact, suggesting a successful shift toward a more aggressive approach aimed at expanding its influence and reach, particularly among young people. This era, made possible by the growing number of fundamentalist institutions and their increasing number of influential alumni, marked a turning point in the history of Fundamentalism, and in the relationship between religion and politics in America.

This third wave of Fundamentalism would also see the quiet inception of Christian radio, the homeschool movement, fundamentalist churches, youth ministry programs, camps, and books all dedicated to the mission of the fundamentalist agenda. A foundation was being laid for what was to come, and though Fundamentalism was relatively demure for now, it would not be long before America would see a fundamentalist resurgence wrought with a political passion not seen since the Scopes trial.

The fundamentalist transition from a quiet religious movement to massive political influence involved three significant developments in the 70s and early 80s. The first was the court case Roe v. Wade, which essentially said that it was lawful under the 14th Amendment to have an abortion. Surprisingly, it was not the ruling itself that caused an uproar among Protestants (not just fundamentalists) and conservative Catholics. Instead, it was the actions of two well-known American fundamentalists tucked into a quiet little nook of Switzerland.

One of these was Francis Schaeffer (1912-1984), an American philosopher and theologian who used his brilliance to further the causes of fundamentalists and evangelicals during the 70s and early 80s. In a conversation I had with Frank Schaeffer (the son of Francis Schaeffer) in 2021 on the UNenlightenment podcast, he recalled how the "pro-life" movement began.[9] His story is also recounted in his bestselling memoir titled "Crazy for God."

Interestingly, many fundamentalists and evangelicals were ambivalent toward abortion at the time. A friend of Francis Schaeffer, Dr. C. Everett Koop (who would one day be Ronald Reagan's chief surgeon) brought up the idea of a video series that discussed the issue. At first, Francis was uninterested, but later his son Frank convinced him that it was a good idea.[10] This resulted in the book "What Ever Happened to the Human Race," which Schaeffer co-authored with Koop. In the book, Schaeffer and Koop begin to articulate a language for Christians to rally around, including phrases like the "value of life," "the murder of innocent children," and "quality of life." The book became a rallying point for Christians. They now had a cause to be incensed over and a strategy that fundamentalists had been utilizing for years; namely, fear-mongering. Fear-mongering had proven successful for years as a way to scare Christians into obedience. The call was simple: Christians must help create legislation that would protect the unborn baby's life at any cost. It is important to note that this was strictly a political movement and not a theological one—theological justification would come later.

The second significant development within Fundamentalism at this time was the establishment of the Religious Right. A man by the name of Jerry Falwell Sr. was responsible for the movement that intended to take over the Republican party. The Religious Right was a very powerful political faction that also utilized fear-mongering as a tactic for complicity. Although the Religious Right is no longer extant, its influence remains perceptible. Several formidable political organizations have emerged to supersede this movement, including the *Conservative Think Tank*, *The Heritage Foundation*, the *Faith and Freedom Coalition*, *Focus on the Family*, and the *Family Foundation*. These organizations, along with many others, persist in advancing the fundamentalist agenda to the present day.

The final development during this period was the publication of a book by fundamentalist Hal Lindsey called *The Late Great Planet Earth*. Few publications have had such a profound and sustained impact on religious culture as this literary work, which became the quintessential book of the 1970s and has since sold an impressive 35 million copies throughout the world and been translated into 50 different languages.

Lindsey's book was a rebranding of the Dispensationalism of the late 19th century and became responsible for creating a new theological industry through the popularizing of apocalyptic literature. This influence can be felt reverberating through authors like Tim LaHaye, Frank Peretti, the Van Impe's, John Hagee, and countless others.

The purpose of Lindsey's book was to establish a correlation between contemporary events and the prophetic verses of scripture, a literary device that still finds resonance to this day. This methodology tremendously augmented the relevance of arcane predictions, rendering them more accessible and ostensibly inevitable to the laity. Additionally, it granted mass appeal upon an otherwise esoteric figure in biblical prophecy: the antiChrist, particularly within the context of the book of Revelation. It is noteworthy that over half a century later, Christian theologians continue to endeavor to decipher the identity of the antiChrist.

Lindsey's book was also responsible for changing certain behaviors among Christians. For example, many Christians became much more informed about the political landscape both in the US and abroad in order to discover the antiChrist. There arose a new urgency within many conservative Christians to help usher in the end times so that they might escape this debaucherous world. Many of these Christians were convinced that Jesus would return in their lifetime (just as every Christian generation before them). This expectancy established a new hope and indirectly a resurgence of faith. We will discuss this in more detail in subsequent chapters.

It goes without saying that by the early 1980s, Fundamentalism had not only been persevered but thrived within American society. It had become a comprehensive political and religious entity, positioned at the forefront of American society, poised to guide the nation into a new era. As long as fundamentalists retained their control over the Republican Party, America would be protected from the worldly temptations and the moral degeneration that accompanied secular values. Ultimately, the more expeditiously fundamentalists succeeded in reinstating America as a God-fearing nation, the sooner Christ would return to establish his Kingdom.

Modern Evangelicalism

Tracing the origins of Evangelicalism is a challenging undertaking. The determination of its inception is often contingent upon the historian one chooses to consult. Our objective is not to chronicle the history of Evangelicalism, but rather, to furnish a contextual backdrop for contemporary Evangelicalism in order to provide sufficient context for its present iteration.

The origins of Evangelicalism can be traced back to the early years of American colonization. Initially, it took on an informal and unstructured form that differed from its present manifestation. It was not until the era of the Second Great Awakening, spanning the years 1790-1840, that most of the doctrines we are familiar with in today's Evangelicalism began to proliferate. This period also witnessed significant growth in denominational membership.[11] Then, with the arrival on the scene of William E. Blackstone (1841-1935), a more refined version of Evangelicalism began to emerge. Blackstone, a prosperous real estate developer from Chicago, was also a devout Christian. In 1889, he authored a book entitled "Jesus is Coming," which went on to sell over a million copies and by 1935 had been translated into over 48 languages.[12]

In the 1930s, the Church faced significant challenges due to the Great Depression. The economic downturn meant that many churchgoers could not afford to tithe and as a result, Churches in nearly every denomination across the country struggled to maintain their operations and provide support to those in need, with one notable exception - the Assemblies of God (AoG).

Despite the challenges, The Assemblies of God managed to maintain its congregation and even grow during the Depression. The denomination's success can be attributed to several factors, including its focus on evangelism, its emphasis on personal responsibility, and its ability to adapt to changing circumstances.

What made this Pentecostal denomination different was the message that it proclaimed. Rather than offering false hope or empty promises, Pentecostalism encouraged its followers to view the economic downturn as an opportunity for growth and spiritual development. Leaders of the Assemblies of God denomination were particularly visionary in framing the depression as a form of suffering for Christ. This idea of suffering provided hope and purpose for those struggling during this difficult time. By embracing their hardships and finding meaning in their suffering, Pentecostals were able to endure the challenges of the Great Depression with a sense of purpose and resilience. This meant that for The Assemblies of God, the Great Depression became a golden age for theological development.[13] In fact, four Pentecostal seminaries were formed during the Great Depression: North Central University (1930); Northwest University (1934); Southeastern University (1935); and Valley Forge Christian College (1939).[14]

World War II followed on the heels of the Great Depression. The war would temporarily unite the American public across denominational and religious lines but it provided very little regarding theological development, with one exception—the creation of the state of Israel.

Israel

On May 14, 1948, the United Nations declared the state of Israel established, marking a significant event that intertwined Fundamentalism, Evangelicalism, and Dispensationalism forever. This historical moment was viewed by many as the realization of a long-foretold prophecy. Despite deviations from the expected timeline claiming that this event was supposed to start the seven-year tribulation period, a notable 80% of evangelicals continue to interpret the re-formation of Israel as a prophetic occurrence.[15] This convergence of religious beliefs and geopolitical events has had a lasting impact on the interpretation of biblical prophecies related to the end times. The primary passage that scholars believe refers to this event is Ezekiel 36:24-26:

> For I will take you out of the nations; I will gather you from all the countries and bring you back into your own land. I will sprinkle clean water on you, and you will be clean; I will cleanse you from all your impurities and from all your idols. I will give you a new heart and put a new spirit in you; I will remove from you your heart of stone and give you a heart of flesh.

The consensus was that Jesus would return within a generation of Israel's statehood. When that failed to happen an entire industry was created to explain how Israel was related to Dispensationalism and the end times. Books like "Dispensationalism" by Charles Ryrie, "Things to Come" by J.D. Pentecost, and numerous books by John D. Walvoord materialized. These authors were not fringe Pentecostals but well-respected evangelical academics.

As time went on, and Jesus continued to elude the predictions of the self-proclaimed experts, new ways had to be created to clarify the relationship between prophecy and reality. The new favorite activity for many end times enthusiasts became identifying the antiChrist. Several candidates seemed plausible, including Hitler and Gorbachev (many thought the birthmark on his head must be the mark of the beast.)

One of the most embarrassing gaffes occurred in 1988 with the publication of Edgar C. Whisenant's *88 Reasons Why the Rapture will be in 1988* by the World Bible Society. Whisenant was a NASA engineer and rocket scientist. His book was his calculation for when the rapture would occur. So confident and arrogant was Whisenant that he was quoted as saying "*Only if the Bible is in error am I wrong; and I say that to every preacher in town.*"[16] Whisenant had predicted that the rapture would occur between September 11 and September 13—Rosh-Hashanah on the Jewish Calendar—exactly 40 years from the date of Israel's statehood.

So popular was the book that it sold over 4.5 million copies. People took Whisenant's book so seriously that some quit their jobs. Even Church attendance rose in some places.[17] When September came and went without the rapture, Whisenant revised his prediction to October 3. Alas, October 3 came and went as well. Although some dismissed the prediction as fringe fanaticism, others, including the publisher, stated that the book was intended to remind people that the rapture was imminent and that we should all be prepared.

1988 did not conclude end times speculation. Eschatology is now a serious industry within Evangelicalism and several books, movies, seminars, etc., are dedicated to its "proper" interpretation. Although end-times speculation was not new at the time of Israel's statehood, it was certainly given a boost as a religious and spiritual phenomenon that has enjoyed a successful run in the marketplace ever since.

It is important to understand that the re-formation of Israel as a state was not just a religious event but also a geopolitical one. The enduring political alliance between the United States and Israel is rooted in the eschatological belief that Israel's reestablishment marked a crucial advancement towards the end times. This event's impact is so profound that ensuring Israel's security has been a key concern for every administration, transcending party lines and garnering bipartisan support. Israel has undeniably served as a unifying force between Democrats and Republicans, emphasizing the enduring political importance of this relationship.

Throughout the years, many Christians have supported Israel primarily due to the belief that Israel plays a significant role in ushering in the end times. This belief is referred to as Christian Zionism (or Christian Restorationism). The name is a direct reference to Zionism within Judaism which was the religious movement that not only fought for the restoration of a Jewish homeland but also helped establish Israeli leadership during the rebuilding process. Despite Zionism's evolution over the years it still plays a significant role in the political life of Israel.

The Three Booms

Following WW2 and the establishment of Israel there were three "booms" that affected Evangelicalism. The first boom that the nation experienced was economic. Following the war, economic stability sharply increased across the nation. This can be attributed to the significant economic boost provided by wartime production, which sent people back to work and took the country from an economic depression to economic wealth. This phenomenon resulted in various social changes, including the rise of consumerism, the increasing emphasis on individualism, and the growing influence of mass media. Overall, it is clear that the post-war economic boom profoundly impacted American society, shaping its values, beliefs, and way of life.

The second boom can be characterized by the emergence of the new middle class. More money meant that contractors could start constructing neighborhoods on the outskirts of the city. More money in the pockets of Americans as well as a new banking system meant that many Americans could afford to move away from the chaos of the city. This new suburban subculture also brought with it an eagerness to spread the Word of God throughout the country. More money in the economy meant that old churches could fix dilapidated buildings and organizations could begin church planting. The physical church was growing, which meant that it needed to be filled with pastors and people.[18] Evangelicalism thrived in this new economy and social order.

The Billy Graham Boom

The exponential growth of the churches throughout America meant that more people were needed to fill the pews. This leads us to the third boom, the Billy Graham Boom. It all began in a small auditorium in Grand Rapids, Michigan between September 13 and September 21, 1947, when a young Youth for Christ evangelist by the name of Billy Graham (1918-2018) made his big debut. It was only three years later that the Billy Graham Evangelistic Association would be created.[19]

Billy Graham's contribution to modern Evangelicalism is incalculable. For better or worse, his impact on the religious and political culture of America is undeniable. Billy Graham was more than just a simple evangelist. He was also an advisor to 12 Presidents, from Harry S. Truman in 1950 to Barack Obama in 2010.

Billy Graham played a pivotal role in fostering a connection between Fundamentalism and Evangelicalism. His staunch support was widely welcomed by adherents of both theological movements, serving as a critical conduit that bridged the divide that had been growing between them since the Great Depression.[20] However, perhaps the most important relationship Graham had was with the American people.

The correlation between Billy Graham's success and the Cold War was not a coincidence. The apprehensions of Americans were amplified by the ideological conflict and the incessant prospect of a nuclear war. Individuals craved hope. This proved opportune for a pastor from a rural area of the country.

Big tent revivals have been a long-standing tradition among fundamentalists, dating back to the 18th and 19th centuries. These revivals have taken various forms, from sweltering outdoor events to packed baseball stadiums. Despite the differences in location and size, the core purpose of these revivals has remained the same—to provide attendees with an emotional experience that leads to conversion. During this communal event, attendees were able to connect with their faith on a deeper level and leave transformed. We can see the lasting impact of these revivals in the continued use of this tradition by religious groups today.

Graham used the big tent format to pack out stadiums. Despite preaching a simple message, common among evangelicals, Graham was able to achieve a level of impact that the average evangelical preacher could not. His success can be attributed to his strategic use of various platforms, which provided him with a wider audience and greater influence. Graham's first platform was the organization Youth for Christ, which was experiencing a period of rapid growth during the 1940s. Graham's involvement with Youth for Christ allowed him to hone his preaching skills and gain valuable experience in front of large crowds. He would later make the most of these skills in his work as a solo evangelist.

In addition to Youth for Christ, Graham also utilized other platforms such as radio and television to reach a wider audience. By appearing on popular radio and television programs, Graham was able to reach millions of people who may not have otherwise been exposed to his message. This allowed him to build a large following and establish himself as a prominent figure in the evangelical community.

The second advantage that Graham had was financial support. Prior to 1957, Graham had received sponsorships from fundamentalists who provided financial backing for his ministry on the condition that he adhere to their doctrinal beliefs. Among his supporters, John R. Rice, a fundamentalist pastor and the founder of the Sword of the Lord, a free newspaper that was widely distributed to the public, was particularly influential. Rice, the son of a Klansman, was a staunch supporter of Graham's ministry and provided significant financial support to ensure its success. This financial backing allowed Graham to expand his ministry and reach a wider audience, ultimately contributing to his success as a prominent religious figure.

In 1957 a rift occurred between fundamentalists and Graham. That year, Graham created an event held in New York City and employed staff members who were not Christian in the eyes of fundamentalists. Both Rice and Bob Jones (President of Bob Jones University) came out in opposition to Graham's decision and eventually removed their support of his ministry.

A few years earlier, a man by the name of Harold Ockenga (1905-1985) had founded a distinct movement meant to provide distinction within Protestantism. Many evangelicals were both embarrassed and disappointed in the fundamentalist's lack of cultural integration so they created the National Association of Evangelicals. And, by 1957 they had found their representative in Billy Graham.[21]

Graham's cultural vision was in perfect alignment with the objectives of the National Association of Evangelicals (NAE). The establishment of the NAE marked the advent of a new era of neo-Evangelicalism. This new alignment allowed Graham to expand the capacity of his ministry. At the same time, the establishment of the NAE also triggered a religious culture war between liberals and evangelicals. Although the issues they debated were not novel, their approach to the defense of their conservative doctrines was. Ultimately, they decided to eliminate the separatism that the fundamentalists had advocated for. They aspired to be in the world but not of it, positioning themselves on the middle ground. Billy Graham was a perfect fit for this model.

During Graham's run as a neo-evangelical, he acquired another platform that was to replace the support he had lost from fundamentalists. There were certain newspaper moguls like William Randolph Hearst who were very sympathetic to Graham's mission and who published "puff pieces" to boost Graham's image with the public. Graham quickly became a media darling and once he began to use television, his ministry took off. In 1957 Graham sold out Yankee Stadium to kick off what would be a significant career of televised crusades. It was reported that 56,000 people converted to Christianity as a result of that crusade—roughly 66% of the people who attended the event.

How Billy Graham Shaped Modern Evangelicalism

There is no doubt that Billy Graham's influence on Evangelicalism was substantial. Graham created the template for evangelicals to use for evangelism. He created a language that evangelicals can still be heard using today.

According to the Billy Graham Memorial Library, Graham preached to approximately 215 million people over the course of 400 crusades across 185 countries. This, of course, does not count the number of people who watched him on television.[22] According to Gallup, Billy Graham was one of the 10 most admired men in the world from 1955 to 2013. This is more than any other man according to Gallup.[23]

Billy Graham is responsible for establishing much of modern Evangelicalism's religious identity, which includes their political participation. Graham laid the foundation for the formation of the Religious Right and helped to establish the presence of the President at the National Prayer Breakfast by convincing President Dwight D. Eisenhower in 1953 to attend. Every President since then has participated in this important political event. For better or worse, this breakfast has nurtured the relationship between the political establishment and Evangelicalism.

In addition to Graham's political participation, he is also the founder of Christianity Today. Christianity Today is a print and online editorial magazine that boasts 4.5 million readers/viewers, not counting the subsidiary companies that they own.[24] Christianity Today has been a significant source of religious news and editorials since 1956.

Graham can also be credited with creating the link between politics and morality within the evangelical imagination. Graham embedded in the religious consciousness the idea that America is punished by God when the nation sins and as a result will receive God's judgment. Similarly, God will bless the nation that follows his statutes.

It could be argued that Graham was not casting a positive influence over Evangelicalism, but rather providing ammunition to weaponize evangelicals to wage a war against culture. For example, Graham is responsible for creating the Communist Fear that still exists today within Evangelicalism. "I believe today that the battle is between Communism and Christianity." Graham once said, "...And I believe the only way that we're going to win that battle is for America to turn back to God and back to Christ and back to the Bible at this hour! We need a revival!"[25]

Graham also wanted to re-popularize the apocalyptic tradition within Evangelicalism. Graham's publication of The Jesus Generation in 1971, a small book on the cultural revolution that was happening at the time, was a significant contribution to this endeavor. Graham's thesis was that the desires of American culture are not the same as those of God and that Christians should be cautious of the various revolutions that are happening. Graham's book is a call for Christians to promote the revolution of Jesus instead. This revolution involves combining the philosophy of Jesus against a transforming culture—a worldview that is still present in the evangelical consciousness today.

Jesus has had various relationships with culture depending on how Christians at the time manifested him publicly. H. Richard Niebuhr identifies 5 major ways that Jesus has been imagined throughout hist ory.[26] Below is a chart that organizes Niebuhr's observations.

MODE	DEFINITION	TRADITION
Christ *Against* Culture	Culture is seen as corrupt and something Christians should avoid so that they are not influenced by their depravity.	Separatists like Amish and Mennonite Communities.
Christ *Of* Culture	In this mode, culture is seen as inherently good and fully capable of moral integrity.	Gnostics and Liberal Protestants.
Christ *Above* Culture	Here, Christ transcends culture. Culture is seen as basically good.	Thomas Aquinas, Roman Catholic, and Eastern Orthodox.
Christ and Culture in *Paradox*	There exists a constant tension between Christians and the culture. Christians live in between Christ and culture.	Martin Luther
Christ the *Transformer* of Culture	The purpose of Christ in this model is the conversion of culture.	Augustine, John Calvin, and the Reformation Tradition

With all of the influence that Graham has exercised over Evangelicalism (and Christianity on the whole), we must ask the question, was all of this positive? Certainly, the pastor of the people was not without controversy.

Graham's White Christian Nationalism

Graham's proximity to the presidential office had been a topic of concern for some. As an evangelist and a player in the game of politics, Graham's nascent Christian Nationalism was a significant aspect of his ministry for many years. However, Graham later reconsidered his beliefs about these things and his role in the acquisition of power. In his 1973 speech in Johannesburg, South Africa, Graham stated that "*Christ belongs to all people. He belongs to the whole world... I reject any creed based on hate... Christianity is not a white man's religion, and don't let anybody ever tell you that it's white or black.*"[27] Despite this change in stance, the damage had already been done and the road had already been paved. Now, evangelicals had access to the President, which not only resulted in the growth of White Christian Nationalism but also increased exponentially the persuasion power this voting bloc had.

There is no doubt that Billy Graham's subtle racism had an impact on conservative Evangelicalism. This is exemplified in his response to reporters who asked him about Martin Luther King Jr.'s famous "Letter from a Birmingham Jail." Graham's suggestion that King should "put the brakes on a little bit" is indicative of a reluctance to take personal risks in the fight for equality. This stands in stark contrast to the assumption held by many within Evangelicalism that Graham was a friend and supporter of Dr. King and the cause of equal rights and highlights the need to critically evaluate the actions and attitudes of Billy Graham regarding issues of social justice.

One of the best examples of Graham's subtle racism was his refusal to take part in any action that would associate him with protests against racism. Furthermore, he rarely spoke about the issue unless provoked. Graham's theology and cultural worldview were heavily influenced by the apocalyptic tradition, which informed much of his thinking. In Graham's response to Martin Luther King's "I Have A Dream Speech," Graham stated "Only when Christ comes again will the little white children of Alabama walk hand in hand with little black children.[28] "This remark, insensitive at best, highlights Graham's lack of empathy for the issue of civil rights and his unwillingness to take a stand in the here and now.

Less nebulous was Graham's anti-Semitism as demonstrated in his recorded conversation with President Richard Nixon in 1972. In 1994 the Haldeman Diaries were published, bringing to light a conversation between Richard Nixon and Billy Graham regarding the Watergate scandal. In that conversation, Graham had made comments about how the Jews had a "stranglehold" on America. When confronted with this information Graham emphatically denied the charge. As retold by Debbie Lord in the Atlantic Journal-Constitution.

> Those are not my words, I have never talked publicly or privately about the Jewish people, including conversations with President Nixon, except in the most positive terms.[29]

Upon the release of the Nixon recordings by the National Archives in 2002, it became clear that Billy Graham had lied regarding his views on the Jewish community. Graham had denied any disdain towards Jews, but the recordings proved otherwise. In fact, Graham referred to Jews as pornographers and claimed that they were responsible for the moral decline of the nation. He also admitted to deceiving the Jewish community into believing that he held favorable opinions toward them. Graham ultimately attributed his controversial remarks to Nixon, stating that he was led into the conversation and did not reflect his actual opinion of the Jewish community. These revelations, however, shed light on his previously unknown views.

Graham later apologized to the Jewish community for his statements. He stated that he did not remember the conversation and insisted that he no longer held those views. But that was not the end of the story. After his death the rest of the conversation was revealed to the public and the additional recording demonstrated that Graham's 2002 apology was nothing more than political spin. The release of the full conversation illuminated the fact that it was Graham who had initiated the conversation about the Jews and it was Nixon who felt noticeably uncomfortable with the conversation.[30] This exposition raises questions about the sincerity of Graham's apology and the true nature of his beliefs. It also highlights the importance of transparency in public figures and the need for individuals to take responsibility for their words and actions.

Ultimately, the conversation with President Nixon demonstrated Graham's lack of integrity and his downright dislike of the Jewish community. Despite all this, his reputation remains elevated among evangelicals. It could be argued that this is due to his significant contributions to the Christian faith, which have been compared to those of the Apostle Paul.[31] However, it could also be argued that Evangelicalism shares in the subtle nuances of racism and antisemitism and continues to protect these positions within its ranks. While Graham's actions may have been morally questionable, his impact on evangelical Christianity cannot be denied.

No doubt a single individual should not be responsible for a movement as large and as complex as Evangelicalism. Billy Graham's countenance, however, beamed brighter than most and his religious stature was as imposing and as influential as the Pope's. His impact was much more significant than that of most other cultural icons within Evangelicalism and it cannot and should not be ignored or minimized. There is little doubt that Graham's legacy will continue to endure, despite the flaws in his character.

The social indifference that existed within Billy Graham is clearly visible within conservative Evangelicalism today. Many within this group display a blasé attitude toward social issues that don't directly impact them. It is important to note that this trend is not unique to evangelicals, but Christians are called to be different and to demonstrate the love of Jesus by caring for the "other" in our society. Unfortunately, both Billy Graham and contemporary evangelicals have failed to fully embrace this calling. Rather, they have positioned Christ against culture, disguising their actions as Christ transforming culture. This approach is misguided at best.

In the next chapter, we will continue to explore the evangelical story. We will see how Billy Graham's influence provided a foundation for subsequent fundamentalists and conservative evangelicals to gain enormous political power and influence as they entered the 1980s.

2

The Decade of the Evangelical

In the first chapter, we looked at the major thinkers associated with Fundamentalism and Evangelicalism through the 1970s. We learned that Fundamentalism was largely birthed out of the scientific revolution and was an attempt by far-right theologians and pastors to exercise control over the culture of their time. As a result, Fundamentalism garnered a militaristic/nationalistic identity that is still present today.

Next, we are going to look at the 1980s, and the role evangelicals played within culture. We will see how the foundations established in the early part of the 19th century paved the way for what we witnessed taking place in the 1980s

It could be argued that the 1980s was the decade of the evangelical. The Moral Majority was in full swing, they had begrudgingly elected their president, Ronald Reagan, and 50 million conservative followers were now ready for battle. The beginning of the decade contained many round table discussions and strategy meetings about how religious morality was going to be restored to American values.[1] One of the founders of the Moral Majority was the Rev. Robert Billings who later joined Reagan on the campaign trail and became an outspoken leader for evangelicals throughout Reagan's presidency.

During the rise of the religious right, the term "family values" was introduced as a means of promoting conservative political beliefs. This term was popularized by James Dobson from Focus on the Family but was already shared by many on the religious right. However, the adoption of this term presented a problem in that it suggested conservative evangelicals were the only ones who believed in family values, or that their beliefs were the only ones that supported such values. While it is true that conservative political beliefs do align with certain aspects of family values, it is incorrect to assume that they represent family values on the whole. The conservative view of family values is inherently narrow and context-specific, failing to advocate for traditionally liberal ideas that could actually strengthen the family unit in America.

Ironically, it was the Democrat Jimmy Carter who initiated the "Return to Families" campaign toward the end of his Presidential term. As a self-proclaimed "born again" Christian, Carter sought to fulfill his campaign promises to his religious constituents by convening the White House Conference on Families. This conference brought together family experts from across the nation to analyze the challenges facing American families. The ultimate objective was to identify policies that could be implemented to alleviate those burdens. Unfortunately, the conference was a wash.

Despite the presence of a diverse panel of experts from various parts of the country, the conference failed to arrive at a unified definition of family. It was observed that some participants were of the view that family should not be defined in strict two-parent heterosexual terms. This brought criticism from other quarters, with Jerry Falwell and his Moral Majority group labeling the conference as "anti-family".[2] Furthermore, the Alabama Governor declined to send delegates to the conference, citing concerns that the conference was in opposition to Judeo-Christian values.[3]

This is precisely when the political pivot happened—the move from Democrat to Republican. Conservative Christians would now look to Ronald Reagan to be their proponent of family values. Although Reagan was always a little hesitant to bring conservative evangelicals on board, he nevertheless provided the support they desired, thus solidifying the marriage between conservative evangelicals and the Republican party.

Ever since conservatives hijacked the term "family values" from the rest of the country, the idea of family has gone through a cultural deconstruction. In recent years, Western culture has begun to shift away from the traditional biological definition of family which refers to parents and their offspring, to a socially constructed definition that focuses more on the emotional commonality between people instead of their biological relationships. The social definition might be considered the more inclusive one, giving permission for the diversity that we see in familial relationships in our country today.

Despite the stereotype, Fundamentalism comes in various shapes and sizes and most often exists on the fringes. But what happens when it is no longer fringe but moves inward to take over part of the center? Like a cancer, growing and devouring everything in its path, destroying a once healthy organism. In today's world, evangelicals have been left with very few options.

In recent years, Evangelicalism has undergone significant changes that have altered its basic principles. The movement has shifted from a redemptive to a retributive approach, resulting in a change in the perception of the Kingdom of God. Furthermore, anti-intellectualism has become a defining characteristic of the movement, leading to a base that associates being Republican with being a Christian. This political ideology has taken precedence over theology, which has further contributed to evangelicals masquerading the Kingdom of God as the kingdom of man.

The Evangelical Soap Opera

It seems almost inevitable that when men obtain power they fall prey to the temptation of obtaining even more. Evangelical leaders were no exception to this rule. With the rise of Evangelicalism's influence within the wider culture came an almost God-like power that could be felt not just in evangelical leadership, but as far down as pastors and church leaders.

If what Plato tells us is true "...the measure of a man is what he does with power," then evangelical leaders would give the world a lot to judge them by. The 80s were an ongoing soap opera when it came to the personal affairs of evangelical leaders. Rumors of consensual and non-consensual sexual indiscretions were not uncommon as church leaders would sometimes use their power to satisfy their sexual urges. Further contributing to the problem, many in leadership also helped to cover up these indiscretions through intimidation and payoffs. These coverups are one of the main reasons this corruption persisted for decades.[4]

Movements like #MeToo have played a crucial role in shining a spotlight on the extent of the sexual abuse problem in the 80s. Figures such as Jim Bakker and Jimmy Swaggart, whose indiscretions were widely publicized, were just the tip of the iceberg. Numerous other religious leaders were engaging in similar behavior, uncovering a pervasive issue within evangelical churches nationwide. The impact of these movements has been instrumental in exposing the larger problem and initiating conversations around accountability and reform.

The increased power and influence of evangelicals had both cultural and theological implications. Evangelicals firmly believed that a wife's role was to support her husband at home, which meant they quickly dismissed the idea of women having a pastoral calling from God. Despite the growing inclusivity in many mainline and liberal denominations, evangelicals remained steadfast in their convictions. In fact, some may argue that they became even more exclusive as they perceived a threat from "liberals" amidst the changing religious culture.

The Emergence of the Religious Right

If Billy Graham granted evangelicals permission to be involved in politics, Jerry Falwell gave evangelicals a way to accomplish it. Another young southern preacher and founder of the megachurch Thomas Road Baptist Church, Jerry Falwell had the passion, entrepreneurship, and zeal that also led him to create the Old-Time Gospel Hour, a nationally syndicated radio and television ministry. The program served as Falwell's primary fundraising tool. In 1980 Falwell raised 90 million dollars for his organization.

Perhaps Falwell's biggest religious achievement was the founding of Liberty University. Falwell's involvement in education began when he founded the Lynchburg Christian Academy in 1967. What made this academy significant was that it was a "whites-only" school.[5] This was the culmination of Falwell's anti-civil rights activities which had been rampant during the 50s and 60s.

Falwell's disdain for Martin Luther King Jr. and the Civil Rights movement as a whole was well-known by many within conservative circles. It was during this time that Falwell gave a famous message at Thomas Road Baptist Church where he responded to King's protest at Selma. Falwell stated,

> Preachers are not called to be politicians but to be soul winners... if as much effort could be put into winning people to Jesus Christ across the land as being exerted in the present civil rights movement America would be turned upside down for God.[6]

In 1971, Reverend Falwell broadened his educational vision by establishing Liberty University, a private Baptist institution associated with the Southern Baptist Convention (SBC). In doing so, he was carrying out the aspirations of early fundamentalists who sought to regulate how Christians were educated. The ideological objective has consistently remained unchanged—to establish educational institutions that can instill evangelical beliefs in young individuals.

Whether intentionally or unintentionally, Falwell created a billion-dollar organization with the establishment of Liberty University. According to the Department of Education in 2017, Liberty University received $773 million in federal aid. This was in addition to the $1.71 billion endowment. Including all assets, Liberty is worth $3.13 billion.[7]

In 1979, the creation of the Moral Majority marked a significant shift in the political involvement of Jerry Falwell. Falwell, a Baptist, had previously been a staunch advocate for the separation of Church and State. However, the allure of political power proved to be too strong for Falwell to resist. Co-created with Paul Weyrich and Howard Phillips, the Moral Majority was a political organization associated with the Republican Party and based on a series of rallies held by Falwell in 1976 called the "I Love America" tour. This move by Falwell went against his previous message that a "preacher should not be a politician," and was antithetical to his opposition to Martin Luther King's political activism. Nonetheless, Falwell justified this evolution by arguing for the greater of two evils. In other words, he believed that capitulating to one ethic was necessary if it resulted in a greater impact. The creation of the Moral Majority was a pivotal moment in Falwell's career and in the intersection of religion and politics in the United States. Ultimately, the Moral Majority was able to create a political army of right-wing conservative Christians to do the organization's bidding. Although the organization has not existed since 1990 its success can be measured through the reverberations that are still felt today.

With Liberty University educating the Christian youth of America and the Moral Majority influencing the American political landscape, Jerry Falwell had an enormous amount of power and influence over the country. However, the question that remains unanswered is to what end Fallwell was willing to go in order to maintain his political and religious influence.

Morality as a Cover for Political Power?

Much of the moral influence that many evangelicals had during this time was simply a cover for a whole host of conservative agendas. Attaching moral arguments to public policy made it easy for evangelical political leaders to influence the legislative process by creating moral outrage in their base. They could also make the argument that supporting a certain agenda was essentially doing God's will. Many leaders within the evangelical community had demonstrated proficiency in generating moral outrage, particularly in their approach toward the AIDS epidemic and the homosexual[8] community.

In 1981, Jerry Falwell wrote a letter titled "The Homosexual Revolution" to justify the continuation of his Old-Time Gospel Hour program. In this letter, Falwell asserts that the homosexual community was responsible for the decline of his program due to their declaration of war against his ministry. He further claimed that his show was actively opposing militant homosexuals and that America is akin to the biblical cities of Sodom and Gomorrah. Falwell characterized homosexuals as dangerous individuals who posed a threat to children, as he believed they were actively seeking to recruit them into their lifestyle and message. These beliefs and attitudes towards the homosexual community continue to shape the perpetuation of harmful stereotypes and discrimination.[9]

Falwell would be in the news again on June 19, 1983, for a comment he made to his congregation that "AIDS was God's punishment for homosexuals." Additionally, he stated that any nation that allowed homosexuality would receive "God's judgment." He re-emphasized this belief in a televised debate he had on July 6th of the same year with gay Reverend Troy Perry. Falwell never backed down from this conviction asserting the same rhetoric again in 2001.

It is important to understand the influence of evangelical leaders like Falwell on the larger base of evangelicals. While some argue that these figures are exceptions, their reach is significant. The rhetoric espoused by these leaders was not limited to public debates but was also present in everyday conversations. Hate and fear rhetoric was not uncommon in evangelical sermons during this time, creating a sense of panic within the community. Homosexual individuals were viewed as dangerous and their perceived depravity was thought to be contagious. This fear was exemplified by the 1985 incident in Queens, NY, where parents kept thousands of students home out of concern that their children would contract AIDS from a second grader with the disease. It is important to understand the impact of such rhetoric on the broader evangelical community and to consider how it shaped attitudes and behaviors towards marginalized groups.[10]

When you add up the influence of people like Jerry Falwell, Pat Robertson, James Dobson, Billy Graham, James Kennedy, and Robert Billings, as well as evangelical politicians, the evangelical impact on the culture is incalculable. These are not just the eccentric ramblings of crazy people but of educated people with huge followings. In fact, you can still hear the echoes of their rhetoric reverberate today.

James Dobson

James Dobson, a trained child psychologist is widely regarded as the nation's most influential evangelical leader today. Between his weekly radio show that brings in an impressive 6 million listeners each week and his some 200 books, Dobson has captivated the attention of evangelicals for over 40 years.

For many years Dobson was known for the organization that he founded in 1977 called Focus on the Family. Focus on the Family was created to "Spread the Gospel of Jesus Christ through a practical outreach to [heterosexual] homes". Despite Dobson's retirement from the organization in 2009 it continues to thrive under new leadership.

Dobson is also known for his hardline stance on corporal punishment as a means of disciplining children. Dobson's work on child discipline came about as the government began to outlaw various forms of corporal punishment. However, what Dobson is most often associated with is his hardline stance against homosexuality. In 1973 Dobson resigned from the American Psychological Association when they removed homosexuality from its mental disorders.[11]

Much of Dobson's career has been practiced behind the scenes but in 2005 Dobson sent a letter to then-President George Bush promising "...a battle of enormous proportions from sea to shining sea" if the President failed to appoint "strict constructionist" jurists or if Democrats filibustered to block these nominees. Dobson threatened to mobilize his million-plus followers if his demands were not met.

Dobson again made headlines when he publicly advocated for Donald Trump in 2015. In an interview with Christianity Today, Dobson was asked why someone should vote for Trump and his response was "I don't vote for candidates or political parties. I support those who will lead the country righteously, honorably, and wisely." It is not entirely clear why Dobson thought any of those attributes fit Donald Trump, but it quickly became clear that the only reason Dobson was going to vote for Trump was that he would elect conservative justices who would overturn Roe V. Wade.

Pro-Life or Anti-Abortion?

The issue of abortion remains to this day the primary issue for evangelicals in America. Unfortunately, conservative evangelicals have been taught many falsehoods when it comes to issues like abortion. The stories that are often recalled from the pulpit or in evangelical books differ greatly from what has actually occurred in history.

Many evangelicals believe that the pro-life movement was ushered in as part of a religious right initiative following the court case Roe v. Wade. Notably, individuals such as Jerry Falwell have contributed to this narrative. In his book: *Strength for the Journey*, Falwell recalls his experience of reading about the Roe v. Wade case, stating that he grew increasingly fearful of the consequences of the Supreme Court's decision and wondered why more voices had not been raised against it.[12]

The truth of the matter is that abortion was not an "issue" for most evangelicals and fundamentalists until it was made an issue after Roe v. Wade. In the years leading up to the Roe v. Wade decision in 1973,

Americans vigorously debated the issue of abortion. A poll conducted in 1972 by Gallup showed that 68% of Republicans and only 59% of Democrats agreed with the following statement, "The decision to have an abortion should be made solely by a woman and her physician."[13]

This is further demonstrated by the Protestant Affirmation on the Control of Human Reproduction by the Christian Medical Society that convened in 1968 to discuss the issue of abortion. In this, they state "Whether or not the performance of an induced abortion is sinful we are not agreed, but about the necessity and permissibility for it under certain circumstances, we are in accord."[14]

What's more, in 1971 the Southern Baptist Convention created a resolution that stated:

> ...to work for legislation that will allow the possibility of abortion under such conditions as rape, incest, clear evidence of severe fetal deformity, and carefully ascertained evidence of the likelihood of damage to the emotional, mental, and physical health of the mother.

This position was reaffirmed in 1974 and 1976.

Additionally, 3 days after the ruling came down, the Baptist Press hailed the decision as a positive step toward religious liberty. The Baptist Press stated:

> ...The reverse is also now true since the Supreme Court decision. Those whose conscience or religious convictions are not violated by abortion may not now be forbidden by a religious law to obtain an abortion if they so choose. In short, if the state laws are now made to conform to the Supreme Court ruling, the decision to obtain an abortion or to bring pregnancy to full term can now be a matter

> of conscience and deliberate choice rather than one compelled by law.[15]

The question that is largely left unanswered is, why then, did abortion become an issue? The answer is that it was about leveraging political power, and when the fight against segregation was lost, they turned to the issue of abortion to gain leverage back. In 1975 Bob Jones University was going to lose its tax-exempt status because, like most religious private schools, it was segregated. It was no secret that Bob Jones Sr. was a racist. In a 1960 radio address, Jones stated that God was the author of segregation and that opposition to segregation was opposition to God.[16] Since most of these religious organizations were anxious about losing their tax-exempt status and felt that it was their right to remain segregated, they argued that it was an infringement on their "religious liberty."

The shift in public opinion towards integration over segregation posed a challenge for the religious right, which sought to protect their religious liberties. In response, a campaign of religious propaganda was launched, with a focus on the issue of abortion. This propaganda machine was spearheaded by Francis Schaeffer, who wrote and toured extensively to rile up evangelicals and fundamentalists about the new issue. Schaeffer's vision and framework continue to be utilized by religious conservatives today. The success of the propaganda campaign highlights the power of persuasive messaging in shaping public opinion and driving political action.

Historian and Episcopal Priest Randall Balmer recalls a conversation he had with Paul Weyrich, considered the architect of the religious right, where Weyrich states:

> ...ever since Barry Goldwater's run for President in 1964 I had been trying to enlist evangelicals in conservative political causes, but it was the tax exemption for religious

> schools that finally caught the attention of evangelical leaders. Abortion had nothing to do with it.[17]

Ed Dobson, Jerry Falwell's chief lieutenant would later confirm that same narrative for Balmer.

There have been unintended consequences as a result of evangelicals going "all in" on issues like abortion. Despite warnings from Christian medical professionals, these groups have continued to push for strict anti-abortion policies. This has resulted in a compromise of the health and well-being of all women, even those within these groups, who may require abortions for various health reasons.

Data from the conservative research group Lifeway Research reveals that a significant proportion of women who seek abortions identify as Christian. More specifically, 7 out of 10 women who get abortions are Christian.[18]

While it is not within the scope of this study to explore the reasons behind this statistic, it shows a clear disconnect between the beliefs of these religious groups and the reality of their members' experiences. This raises important ethical and moral questions about the role of religion in shaping public policy on issues such as abortion and about the attitudes toward abortion within evangelical and fundamentalist churches.

When reading statistics like these, it is important not to simply think of these women as hypocrites. Instead, they reveal a deeper problem within Evangelicalism; namely, the general treatment of women and the fear and shame produced around this issue.

As many outside of the pro-life movement argue, a woman who seeks an abortion is not just terminating a pregnancy as a means of birth control (as many stereotypes out there proclaim); instead, every woman has a story—a circumstance within which they have to make this difficult decision. Evangelical women (who are oftentimes pro-life advocates) are no exception to this rule. Therefore, it is important to step back and ask the question: what does this tell us about evangelical women?

Unfortunately, this is an issue that has deep theological roots. There has been a lot of work done by evangelicals to maintain a theological fallacy that maintains women should be subjugated to men. As we will see in the next section this doctrine is not only inaccurate but dangerous for women and has acted, throughout the years, as the basis for their terrible mistreatment.

The Dangerous Doctrine

Many people only think of theology as something that professors and pastors study and that has very little practical impact on the everyday lives of congregants. This fallacy can be illustrated by the evangelical theological perspective on the role of women in the Church and society and how that has affected the lives of conservative women.

Oftentimes, various biblical passages have been used to justify the unhealthy treatment of women. Some of those passages include:

> I do not permit a woman to teach or to assume authority over a man; she must be quiet. (1 Timothy 2:12)

> But I want you to realize that the head of every man is Christ, and the head of the woman is man, and the head of Christ is God. (1 Corinthians 11:3)

> Wives, submit yourselves to your own husbands as you do to the Lord. For the husband is the head of the wife as Christ is the head of the church, his body, of which he is the Savior. Now as the church submits to Christ, so also wives should submit to their husbands in everything. (Ephesians 5:22-24)

> Then they can urge the younger women to love their husbands and children, to be self-controlled and pure, to be busy at home, to be kind, and to be subject to their husbands so that no one will malign the word of God. (Titus 2:4-5)

It is not the purpose of this book to go through and dismantle these passages.[19] Instead, I want to briefly summarize the issue and show how it impacts women and their relationship to conservative Evangelicalism. I contend that it is precisely this theology that causes not only the aforementioned issues surrounding abortion but other tangential issues as well.

A role-based philosophy for the family has been in existence for thousands of years and has served humanity well in agricultural societies, where expectations and roles within the family unit were necessary for survival. However, in the modern era, intellect has become the primary source of capital, rather than agriculture, and we must recognize that the role-based family structure which was beneficial in agrarian societies is not necessarily beneficial in the modern world.

In fact, when we unquestioningly apply an ancient practice within a new context without considering its original context and implications, we can end up causing significant damage, and in this case, the result has been the subjugation of women. Granted, evangelicals are not trying to make a cultural argument from the Bible when they argue for complementary roles, but they should be if they want to reflect what Scripture says in its proper context. The most significant mistake people make in trying to understand these "problem passages" is that they strip the original context away from scripture, which then allows them to apply them universally.

A good example of the incongruence in evangelical hermeneutics can be seen in the use of 1 Timothy 2:11-12, which is quoted above. If taken propositionally, one can see how easily one can use these two verses to promote a particular theology. However, if we look at the previous verses, 8-10 we read:

> Therefore I want the men everywhere to pray, lifting up holy hands without anger or disputing. I also want the women to dress modestly, with decency and propriety, adorning themselves, not with elaborate hairstyles or gold or pearls or expensive clothes, but with good deeds, appropriate for women who profess to worship God.

Unless you belong to a strict Mennonite community, these verses are often ignored or rendered contextual and not universal. It's a mystery how these verses are considered contextual, but the next two verses are universal.

A similar argument can be made about 1 Corinthians 11:3 "But I want you to realize that the head of every man is Christ, and the head of the woman is man, and the head of Christ is God." In this verse, the comparison being made is between the subordination of Jesus to the Father and the subordination of women to men. However, it is important to note that the concept of eternal subordination between members of the God-head is not supported by scripture and is in fact an ancient heresy. Despite this, many complementarians have recently been advocating for this idea in order to *align their ideology with their theology*. This problem has been present within Evangelicalism for quite some time. It is the theologian's duty to remain vigilant against the misrepresentation of scripture regardless of any alignment with political ideologies.

The passages that address female subordination in the New Testament are based on the cultural context of the time. During the Roman Empire, women were viewed as second-class citizens. However, the women within the early Christian churches felt the freedom to break through those stereotypes. This is because Jesus, during his time on earth, was accepting of women, and in the earliest church movements, women were seen as leaders.[20] Therefore, the New Testament's insistence on women being subordinate to men is not a universal axiom, but rather a reflection of the cultural norms of the time. Ultimately, it is important to understand the historical context in which these passages were written in order to interpret and apply their teachings properly.

This is the historical context that women continue to contend with today. Instead of male Christian leaders coming to the theological rescue of their sisters, they have perpetuated lies in order to maintain their power and authority over women. This may provide the best explanation as to why Christian women feel powerless to speak up when issues arise, including when they face unplanned pregnancies and sexual or other types of abuse. Women in these churches are afraid. They are afraid of being misunderstood, judged, shamed, and ostracized. It speaks to a Church that is not caring for the women within its congregation and to the general disregard evangelicals have traditionally had for the needs of their sisters.

There is an apparent agenda that dictates both public policy and theology within these conservative evangelical circles. In the upcoming sections, we will explore some of these agendas in order to understand why they continue today.

Evangelicalism & Race

There is an unexpected relationship that many of the social concerns surrounding Evangelicalism have in common. For example, even today, groups like the American Center For Law and Justice (ACLJ) and their promotion of anti-abortion and anti-gay policies in Kenya are having a detrimental impact on their culture. The ACLJ's lack of cultural sensitivity and neocolonial approaches are leading to the establishment or defense of laws that infringe on the rights of Africans and their sexuality. These infringements on African culture are reminiscent of early colonial times, where African ideals were subjugated to those of the colonizers.

By attempting to impose their own beliefs and values on the people of Kenya, and of other similar African countries, the ACLJ is implying that their ideals are superior to those of the African people. This lack of cultural sensitivity goes beyond simple disrespect but also undermines the cultural heritage of the country. However, this problem extends beyond the ACLJ simply being more culturally sensitive. What they are doing in Kenya is intentional. Not only do they feel that their ways are far superior to those of the Kenyans but they are trying to establish roots that allow their ideals to gain power for Western control. Their interference is an attempt to systematically eradicate and replace Kenyan cultural identity. The African people and their country deserve better, not only because they are fellow humans but because those who claim to be helping are followers of Jesus Christ.

One might argue that if Kenyans did not want the assistance, their government could easily ask them to leave. That might be true if the leaders who have enacted these laws weren't incentivized to believe that the American Christian way is the right way. Kenya's leaders know that Western Christian values are what got them into power; relinquishing those values means relinquishing that power.

The lengths to which the Kenyan government has gone to propagandize their people are outrageous. Additionally, because they have criminalized certain "sins" like homosexuality; the government actively seeks out those "sinners" through various types of stings in order to round them up for prosecution.

Despite how surprising (or unsurprising) this might be, this is not an uncommon evangelical practice. Evangelicalism and Fundamentalism have a long history of pro-slavery, segregation, and racism that has provided a foundation for its white Christian influence over these countries. For example, Southern Baptist Theological Seminary was started as a pro-slavery seminary. In 2009 Albert Mohler wrote that the founders of the seminary were "products of their time."[21] However, it took 160 years for the school to confront and apologize for its role in the propagation of slavery.[22]

The lack of racial diversity in many evangelical and fundamentalist churches demonstrates to what extent racism and segregation have been a part of their culture. It could be argued that the composition of a church is merely a reflection of the community it is situated in. However, the dearth of diversity in suburban communities, where most of these churches are located, is a direct consequence of the segregation and racism that influenced public policy in the mid-20th century when these areas were being populated. Policies such as the New Deal and Redlining facilitated the migration of whites to suburban areas, while African Americans who migrated north were limited to poor-quality housing in inner-city ghettos. This separation was further reinforced through Eisenhower's infrastructure plan, which led to the displacement of 475,000 people, mostly people of color and other minority groups.[23] This allowed whites to commute from the suburbs to work more efficiently.

Some of the influential evangelicals and fundamentalists at the time were people like John Rice, Baptist pastor and founder of the highly influential Baptist newspaper, The Sword of the Lord, who made statements during WWII, like "...how wicked the Japanese are." And many others have been documented in Alan Cross's book, *When Heaven and Earth Collide: Racism, Southern Evangelicals, and the Better Way of Jesus.* Christians today often argue that those were different times or that it was just an issue for the South. As Cross points out, much of what we saw back then still exists today, it simply manifests differently.

Notably, slaveholders in early colonial America identified as "Christians." This fact is corroborated by the exhibit at Harvard University titled "The Yoke of Bondage: Christianity and African Slavery in the United States," which explores how Christianity shaped slavery in the South. However, it is important to note that not all Christians supported slavery. The Church was deeply divided on this issue, with the divide mostly falling along the North/South line.

It is clear that the history of racism within the Christian community is a complex one, with many factors contributing to its persistence. If conservative evangelicals want to hold to a "biblical faith," it will be important for them to re-evaluate their role in perpetuating certain racist perspectives. Resolving this issue is a difficult but necessary endeavor for those who follow Jesus.

One of the chief aims of this book is to address the question of how adherents of this faith justify engaging in certain behaviors that are seemingly at odds with biblical teachings on social issues. The key factor that contributed to this phenomenon was the shift in the narrative that was engineered by evangelical and fundamentalist leaders. Specifically, these leaders sought to politicize certain social acts that were previously viewed as religiously immoral. By doing so, they were able to create a sense of polarization that allowed individuals to manipulate their moral obligations in a way that aligned with their political beliefs.

For example, arguing that slavery was an economic necessity for the country switched something that was a religious moral issue (the humane treatment of Africans) to a political one, thus negating the religious person's biblical responsibility. It was this line of thinking that also perpetuated subsequent Jim Crow laws and segregation. Even though the freeing of slaves proved the argument for slavery's necessity to be false, conservative Christians and non-Christians alike continued to discriminate. Many of these social issues are not as political as they are moral. They are moral because they speak directly to our humanity.

To Be or Not to Be Homeschooled, Is that the Question?

Homeschooling has been a part of the evangelical ethos for nearly as long as Evangelicalism has been around. However, in the 1980s, homeschooling became a significant aspect of evangelical culture. Evangelical leaders realized that they could exercise a substantial amount of control if they were in charge of what children were learning. Evangelical kids could be bred to be the types of leaders needed for the future of the movement.

As a result, an evangelical homeschooling empire was created. Under the guise of "family values," Evangelicalism has been concerned about the public school system ever since the first culture war over evolution in the 1920s. That is the narrative that has been presented both to evangelicals and the general public. Although this may be true in part, it is not the full story.

The story begins in the 1950s with the Civil Rights Movement and the desegregation of public schools. In his book, the Bible Told Them So, historian and Dean at John Wesley Honor College, J. Russell Hawkins demonstrates, through statistics gathered in South Carolina between 1955 and 1970, that white southern evangelicals were convinced that segregation was a divine delineation between the races. This segregationist theology was popular in the South. Since at least 80% of South Carolinians were either Methodist or Baptist during this time the sample size for Hawkins' research was bountiful, providing him with significant accuracy. Hawkins goes on to argue that this type of theology is still present throughout much of the South today.[24]

The theological justification for segregation among southern evangelicals was largely driven by the fear of racial intermarriage rather than sound theological principles, as evidenced by Hawkins' research focused on South Carolina. This mindset was not limited to a specific region but rather reflected a broader perspective among Southerners. A notable example of the extent of this sentiment was observed when Baptist and Methodist colleges like Furman University and Wofford College faced funding repercussions from their parent denominations for their integration efforts, highlighting the deep-rooted resistance within their denominations.

Enter R.J. Rushdoony, a former missionary and founder of Christian Reconstructionism, the belief that the American government should be run theonomically (under God's law). Rushdoony is the primary actor responsible for bringing the homeschooling movement legitimacy within Evangelicalism. Rushdoony argued fervently in his writings and within the government to reform education away from "progressive liberalism" and toward theonomy. His failure to accomplish those reforms led to his involvement in the homeschooling movement. His central argument was that education should not be a task of the government but should be solely in the hands of parents.

Rushdoony's philosophy of education was a subversive attempt for white middle-class parents to educate their children in a way that allowed them to control the knowledge their children inherited. But perhaps more important to Rushdoony were his attempts to segregate whites from blacks. Rushdoony was a well-known Holocaust denier and racist who often defended slavery. Rushdoony believed that when schools became integrated this would create a breeding ground for inter-racial relationships; something Rushdoony was outspokenly opposed to.

White evangelicals were eager to get involved. According to the Home School Legal Defense Association (HSLDA) by 1990, it was estimated that 85%-90% of homeschoolers were conservative Christians—specifically evangelicals.[25] Additionally, the most powerful homeschooling lobbying organization (HSLDA) is run exclusively by white evangelical men.

By the 1990s Rushdoony's vision was successful. Joseph Morecraft, who is a significant contributor to homeschooling curriculum, revealed the true motives of Christian Reconstructionists and the homeschooling movement when he stated in 1987:

> I believe the children in the Christian schools of America are the Army that is going to take the future. Right now... the Christian Reconstruction movement is made up of a few preachers, teachers, writers, scholars, publishing houses, editors of magazines, and it's growing quickly.

> But I expect a massive acceleration of this movement in about 25 or 30 years, when those kids that are now in Christian schools have graduated and taken their places in American society, and moved into places of influence and power.[26]

Morecraft's statement was prophetic. These children are now adults and are working throughout the country as pastors, politicians, and other community leaders. They are the influencers within the current culture.

Is Any of this Real?

At the end of the day, evangelicals must ask themselves the question, is any of this real? Is the hope that they have in our religious political leaders based on genuine faith and conviction? It's one thing to believe that an individual's intentions are based upon sincere religious convictions. It is another to believe in this fact so much that this trust necessitates naivety. In an interview by Vanity Fair in January of 2022, Jerry Falwell Jr., the now disgraced son of Jerry Falwell Sr., revealed that the whole world of evangelical politics is nothing more than an act. It is an act meant to stoke the fire within evangelicals. The farce is meant to be the common ground through which evangelicals can trust that their leaders are one of them. The fact remains, that many evangelical political leaders are simply actors playing a role to command attention and influence.

As a community, evangelicals must strive to hold their leaders accountable and demand authenticity in their actions and beliefs. Blindly trusting in the sincerity of their leaders can lead to disastrous consequences. It is only through a critical examination of the actions and beliefs of those who represent evangelicals that they can ensure that their faith and convictions are upheld in the realm of evangelical politics.

When discussing the faults of certain leaders, it is important to understand that this is not about casting aspersions. It is not about holding people to an untenable standard. Instead, there is a specific type of sin being called out, one in which leaders arrogantly condemn others for actions that they themselves engage in. This behavior is particularly egregious given the lack of consequences faced by these leaders, who often believe themselves to be above the law. Such entitlement is fueled by a desire for power, rather than mere temptation. These actions are indicative of a dangerous level of hubris, and it is important to recognize the extent to which this behavior can undermine the foundations of leadership and authority. Unfortunately, the ones who pay the most for these actions are those to whom Christians are supposed to be ministering.

Political leaders—especially those claiming to be religious—have to be held to the highest standards. Not just because people are watching, and not for show, but out of conviction for the Gospel of Jesus Christ. Church leaders must ask themselves whether or not their permissiveness of political leaders is because the acts they are tolerating reflect things they participate in within their own lives. Or, are they being permissive out of fear of losing influence with their congregations? Either way, not taking action to quell the overzealousness of our leaders makes those who tolerate the acts accomplices to their indiscretions.

Many of the men discussed in this chapter had significant influence over a large swath of evangelicals. These figures, whose names are listed on TheKingdomOfMan.com, wielded significant power and used it to propagate falsehoods in order to maintain their hold over their followers. This insidious behavior has had a cancerous effect on the evangelical movement, gradually infiltrating their beliefs and shaping their worldview. As we will demonstrate in the forthcoming chapters, it is this pervasive influence that has led to poor decision-making not only among evangelical leaders but among their followers. Many of these followers have been unwittingly manipulated—becoming pawns in a game they were unknowingly participating in.

3

The Hearts & Minds of the Evangelical Youth

The 1990s was a decade of change in American culture. With the emergence of new music genres like Gangsta Rap and Grunge, young people now had a voice to express the general frustration they felt toward the direction America was heading. It was a decade defined by anarchism and the family values that once defined the 1980s were being challenged by the anti-authoritarianism of America's youth.

The emergence of this new youth culture led Evangelicalism to shift its focus towards its young people. Evangelical leaders believed that the prevailing secular culture posed a threat to a previously thriving Christian culture. Recognizing the urgency, the Church sought to shape the hearts and minds of their youth. Unfortunately, this effort had unintended consequences, resulting in significant damage and lasting trauma for an entire generation of Christians.

Many individuals from this generation continue to face ongoing challenges as adults. Women, especially, struggle with the profound impact this era had and continues to have on their self-perception. This struggle has extensive consequences, including strained relationships with loved ones and mental health problems. Despite the various ways it manifests, a common thread among both men and women from this generation is that their sense of identity has been damaged.

The evangelical youth of this era have now transitioned into middle age, and have inevitably, as each generation before it, taken the reins of leadership. Once known for their rebellious spirit, characterized by baggy pants, mohawks, and skateboards, they have evolved into parents, educators, religious leaders, and policymakers—the very leaders shaping our nation today. Yet, America, much like its current leaders, grapples with its own identity crisis, often failing to recognize that it is not the moral compass of the world, particularly given its numerous moral shortcomings. These leaders inherited a nation already entrenched in internal strife, a conflict destined to escalate in the coming years. However, many among this generation remain unaware of the challenges looming ahead; challenges that will go on to shape their lives and the country.

Creating a Culture of Purity

It's 1994 and Amy was a sophomore in High School when her parents decided to send her to a Baptist camp across the state. This was not unusual as Baptists in particular are quite fond of their camps and have made them an integral part of their youth ministry. This particular camp was promoted by the youth pastor for months leading up to Summer break. Many of the kids in the youth group planned on going. When Amy and the others arrived at the camp she was greeted by eager young college-aged counselors and the camp director. Amy was looking forward to participating in all of the upcoming activities.

The theme of the camp was a slogan that was very popular in the '90s: "True Love Waits." The camp even brought in a guest speaker who was a part of the True Love Waits organization. Each day the counselors would divide up the boys and girls to discuss the significance of abstaining from sexual activity until marriage. The counselors utilized a plethora of scripture to emphasize the concept of sexual immorality and its correlation with pre-marital sex.

While at camp a young boy caught Amy's eye. Amy did not care much for boys up to that point, but there was something about this one that she could not resist. Her heart raced every time she saw him and unbeknownst to her, he did the same. The two began hanging out during their free time. One night while sitting in front of the camp's lake, they kissed. A tiny peck on the lips. Amy admitted to the boy that she had never kissed anyone before. The boy admitted the same.

After sunset, the two returned to their cabins. Both were so excited, they could not help but tell their friends what happened. The next afternoon Amy was called into the camp director's office along with one of the boy's counselors. The director began to inform Amy that a boy had come forward to inform one of his counselors that she and one of the other boys had kissed yesterday. The director asked Amy if that was true.

Unsure whether or not she should tell the truth, Amy said with a shy voice that she had. It was then that the counselor told Amy that her actions could have led to the two of them having sex. The director went on to inform her that she could not stay at the camp anymore and that her parents were already on their way to pick her up.

The boy whom Amy had kissed was sentenced to extra chores around the camp as penance for his indiscretion. Ultimately, he got to stay while she was forced to leave. Amy later admitted that she never understood the double standard. She never understood why she was considered the perpetrator; why she was more guilty than the boy.

Amy's story was not uncommon at that time. Evangelicalism in the 90s became synonymous with purity culture. In Linda Kay Klein's book, Pure: *Inside the Evangelical Movement that Shamed a Generation of Young Women and How I Broke Free*, she offers insight into the experiences of women who grew up in this culture. Through Klein's work, we gain insight into the various ways in which these women suffered as a result of the purity culture. Klein provides a glimpse into the extreme measures taken by Church leaders and families to ensure the purity of these girls. Klein also gives us insight into how these measures not only damaged the personal identity of these girls but also led many of them into toxic relationships and marriages. Klein refers to this as Religious Trauma Syndrome (RTS) and says there are many women today who may have RTS and don't realize it. Unfortunately, many of these women chalk up their relationship problems to some deficiency in their character and are never able to get to the point where they realize that much of their problems stem from their religious experiences as teenagers.

Klein also informs us that in her experience as well as those she interviewed, there is a deeply spiritual component underlying the purity system. Klein argues that many girls grew up in a shame-based environment. This shame was brought about by the extreme pressure girls were under to not only maintain their own purity but also the purity of their brothers in Christ.

In a recent article published by The Society For The Psychology of Women, the authors summarized the nature of the trauma that was induced through purity culture.

> Extant research illuminated the ways these teachings have harmed women by normalizing the oppression of their bodies, restricting sexual agency, teaching a shame response to pleasure, and perpetuating rape culture.[1]

Ultimately, purity culture provided a way for fathers to control their daughters. It also created a way for the church to reign in their children in a culture that was undergoing another sexual revolution.

Girls were not the only ones affected by purity culture. Boys were undergoing their own training in masculinity. With the emergence of groups like Promise Keepers, men were being trained to see themselves as knights needing to protect their weaker sisters in Christ. In her book Jesus and John Wayne, historian Kristin Du Mez provides the historical context for how toxic masculinity has spread throughout Evangelicalism. Speaking in the context of a speech from Eric Metaxas, Du Mez writes:

> What is a man? And what makes a man great? The answer started with none other than John Wayne. Wayne was the 'icon of manliness.' He had 'toughness and swagger,' but

> he used his strength to protect the weak. Generations of men were inspired by his model of masculinity...[2]

In addition to events like Promise Keepers, there was also an abundance of reading material. Books like I Kissed Dating Goodbye by Joshua Harris; Passion and Purity by Elizabeth Elliot; Wild at Heart by John Eldredge, and the list goes on and on. Purity culture became a commercial empire and many of these books were soon accompanied by study guides and conferences in order to meet church demand.

Much of what could be seen developing among the evangelical youth was based on significant changes that took place a few years earlier with their parents. By and large the role of women in the evangelical Church and home was based upon a hierarchical system where the man was the head of the home and the "breadwinner." This has been the predominant view within Evangelicalism for as long as people have called themselves evangelical. However, in the late '80s, a group of scholars and pastors came together to solidify this perspective in what has become known as Complementarianism.

The Council on Biblical Manhood & Womanhood

In 1987, a group of evangelical leaders, including John Piper, Wayne Grudem, Wayne House, S. Lewis Johnson, James Borland, Susan Foh, and Ken Sarles, gathered in Dallas, Texas. Their concern was that the Church was allowing secular culture to shape their understanding of manhood and womanhood. More specifically, these evangelical leaders were trying to address what they perceived to be the theological intrusion of Christian feminism.

To address this, the Council on Biblical Manhood and Womanhood (CBMW) was formed. In order for Christians to understand the nature of manhood and womanhood as God had defined it, CBMW set out to develop a theological framework called complementarianism. Complementarianism asserts that "men and women are complementary, possessing equal dignity and worth as the image of God, while also having different roles that bring glory to Him." This perspective not only played a significant role in shaping gender roles within Evangelicalism but also provided a theological foundation for the purity movement.

Unsurprisingly, Complementarianism often posits itself as a "traditional" ethical perspective. This term is often used synonymously with "orthodox." Additionally, much of their writings include loaded subliminal language like "biblical" and "truth" in order to subconsciously bolster their impact upon their followers.

Complementarianism is largely based upon two biblical arguments. The first argument has to do with the created order of humanity. The second is based upon what is referred to as the household codes.

The first argument claims that since Adam was created first he was the primary human. Eve was created as one who was to assist Adam as he worked. This is where the term complementarian is derived from. Adam and Eve had roles that complemented one another. Additionally, it is argued that God could have created them at the same time but chose to create them at different times in order to establish their differences.

Complementarians will often cite 1 Timothy 2:13 to bolster their authoritative claim.

> A woman should learn in quietness and full submission. I do not permit a woman to teach or to assume authority over a man; she must be quiet. For Adam was formed first, then Eve. And Adam was not the one deceived; it was the woman who was deceived and became a sinner. But women will be saved through childbearing—if they continue in faith, love and holiness with propriety.

The key to the complementarian argument is that these delineations were a part of original creation and not a result of the fall and therefore reflect what God desires and not some misplaced notion of power.

The second argument refers to the "household codes," which are instructions in the New Testament (associated with the Apostles Paul and Peter) for how Christian couples should exist within a typical Roman household. There are several passages that complementarians put forth from the New Testament to demonstrate what a biblical relationship between a man and woman looks like, including: Colossians 3:18-4:1, Ephesians 5:21-6:9, Titus 2:1-10 and 1 Peter 2:13-3:7. This allows complementarians to create a more comprehensive expression for their position.

These codes were not exclusive to the New Testament but reflected the larger cultural norms within the Grecco-Roman empire. The reason behind the development of the household codes had to do with managing the large contingent of people contained in a typical home. These households would often consist of children, slaves, and extended family members. This meant there needed to be a practical way to organize households for legal matters. Household codes were not a product of an overnight senate discussion but something that evolved over many years of debate.

One of the first major articulators of the codes was the Greek philosopher Aristotle.

> Of household management we have seen that there are three parts—one is the rule of a master over slaves... another of a father, and the third of a husband. A husband and father rules over wife and children, both free, but the rule differs, the rule over his children being a royal, over his wife a constitutional rule. For although there may be exceptions to the order of nature, the male is by nature fitter for command than the female, just as the older and

> full-grown is superior to the younger and more immature...[3]

Additionally, you can even find these household codes in Cato[4] and Seneca[5] as well as among Jewish thinkers such as Philo and Josephus. For example, Philo states:

> Wives must be in servitude to their husbands, a servitude not imposed by violent ill-treatment but promoting obedience in all things. Parents must have power over their children... The same holds for any other persons over whom [the man] has authority.[6]

In other words, the household codes were an integral part of society for the ancient Greco-Roman culture and there is no doubt that this is the context that the New Testament writers are referencing when they talk about roles within the household.

However, the question remains as to whether or not this sort of household code is simply contextual or a universal axiom. Complementarians argue its universality based upon its link to the creation story and the created order. But there are many today who not only doubt these passages are applicable for today but question the motives behind their agenda.

Consider David Shaddy, a complementarian who, writing for the Missouri Synod on having a Christ-centered marriage (the article has been subsequently taken down), states the following: "*God's purpose was to give the man someone to love.*" This of course implies that the only purpose a woman has is to serve man; and only through serving man is she serving God.[7]

Or consider James Fowler, former professor of theology and human development at Biola University, who has famously stated:

> The Holiness of God is not evidenced in women when they are brash, brassy, boisterous, brazen, head-strong, strong-willed, loud-mouthed, overly talkative, having to have the last word, challenging, controlling, manipulative, critical, conceited, arrogant, aggressive, assertive, strident, interruptive, undisciplined, insubordinate, disruptive, dominating, domineering, or clamoring for power. Rather, women accept God's holy order and character by being humbly and unobtrusively respectful and receptive in functional subordination to God, church leadership, and husbands.[8]

Additionally, in a fundraising letter for his Christian Coalition in 1992 Pat Robertson stated:

> The feminist agenda is not about equal rights for women. It is about a socialist, anti-family political movement that encourages women to leave their husbands, kill their children, practice witchcraft, destroy capitalism and become lesbians.

To be fair, the CBMW would argue that these quotes reflect extreme versions of Complementarianism. However, there is a disconnect between theory and praxis. What is clear is that there are many men within Evangelicalism who use Complementarianism as a way to exercise power and control over others. These claims are not just anecdotal but are also based on science.

In their 2021 study, sociologists Homan and Burdetter argue that theories like Complementarianism can be categorized as forms of "structural sexism."[9] They assert that homes and religious institutions that uphold such forms of structural sexism have detrimental effects on women's physical health. The researchers collected data that revealed that women within structurally sexist religious environments reported poorer health compared to those in egalitarian religious environments. Interestingly, the same was not true of men's health.

The report indicated that there exists an element within religiously conservative churches that contributes to poor health outcomes based on women's perceptions of their own health and well-being.[10] Complementarian churches, Homan and Burdette argue, sanctify traditional gender rules by imbuing them with a sacred quality.[11] The final measure the authors of the study used was the perceived health of non-church-attending women. Those women perceived their health to be significantly better than women attending complementarian churches. Ultimately, the study concluded that the Church does have a positive impact on women's health, but only in congregations that do not limit their role and function.

Though studies like this do not prove the invalidity of a theory like Complementarianism, they do indicate that it is detrimental to women's health - both physically and psychologically. And if this is the case, then one should, at the very least, question it. Is Complementarianism simply a theology by men for men? I explore this question further in part two of this book but for now, consider that in 1991 when CBMW published their complementarian argument in a book called "Recovering Biblical Manhood and Womanhood," Christianity Today named it their book of the year for 1993.

The Sacred Silence of Domestic Violence

Pat Robertson was known for making controversial and offensive statements. Robertson was also a fringe element when it came to evangelical theology and was well within the fundamentalist camp. Nevertheless, a statement he made in 2012 on his program, the 700 Club, made many of those previous offenses seem insignificant by comparison. In a segment where he addressed letters from his viewers, he responded to a letter from a man named Michael who said:

> My wife has become a real problem. She has no respect for me as the head of the house. She insults me and she even went as far as stretching her hand to beat me. I've lost my self-confidence. Her words hurt so much and she refuses to talk through our problems.[12]

Robertson was visibly angry after reading the letter and his first response was: *"Well you could become a Muslim and beat her!"* After a long pause and an awkward giggle from his female co-host, he continued: *"...he has to stand up to her and not let her get away with this stuff. I don't think we condone wife-beatings these days but something has got to be done."*[13]

Despite the awkwardness of the situation, the message was clear, Michael should take control of the situation even if that meant assaulting his wife into obedience. Although the majority of evangelicals would never condone such behavior either publicly or privately, it gives insight into aspects of the subliminalism that is applied across Evangelicalism. Sometimes these impulses of white men lay dormant until they're put in a situation that activates them. While most of the time those impulses are mental; they can also be physical. In either case, they are a problem.

There is subliminal messaging taking place with both Robertson and Michael that demonstrates how deeply this worldview is ingrained in the evangelical consciousness. First, looking at the wording of Micheal's letter can give some insight into his subconscious. The letter begins by not only presupposing that his wife is unequal but that she is the singular cause for his consternation. The way his wife and the issue are presented is similar to how a parent might talk about a problem child. The letter also assumes that he is entitled to respect simply because he is a man instead of having to earn the respect of his partner. These insights are important because they may indicate how many evangelical men think, regardless of whether or not they act on those feelings - including those men who are responsible for theologies that perpetuate this behavior.

Second, Robertson's response is also indicative of how men might react, at least internally, in a situation like this. Appropriate counsel should have involved an inquiry into why his wife was unwilling to do counseling with him. Instead, Robertson's first response was to be violent. Moreover, his follow-up response of clarity did nothing but confirm this initial bias.

It is easy to simply dismiss occurrences like this as the ramblings of a crazy man who does not speak for mainstream evangelicals. And that is part of the problem. Despite his lunatic ramblings, Robertson was an influential leader who had millions of followers and whose words were often taken seriously.

Many evangelicals think that because their leaders may publicly denounce violence against women, the matter is closed. Even having a zero-tolerance policy is ineffective if the person or organization fails to address it properly. Additionally, participating in concealing abuse is the same thing as promoting it.

According to Vicki Lowik and Annabel Taylor, researchers at the Queensland Institute of Technology (QIT), evangelical men in Australia are more likely to commit physical violence against their partners than non-evangelicals. Lowik and Taylor describe it as enablement through concealment.[14] ABC Australia confirmed their findings through their investigations into domestic violence and religion.[15]

Several studies exist on domestic violence (AKA, Intimate Partner Violence) within conservative Christian households in the United States. The majority of these studies indicate that violence in these homes is not necessarily greater than that in non-religious environments. However, since domestic violence is drastically underreported it's likely that phenomenon is skewing the results significantly. Also, many of these studies do not differentiate between evangelical and mainline beliefs. With that said, it may be even more likely to occur within conservative religious homes than non-conservative ones. There are several factors at play when attempting to measure Intimate Partner Violence.

First, women who have suffered IPV are likely hesitant to come forward out of fear that it will make their religion look bad. Especially if it is a religious institution or doctrine that perpetuated the violence.

Second, it is highly likely that there is a greater stigmatism surrounding a woman's social status within her church than there would be within a secular community. The fact that she would be unwilling to protect her family and the Church's reputation may play a part in that. In other words, violation of a sacred silence is punished in that culture.

Third, and perhaps most damning, is the lack of reporting by third-party individuals within these churches, such as Pastors. Historian Kristin Du Mez poses the question "Why do evangelicals have such a difficult time condemning sexual assault, harassment, and domestic abuse?" She reasons that "since much of Evangelicalism's political identity was formed around opposition to feminism it makes sense that an initial reaction might be to deny, dismiss, or excuse such behavior."[16]

It does seem to be the case that there is more going on behind the scenes than is known by the public. Interestingly, in the CBMW Danvers Statement there is a line that reads "In the family, husbands should forsake harsh or selfish leadership and grow in love and care for their wives..." The statement is clear that husbands have to treat their wives with respect and not as an authoritarian. It does beg the question of why such a statement is necessary if there has not been a history of violence within conservative religious homes.

Additionally, In 2011, Michelle Louise PonTell from California State University, San Bernardino, performed a study about the domestic abuse of conservative religious women. These were the findings of that study:

> This study found that the biblical teachings on divorce and submission were two primary factors contributing to Christian women staying in abusive marriages. In addition, the results supported existing data suggesting that

> often the Christian community encourages the abuse victim to stay in the relationship, and that clergy tend to be ill-equipped to handle domestic abuse.[17]

There were several interesting aspects to this study. One, in particular, demonstrated that religion both contributed to, as well as helped victims of domestic violence. For example, the altruistic nature of the Church supports donations and volunteering for charities like women's shelters. Additionally, the Church provides spiritual support through Scripture. But it is also clear that although evangelical theology may not directly contribute to the violence towards women, it does in many cases enable the perpetuation of the behavior by pressuring women to stay married to abusive men and not report abuse to the authorities.

It's a slippery slope that can also lead to non-domestic violence towards women. Much of this abuse happens by Church leaders who use their power to take advantage of women in vulnerable states. In 2019 the floodgates were opened by the Houston Chronicle which published their article Abuse of Faith, which revealed a database that records the instances of abuse by Church leaders within the Southern Baptist Convention (the largest single denomination in the United States). It led to an FBI investigation and the establishment of the church predator database. The resulting investigation located over 700 victims spanning 20 years.

Ultimately, this has resulted in a significant increase in women from various denominations worldwide who have come forward to acknowledge their experiences of sexual abuse. This surge in disclosures can be attributed to the #MeToo movement, which aimed to shed light on the prevalence of sexual violence against women. Additionally, investigations into violence perpetrated by church leaders have also played a role in encouraging women to speak out. It is important to note that while these incidents are not exclusive to conservative churches, a considerable number of victims have been identified as evangelicals or members of non-denominational megachurches. This pattern highlights that it might be the case that theological ideas about the nature of men and women in the church do play a role in how both groups are treated.

Ultimately, the study concluded that although religion is not necessarily the direct cause of violence against women, conservative Evangelicalism does provide a breeding ground when it fails to address the issue properly and works instead to conceal the abuse. There is a spiritualization of abuse that acts as a common thread for its propagation. Compounding the issue is the shame that one experiences in abusive relationships. This shame is heightened in religious contexts when God is used as justification for its perpetuation.

Piety is a mask that many of these abusers wear. Their outward devoutness acts as an extreme cover for the greater sin taking place behind the scenes.[18] Similar to a cult leader, their perceived piety allows them to justify or excuse certain behaviors that in any other context would not be tolerated. It is important to recognize that abuse manifests in many different ways and the reasons meant to justify these acts are mere attempts at scapegoating accountability.

The Experiment Called "Youth Ministry"

The evangelical youth of the '90s were all in. With youth ministries across the nation growing by leaps and bounds, there seemed to be no limit to the production that was known as Youth Group. Youth ministries around the nation had become so successful that churches began to apply the same entertainment-type model to attract unbelievers - later to be referred to as the attractional church model. This model worked perfectly for a burgeoning megachurch movement that had begun in the 1980s.

Although youth ministry had always been a part of Evangelicalism, it had not always been the priority for the Church. Throughout Evangelicalism's history, youth-coordinated events and meetings periodically took place and there were certainly times when they were more of a priority, but, up to this point, most youth ministries across the nation were staffed by volunteers and were primarily a way for parents to send their kids to church for wholesome entertainment. In the '90s, however, being a Youth Pastor suddenly became a serious vocation and career, with Christian Universities across the country adding youth ministry classes and majors to their growing catalog of degrees.

Youth groups had become, as Joseph Kett rightly described, "fortresses of morality" whose goal was ultimately to continue the domestication of the Christian faith for future generations. Youth ministry created a new form of cultural Christianity that mimicked the larger American culture—albeit a sanitized version of it.

Although many youth groups were created to be entertaining and educational outlets for evangelical youth, they also became the primary channel for the transmission of purity culture. You would be hard-pressed to find a youth group meeting, conference, or camp that did not integrate thinly veiled moralizing about sexuality. Sometimes this was subversive but not always. Organizations like True Love Waits were formed in order to bring the purity conversation to the forefront. No longer would being a virgin have a cultural stigma attached. The aim of these organizations was to make it cool to be a virgin. No longer were virgins shy outcast church girls in long dresses, but large groups of young people—particularly girls—would sign purity pledges and wear purity rings to signify to their peers that they were saving themselves for marriage. Abstinence had become a full-fledged, popular movement.

The seemingly well-timed AIDS epidemic (or perhaps the misinformation surrounding the epidemic) helped provide the fear that leaders could utilize to frighten their youth into compliance. Misinformation surrounding AIDS spread rapidly and caused hysteria in some cases. Although health officials tried to educate the public, the simple truth was that not much was known about the virus. In 1985, a notable incident occurred in a New York school system, where a school board decided to allow a second-grade student with AIDS, who had contracted it through a blood transfusion, to attend classes. Despite reassurances that the student posed no threat, around 2,000 parents protested by keeping their children home.

God Save the Virgins?

There is no doubt that purity culture was much more demanding and devastating for girls than for boys. The importance of female virginity has been significant for most of recorded human history. You need not look any further than the most famous virgin in history—the Virgin Mary. Some cultures have gone to extreme lengths to test the virginity of their women. Even marital contracts were made based on the "bloody bed sheet" that could be shown as proof of the woman's chastity. In some cultures, virgins even had special abilities. In Chinese culture, for example, it was believed that naked virgins in the forest could summon unicorns. Similar ideas can be seen in Greek and Persian cultures.

Societies have long assigned different meanings to sexual activity for men and women. In numerous cultures, a woman's body was viewed as the possession of her husband, and most men did not wish for their property to have been previously owned by another. At the same time, sexual activity had a different meaning for men. The sexual prowess of men was largely associated with power and influence. Consequently, men who liberally engaged in sexual activity were regarded as dominant and influential, thus elevating their social status. It is worth noting that men aspired to be perceived as sexually active, even if they weren't, while the typical standard for women was to be chaste.

Although the importance of sexuality ebbed and flowed throughout history it was largely understood that marriage was about producing offspring and securing a lineage for inheritance purposes. In these cases, wives had very few social, economic, and legal rights and they were almost always viewed as the property of their husbands. Chastity was often used as a way to restrict women and keep them focused on their duties as wives, mothers, and household overseers. Sex was seen as an unwelcome distraction. This idea was later transferred into early Christianity and turned into a liberating choice that a woman could make as a sign of dedication to God.

Virginity became not just something a woman was expected to possess prior to marriage, but an elevated, socially acceptable status a woman could choose for herself. Upon the rise of Medieval Christianity, the Virgin Mary became a token of devotion and purity. That meant sex and sexuality were seen as antithetical to those values and deemed sinful. The importance of purity represented demurity and passiveness and was believed to make women better mothers as a result. The idealization of Mary created religious symbols that are still held today such as the purity of the womb.

The veneration of virgins was not just a Christian attribute. Many other religions sacrificed virgins because they believed that this was the purest sacrifice they could offer their gods. In some cases, women would abstain from sex for that sole purpose.

It was not until the Reformation that human sexuality saw redemption. In contrast to their Catholic counterparts, the reformers emphasized marriage over abstinence and not only allowed but encouraged their clergy to be married and have children. Nevertheless, in the time following the Reformation, a puritanical culture developed that reimagined sexuality in terms of the image of God. The body is God's temple—an icon representing the pure goodness of God's creation. Sex outside of marriage was seen as whimsical, uncontrolled, and unfocused from the more important spiritual matters. Even within the confines of marriage sex was viewed as something for procreation and not for pleasure.

Although Protestants argue that the importance of virginity is not exclusive to women, the evidence for that belief remains scant. The evidence suggests that women have always been treated more harshly than men. This is often based on the idea that men are "wired" as highly sexual beings whereas a woman's nature is much more chaste. In the religious mentality, there is something lost that can never be regained when a woman has sex outside of marriage. In contrast, although men also sin when they engage in extra- or premarital sex, they are considered to have simply given in to their innate desires, and therefore cannot be judged as harshly.

Puritanical Christianity tends to idealize female sexuality and hold women to an unreasonable and extra-biblical standard. Condemnation for sex before marriage is not found in Scripture, but rather a focus on the intentionality behind the act. Evangelicals have long equivocated between generalized statements regarding sexual practices and the specificity of chastity before marriage.

Additionally, the same equivocation has been made between marriage and sex. Is sex only "good" because it happens between two people who have a piece of paper that indicates that commitment? No. It is about the commitment itself. What the Bible speaks against is having a frivolous attitude towards sex. This is especially true in the New Testament as it is a direct response to the passiveness with which Romans participated in sex. Paul puts forth a sexual ethic that reimagines sex as a spiritual act between two committed people. It is quite beautiful when understood correctly. Unfortunately, it has been largely distorted by those who prefer to use it as a way to control women.

Today's continued emphasis on female virginity as a symbol of morality and honor can be traced back to biblical teachings and societal norms that had their place in their respective historical and cultural contexts. Female chastity and fidelity were no doubt important at a time when family lineage determined inheritance rights and kept society stable and orderly. Modern society, however, has made significant strides in reorganizing women's legal rights and autonomy, and these historical, cultural, and social contexts no longer apply. Meanwhile, the religious obsession with female virginity in some circles continues to perpetuate the notion of women as possessions or objects of value in a way that is inappropriate and dehumanizing in today's context. Regardless of what male leaders within Evangelicalism may argue, purity culture demonstrates that men still view women as property and not co-equal in worth.

Does True Love Really Wait?

Youth groups, camps, seminars, conferences, and even concerts became the central hub of this new religious consumerism called purity. Authors from around the world came out and began publishing multitudes of books, studies, and curricula aimed at motivating young people to stay pure.

The '90s marked a significant era for purity culture, largely influenced by Evangelicalism and Christian pop culture. The lasting effects of this cultural phenomenon have been extensively analyzed by various authors. One observable consequence today is the decline in evangelical church attendance over the past two decades, with Protestantism experiencing a notable decrease overall. While multiple factors contribute to this decline, it is evident that the impact of purity culture on the youth of the '90s played a significant role in shaping current trends within the larger religious landscape.

In 2019, former Lutheran pastor Nadia Bolz-Weber attracted widespread attention when she unveiled a "golden vagina statue" as a symbolic gesture against the purity culture prevalent in the 1990s and early 2000s. Bolz-Weber's initiative involved collecting old purity rings from her social media followers to create the statue, highlighting the detrimental effects of idolizing purity within Evangelicalism. This culture of purity has been linked to lasting emotional scars and shame among a generation that was ill-prepared to navigate relationships, leading to issues such as troubled marriages, increased divorce and abortion rates, and a lack of self-worth. The aftermath of purity culture continues to haunt Evangelicalism, prompting ongoing efforts toward recovery and healing by those affected.

Meanwhile, as theologians and other Church leaders were convincing a generation of young people that "True Love Waits," conservative religious and political leaders were gearing up for their own battle. It was not a war of bloodshed but a war of ideals fought on the front lines of American culture. It was a war whose objective went beyond just winning the hearts and minds of evangelical youth; it was a battle for the soul of the nation.

The Culture War: Part Deux

The youth's involvement in politics during the '90s provided an outlet for them to express their frustrations with home life and culture. Movements like "Rock the Vote" were meant to motivate young people to get involved in politics, encouraging them to express their opinions on a whole range of political topics.

The young people of the '90s gravitated toward social issues. One such issue was the growing importance of LGBTQ+ issues. In 1998, the brutal murder of Matthew Shepard, a young gay student at the University of Wyoming, served as a wake-up call to galvanize a generation that had been largely tacit towards this community. This hate crime coupled with the never-ending attacks by social conservatives and religious leaders resulted in a backlash against the hyper-masculine religious culture that had endured for decades. Shepard's death became a transition point from an age of innocence and ignorance to one focused on tolerance and understanding.

As the LGBTQ+ community gained increasing acceptance and their concerns moved into the mainstream, it inevitably sparked tension with Evangelicalism. Yet, what evangelical leaders failed to anticipate was the extent to which their animosity toward the LGBTQ+ community would create a backlash, turning much of American culture against them. Rather than maintaining a significant influence over culture, evangelicals found themselves increasingly perceived as judgmental homophobes, alienating themselves from broader societal acceptance. This tension would create a significant barrier between society and much of the Church and ultimately, this clash would result in a culture war between traditional "family values" and society, and divide the country for years to come.

The Emergence of a New Kind of Church

The '90s witnessed not only a significant culture war between evangelicals and society but also an internal Church conflict that saw many heading for the door. This conflict was more than the typical spat between liberal and conservative ideologies, these were deep disagreements that challenged the very foundation of Evangelicalism. A new type of culture war was emerging and with it came the rise of the Emergent Church.

Throughout the '90s there was growing frustration among some pastors, youth pastors, and other Church leaders within Evangelicalism.[19] Like many movements, this one began as a simple conversation between pastors whose desire it was to make the Church a vessel of Christ for the poor and downtrodden. Wishing to do more than just carry on with business as usual, they quickly consolidated their efforts and launched a movement that became known as the Emergent(ing) Church.

Many of the early leaders such as Tony Jones, Doug Pagitt, Chris Seay, et al., were part of the larger philosophical evolution that was taking place concurrently called postmodernism.[20] Although postmodernism had been around since the '70s, it wasn't until the '90s that its philosophical ideals created practical implications for the Church. Postmodernism had, up to that point, been largely equated to theological liberalism and the various forms of liberation theology. Now that was all changing and postmodern thinking was reaching more mainstream parts of the Church.

Postmodernism was the philosophical reaction to modernism, which we discussed in Chapter 1. Postmodernists believed that modernism's absolutism and idealism made promises that were never realized. In response, postmodernists wanted to understand the world and the human experience as it truly was, without modernism's preconceived notions of how it should be. Many Christians in the '90s seemed to grasp the theological problems plaguing the Church due to the influence of modernism and wanted to see change. Change, however, would not come easily and would require undoing much of what modernism had built.

Although by nature postmodernism is acategorical we might be able to capture its intent in a single word: skepticism. Questioning everything became its predominant theme and the preferred method for capturing truth - if truth even existed. In one sense this was a throwback to Descartes's *cogito ergo sum.* In another and perhaps contradictory sense, postmodernism was also skeptical of doubt itself. For modern thinkers, this contradiction was proof that postmodern thinking was not only flawed but entirely illogical. The postmodern response to this critique was largely indifference but at a more fundamental level, postmodern thinkers questioned whether logic itself was flawed. After all, who is to say that nature always obeys logic?[21]

The Megachurch: An Exercise in Futility

Evangelicalism developed its own response to the emergence of relativistic postmodern thinkers. Its attempt at wrangling this generation included establishing large, Hollywood-style megachurches[22] which resembled scaled-up models of the highly successful youth ministries that existed throughout the country. Organs, suits, dresses, hymns, and pews were no longer considered sacred and were replaced by full bands, casual clothing, emotional songs, and comfortable seats. It was this "seeker-sensitive" model that evangelicals thought would help propel their churches into the new millennium.

It bears mentioning that the seeker-sensitive model was not strictly a megachurch model, nor exclusive to evangelicals. Nevertheless, it was the primary model for developing megachurches across the country, and it was quickly adopted and perfected by evangelicals.

For emergent Christians, the creation of seeker-sensitive churches full of entertainment and superficial teaching further illustrated the problem they saw in the mainstream evangelical Church. The ideas employed to build megachurches were not new or innovative, but simply recycled and modernized methods from the time of the big tent revivals. Emotional worship music tapped into people's most primal desires. Highly persuasive and engaging preaching always came with a hook that people could not easily resist. These methods continued to draw people into churches in large numbers, just as they had done during Billy Graham's heyday.

Was the Holy Spirit attracting all of these people in droves? Maybe. It's also possible that many of these people were falling prey to the old subversive tricks that had made the tent revivals and sold-out stadiums so popular. Was innovation simply a disguise for pretense? In the business world, they call this "rebranding." Rebranding allows a company to change its identity in hopes of rehabilitating the public's perception of it even though nothing about its services or products has changed. This is precisely what the seeker-sensitive approach was. It was an attempt at making Christianity fashionable and appealing while still perpetuating the deceptive guise of modernity with all of its absolutism and idealism.

For those within the emergent church movement, the growing practice of megachurch fabrication was a perfect example of not only how out of touch evangelical leaders were with culture but also how much the modern church was missing the point. What the megachurch model perpetuated was this idea that the church was like a country club where the privileged could gather in the comfort of superficiality. Doing church this way meant that people had to come *to* the church, as opposed to the church *going* to them. By their nature megachurches also allowed for people to be invisible if they wanted to be due to the sheer volume of people attending these churches.[23]

The Problem with Modernism in a Postmodern World

The Emerging Church understood something that Evangelicalism still struggles to grasp to this day. That is, you cannot manipulate culture into something you wish it to be, you have to engage it as it is. Due to modernism's influence, Evangelicalism largely views people categorically, reducing people to concepts, numbers, groups, and labels. Unfortunately, people are not so easily reduced. They are individuals with unique personalities, stories, and experiences. If the Church wishes to understand and meet the spiritual needs of its people, it must engage with sensitivity and nuance and accept them as they are, not as they wish them to be. Although we will delve deeper into this topic in the second section, it is important to note here that many evangelicals struggle to comprehend certain social issues like women's rights and racism due to their tendency towards idealism and reductionism. Their modernist approach leads them to view individuals solely through limited categories and stereotypes.

For example, some evangelicals—particularly white evangelicals—find it challenging to acknowledge the existence of systemic racism because they cannot envision a scenario where law enforcement officers would intentionally inflict harm on others. From their perspective, the primary role of the police is to safeguard individuals rather than cause harm, which is what they experience in their own context. Consequently, when confronted with instances of police brutality in the media, they often dismiss such occurrences as isolated incidents rather than recognizing a larger issue within policing practices, particularly in black communities. Additionally, when confronted with repeated instances of police violence in the news media, they are inclined to dismiss it as biased reporting rather than considering the possibility of underlying problems. This mindset can even lead them to entertain more extreme notions, such as believing in conspiracies orchestrated by media conglomerates to perpetuate falsehoods. This perspective is the direct result of a combination of their religious leaders planting seeds of propaganda in their minds and the unconscious bias that is the result of ongoing exposure to books, news, and radio media that perpetuate the conspiracy.

They have been primed for this worldview by a modernist Church that has elevated absolutism and idealism above reality. The lack of nuance in evangelical thinking is the direct result of being taught to think in black and white. This is referred to as binary thinking and is a significant problem for many evangelicals, especially when it comes to social and theological issues that don't fit neatly into an idealized worldview.

The early success of the Emerging Church can be attributed to their ability to recognize the nuance associated with individuality. By focusing on personalized interactions and relational discipleship, the Emerging Church was able to cultivate a more dedicated and engaged community. This approach allowed for deeper connections and a more meaningful impact on individuals, leading to a stronger sense of commitment among the members.

The theatrical nature of megachurch services, characterized by elaborate performances and entertainment-driven presentations, replaced traditional religious practices with elements of pop culture. This shift towards a more consumerist approach to evangelism has transformed the Church into a spectacle rather than a place of genuine spiritual connection. Consequently, the emphasis on entertainment and superficial engagement has led to a perception of inauthenticity that began alienating congregants seeking a more meaningful religious experience.

What the emerging church capitalized on was its ability to understand culture. The leaders understood that people did not want to be entertained, they wanted deep meaningful relationships. This meant that the Church did not need to become bigger, but smaller.

It quickly became apparent that in order to make this change it would be necessary to reimagine what it meant to be a part of a local church. "Church" needed to look less programmatic and more organic and personal. Pastors needed to be less about hierarchy and power and more about accessibility and humility. Evangelism needed to be less about giving people information and more about establishing communal relationships.

There are many theological and ecclesiastical differences between Evangelicalism and the Emerging Church. Therefore, I have included a chart below that distinguishes some basic differences between the two groups. See Appendix B for a more comprehensive version.

BELIEFS/PRACTICES	EVANGELICALISM	EMERGING CHURCH
Philosophical Context	Modernism	Postmodernism
Theological Methods	Systematic	Contextual
Missions	Informational	Communal
Church Form	Institutional	Missional
Main Focus	Bible and Salvation	Community and Incarnation
Hermeneutics	Inductive	Narrative

The emergent church movement, initially perceived as a minor annoyance by evangelicals, started to gain momentum as the new millennium approached. Tensions escalated over time between evangelicals and followers of the Emerging Church. Younger evangelicals became increasingly intrigued by the authenticity of the Emerging Church, prompting some to transition from their conventional congregations to join the emerging church community and stoke the embers into flame.

4

For God & Country

Throughout history, there have been significant events that have had a profound impact on American culture. The death of Abraham Lincoln altered the course of the nation's recovery from the Civil War and slavery. The assassination of John F. Kennedy led to reforms for how the President would be protected in the future. The fall of the Berlin Wall marked the end of the Cold War and brought about a new era of peace. Similarly, the terrorist attacks on September 11, 2001, defined a new era and had a lasting impact on culture, its memory forever embedding itself upon America's consciousness.

9/11 would not only define this new cultural era but also define a President who believed that his timely ascension to the presidency was divinely orchestrated. In the eyes of this newly-minted President and the millions of evangelicals who supported him, only someone with the faith and fortitude of George W. Bush could handle such a difficult time. God had his hand upon America and Bush would be the executor of His Will.

Bush's story doesn't start on September 11, 2001, but in 1985, when a young 39-year-old George W. Bush had a fateful encounter with Billy Graham. It was during this time that, under the guidance of Graham, Bush became a "born again" Christian. This event would later prove to be a pivotal moment in Bush's political career, as he was subsequently elected as Governor of Texas and later, as President of the United States. Neither Billy Graham nor George Bush could have known at the time how much this moment would define his political career and the future of America.

To Err is Human, To Forgive is Divine

The importance of the sense of "divine" appointment felt by Bush can not be overstated. In his 2003 biography, Stephen Mansfield recounts several stories about how Bush perceived his appointment as President. According to Mansfield, in the days leading up to Bush's decision to run for President, he confided in a friend, Texas evangelist, James Robinson, that he had a premonition about a national tragedy.

> I feel like God wants me to run for president. I can't explain it, but I sense my country is going to need me. Something is going to happen. I know it won't be easy on me or my family, but God wants me to do it.[1]

In 2000 George Bush would use his story of redemption from hard living and alcoholism to run for President of the United States. When asked in a debate who his favorite thinker was, Bush replied "Christ, because he changed my heart." A few years after 9/11 in his State of the Union Address and in the context of the war on terror, Bush stated: "This call of history has come to the right country. The liberty we prize is not America's gift to the world, it is God's gift to humanity."

President George W. Bush's strong sense of divine calling was demonstrated during his presidency through the daily prayer meetings he held with his staff, regardless of their personal beliefs. Additionally, he would go on to allocate billions of dollars to benefit faith-based groups, considering them essential for fulfilling the country's social responsibility. This approach resonated with white evangelicals, as evidenced by his 75% approval rating among this group at the end of his first term in 2004, according to the Pew Research Center. It is clear that President Bush's religious convictions significantly shaped his policies and governance style. However, the implications of his election for an increasingly secular nation raise questions about the intersection of religion and politics in the rapidly changing societal landscape.

Religion & Politics at the Crossroads

For evangelicals who, as Kristin Du Mez says, were grateful to have another "cowboy in office" there was no one better to run the United States and protect their interests than Bush. He was one of them. He understood their issues, passions, and purpose. This was proven on September 11, 2001, when the United States was attacked by Muslim extremists.

The events of September 11, 2001, significantly heightened the awareness of religion in the cultural sphere. The tragic occurrences of that day, witnessed by many across America via live television broadcasts and subsequent news coverage, left a profound impact. The sight of two of America's iconic buildings collapsing, coupled with the realization that individuals were still inside, evoked strong emotions. Consequently, religious institutions faced an increased demand for guidance and support, resulting in a surge in church attendance, as reported by Gallup, with a six percent rise the week following 9/11.[2] However, this uptick was short-lived, as the nation grappled with the implications of a transformed reality in the aftermath of the attacks.

Regardless, the events of 9/11 ignited a fire under evangelicals who shifted their apocalyptic nemeses from the typical suspects to a group they had been fighting with for centuries. The religious nature of the events coupled with the historical context between Islam and Christianity helped to fuel an anti-Islam phobia. Luckily, evangelicals had George Bush at the helm and there was no way he was going to let those responsible go unpunished.

For most Americans, evangelicals included, revenge for the senseless attacks quickly superseded geopolitical concerns. Every evangelical's eye was on the new President to see how he would respond. Ultimately, they were unprepared for and unhappy with Bush's mild response, particularly as it related to the nature of Islam.

> The face of terror is not the true faith of Islam. That's not what Islam is all about. Islam is peace. These terrorists don't represent peace. They represent evil and war... America counts millions of Muslims amongst our citizens, and Muslims make an incredibly valuable contribution to our country. Muslims are doctors, lawyers, law professors, members of the military, entrepreneurs, shopkeepers, moms and dads. And they need to be treated with respect. In our anger and emotion, our fellow Americans must treat each other with respect.

As outrage grew, American followers of Islam were in danger. Reminiscent of what the Jews experienced in America during WWII, some evangelical leaders were quick to ostracize. Evangelicals like Pat Robertson stated on The 700 Club "Adolph Hitler was bad, but what the Muslims want to do to the Jews is worse." Robertson also characterized the Prophet Mohammad as a "robber and a brigand. And to say that these terrorists distort Islam? They're carrying out Islam!"

According to an ABC/Belief.net poll, anti-Islamic attitudes increased 9% in the aftermath of 9/11 indicating that 33% of Americans held such views. Prominent evangelical figures other than Robertson stoked Islamophobia further. Jerry Falwell stated in a television interview that "Mohammad was a terrorist," and Rev. Jerry Vines claimed that "Islam was founded by Mohammed, a demon-possessed pedophile who had 12 wives, and his last one was a 9-year-old girl." It is worth noting that biblical figures like the Virgin Mary, who was married around 13, and King Solomon, who had around 1,000 wives and concubines, are considered heroes of the Christian faith. These assertions, despite their inflammatory nature, were made in public forums such as Fox News and the Southern Baptist Convention. Even Jimmy Swaggart, former head of the National Association of Evangelicals, opined in a 2019 sermon: "You know what we ought to do? We ought to take every single Muslim student in every college in this nation and ship them back to where they came from." [3]

While true that Islamophobia has been common within Christianity since the Crusades, these public comments made by evangelical leaders gave permission for others to speak and act accordingly and unleashed vitriol among the masses. Although Islamaphobia in recent years has been primarily cultural, anti-Islam sentiment is largely a "theological one" says Todd Green, former professor of religion at Luther College and current director of Campus Partnerships at Interfaith America. Green explained how its development began in the early Middle Ages:

> Christians in this era became familiar enough with the basics of Islam to recognize it as a monotheistic religion that shared common figures and overlapping vocabulary with Christianity. This theological overlap led Christian theologians to categorize Islam as a perversion of the true Gospel. While few of these theologians engaged in any in-depth study of Islamic texts and traditions, they were nonetheless quick to view the Prophet Muhammad (PBUH) as a false prophet, one who deliberately corrupted the witness of the Old and New Testaments to spread false messages and usurp power. These same theologians also developed a cadre of shallow stereotypes of Islam that persist to this day, including the notions that Islam is violent and harmful toward women.[4]

9/11 simply stoked a fire that was already smoldering under the surface of the evangelical consciousness. From the persecution of Middle-Eastern citizens to the illegal detention of Muslims at Guantanamo

Bay, 9/11 seemed to grant permission for Americans to be overtly xenophobic.

The Impact of 9/11 on Evangelical Identity

For end-times enthusiasts, 9/11 was seen as a punishment for the United States, which seemed to be moving away from God. In stereotypical fashion, these evangelical leaders were making the argument that has been made countless times before: God punishes America for its sins! Jerry Falwell appeared as a guest on the 700 Club on September 11th and offered this explanation for why terrorists attacked the United States:

> Throwing God out successfully with the help of the federal court system, throwing God out of the public square, out of the schools... the abortionists have got to bear some burden for this because God will not be mocked. And when we destroy 40 million little innocent babies, we make God mad.
>
> ...[T]he pagans and the abortionists and the feminists and the gays and the lesbians who are actively trying to make that an alternative lifestyle, the ACLU, People for the American Way—all of them who have tried to secularize America... I point the finger in their face and say you helped this happen.

Did this mean that 9/11 was something different from the end times? Was this just a punishment for America in the interim? In 2022, Pew conducted a survey surrounding belief in the end times. Although their study was specifically centered around how belief in the end times impacted views about the environment, their results were insightful regarding religious beliefs as well. In their survey, they noted that 39% of

Americans believed we were living in the end times; while only 31% of mainline Christians believed we were living in the end times. However, an astounding 63% of evangelicals believed we were living in the end times.[5]

Despite how high these numbers are, they are still considerably lower than a Barna omnipoll that was conducted in 2013. Those results showed that 77% of evangelicals believed they were living in the end times. This may have correlated to rising tensions that existed in Syria at the time but it was mostly a quiet historical period and yet belief in the end times seemed to be growing.

Although most Christians believed that the terrorist attacks were political and not religious in nature, some evangelical leaders could not help but perpetuate the "punishment" narrative. In a rare show of disagreement between laypeople and their leaders, 63% of evangelical Christians did not believe that the terrorist attacks were a result of God punishing the United States, according to Pew.[6]

Oftentimes there are one of two directions that Christians usually head during a catastrophe. They either move outward to confront the issue or they remain passively antagonistic. In an unpredictable move, many evangelicals turned inward after 9/11, which was both unexpected and significantly different from many of their leaders.

Richard Cimino of the New School for Social Research performed an interesting study. He surveyed evangelical writings pre and post-9/11 and analyzed the difference in rhetoric toward Islam. His research revealed that there was a significant rise in anti-Islamic attitudes in post-9/11 literature, particularly within evangelical and charismatic literature. Cimino argued that 9/11 helped to foster a more pluralistic society and in so doing naturally clarified the resolve and identity within Evangelicalism. Ultimately 9/11 led to evangelicals reasserting themselves and becoming more unified than ever before.

This unification was specific to white evangelicals and this demographic witnessed further growth within Evangelicalism throughout the 2000s and 2010s, culminating in the election of Donald Trump to President of the United States. The mid to late 2000s also turned out to be a dark time for evangelicals. Although much of what was happening during this time was not made known until much later, power dynamics among some of the old guard were in full swing, leaving a host of victims in its wake.

Ted Haggard

Ted Haggard is what you might call an evangelical of evangelicals. Haggard was a former SBC minister and he founded both the megachurch New Life Church and the evangelical denomination Life-Giving Churches. Haggard also served as the President of the National Association of Evangelicals from 2003-2006. However, like many of the evangelical leaders that have been profiled in this book, Haggard had another side to him.

In 2006 allegations of drug use and sexual misconduct surfaced. It was Haggard's preaching against gay marriage that became his undoing when the male prostitute he was having an affair with came forward out of anger at his hypocrisy. The allegations were originally explained away as political retaliation, a strategy that is right out of the evangelical political playbook. Even James Dobson came to Haggard's defense. However, upon Haggard's admission, church leaders began to distance themselves. In an attempt to spin the story, they would often describe Ted as having very little influence across Evangelicalism.

This, of course, was categorically untrue as he was not only the President of the National Association of Evangelicals at the time but also the pastor of a 14,000-person church, which he had led for over 22 years. Furthermore, just the previous year, Haggard was listed by Time as one of the top 25 most influential evangelicals in America.[7] Author Jeff Sharlet reported in 2005 that Haggard spoke with President Bush about once a week and that no other pastor in America held more sway over the political direction of Evangelicalism. Haggard is sometimes credited with being the unified factor in Bush's re-election campaign in 2004. In other words, Haggard's influence was profoundly significant.

Ultimately, Haggard was sentenced to three weeks of counseling and received a "completely heterosexual" diagnosis from his pastoral guidance team. Despite being declared free of homosexuality, subsequent abuse continued. In 2022 Religion News Service reported that Haggard had an inappropriate sexual relationship with an underage boy and with another adult in 2009.[8]

Haggard's situation is interesting in that it demonstrates to some extent the amount of homophobia that exists within Evangelicalism. Haggard's indiscretion was largely viewed as a compromise of his values because he participated in a homosexual relationship. The fact that he was having an affair was barely addressed, much less corrected. Haggard's affair was part of a pattern that had become prevalent in Evangelicalism where various leaders were participating in either acts that they were preaching against or sexually abusing their parishioners. Many cases from the '80s and '90s had come to light, but it would be several more years before the full picture and extent of the abuse would be revealed.

Power & Abuse

The prevalence and impact of abuse in the 2000s sheds light on a troubling aspect of the evangelical community's religious leadership. During this era, numerous cases of abuse surfaced, revealing a dark underbelly within some evangelical circles. These abuses ranged from emotional manipulation and spiritual coercion to physical and sexual misconduct, with victims often silenced or disbelieved due to the authority and stature of the perpetrators.

The impact of abuse has reverberated throughout the evangelical community and further tarnished their reputation and influence within the wider culture. The victimization of evangelicals is complicated as it involves various aspects of the individual's identity, including the added dimension of their faith.

An individual's faith can be a double-edged sword as it can both help and hinder. It can help the individual through recovery but it can also prevent them from reporting their abuse. Often victims rely on their religious leaders to help guide them, but in many cases, it is the leaders who are the abusers. This results in a drastic underreporting of the crime to authorities—perhaps even more than is typical.

Power dynamics and organizational structures played a crucial role in enabling abuse within evangelical communities. In many cases, leaders within religious organizations were seen as figures of authority and trust, which created an environment where abusive behavior went unchecked. The hierarchical nature of many evangelical churches can contribute to a culture of silence and fear, where victims may feel powerless to speak out against their abusers.

Moreover, the lack of accountability mechanisms that existed in some evangelical organizations at the time contributed to ongoing abuse. Leaders used their positions of power to manipulate and control their followers, creating a toxic dynamic where dissent was discouraged and loyalty was valued above all else. In some cases, the emphasis on forgiveness and redemption within evangelical theology was weaponized to silence victims and protect abusers.

Addressing abuse within the context of evangelical leadership in the 2000s requires a deep exploration of the intricate relationship between faith, power, and accountability. The intersection of these dynamics sheds light on the systemic issues that allowed abuse to persist and perpetrators to evade consequences.

Faith, as a foundational aspect of evangelical leadership, can sometimes be manipulated to justify abusive behavior and shield abusers from scrutiny. The trust and reverence placed on religious figures can create a power dynamic that empowers abusers and silences victims. This misuse of power highlights the need for increased transparency and accountability within religious institutions.

Fortunately, a new movement was on the horizon that would empower victims to come forward. This movement would open the floodgates of disclosure, not just about abuse taking place in the Church but all across society. It was a movement that gave victims permission to say out loud #MeToo.

Since sexual abuse is almost always about power and control, we must consider where these leaders get their empowerment from. Is it due to churches' centralized and hierarchical power structures? Or, is it due to something inherent within their beliefs?

Mark Driscoll: The Embodiment of Complementarian Christianity?

In the midst of these tumultuous times, a large church in one corner of the country was celebrating 15 years of successful ministry in Seattle, Washington, and a new up-and-coming superstar pastor was making headlines. Mark Driscoll was unapologetically brash and had a specific vision for the Church. In Driscoll's early days, he participated in emerging church conversations and conferences. However, he had been largely disappointed in the direction that both the Emerging Church and Evangelicalism were heading. This led Driscoll to start his own church in the context of his vision. Driscoll's vision was called Mars Hill.

Mars Hill, also known as the Hill of Ares or the Areopagus in Athens, Greece, holds historical significance as the site of one of the Apostle Paul's pivotal presentations during his second missionary journey (Acts 17:19,22). This particular address by Paul directly confronted the prevalent religious idolatry among the Greeks. However, Mars Hill has another meaning too as it represents the hill of Ares. Ares was one of the 12 Gods of Zeus and the God of war.

This name would become prophetic as Driscoll and his leaders would go to war with culture over their hyper-evangelical beliefs. Driscoll would act more like a dictator and less like a pastor as the years went on. He would surround himself with "yes" men whose job was to help manifest his will upon the congregation. Ultimately Driscoll was able to create a megachurch of devoted followers that spanned 13 different locations.

Driscoll's followers were enthralled with the rock-style atmosphere and the rebellious nature of the church. They were even more enthralled with the hard-core preacher who was guiding this ship of rebellion. A pastor that was unafraid to talk about provocative things. A pastor whose passions were Mixed Martial Arts and beer. A pastor that might swear from time to time from the pulpit. For Driscoll's followers, he embodied a type of Christianity that was hyper-masculine and hyper-evangelical. Driscoll was a new type of hellfire preacher who was counter-cultural to the evangelical megachurch - which, in Driscoll's eyes, had become soft.

But make no mistake, Driscoll was not anti-evangelical; he was hyper-evangelical. To Driscoll's credit, he was the full embodiment of what evangelical Christianity, and in particular complementarianism, believed. From this perspective, Driscoll was not an extremist but a bold preacher willing to live out evangelical ideals in the real world regardless of who they might offend.

To be fair, Driscoll does not represent the majority within Evangelicalism and he was certainly an acquired taste even among evangelicals. However, he does exemplify how radical some evangelical beliefs are. Moreover, Driscoll is an example of why current power structures and complementarianism are both theological and practical failures.

One of Driscoll's primary methods for enforcing complementarian beliefs in his congregation was through his theories on masculinity. Sometimes this even resulted in him insulting the men in his church from the pulpit. Perhaps the most infamous story associated with his tenure was a blog post that he wrote using the pseudonym of the famous Scottish warrior William Wallace (as in the movie Braveheart). It was under this pseudonym that Driscoll created the topic called "A Pussified Nation." In his post, Driscoll scolds men not only in his own church but across the world.

> We could get every man, real man as opposed to pussified James Dobson knock-off crying promise keeping homoerotic worship loving mama's boy sensitive emasculated neutered exact male replica evangellyfish, and have a conference in a phone booth. It all began with Adam, the first of the pussified nation, who kept his mouth shut and watched everything fall headlong down the slippery slide of hell/feminism when he shut his mouth and listened to his wife who thought Satan was a good theologian when he should have led her and exercised his delegated authority as king of the planet. As a result, he was cursed for listening to his wife and every man since has been his pussified sit quietly by and watch a nation of men be raised by bitter penis envying burned feministed single mothers who make sure that Johnny grows up to be a very nice woman who sits down to pee.[9]

The post continues with a comment thread spanning 140 pages. Although this provocative post shocked people, his position was not surprising. In fact, it was this posture that would help usher in another individual's later rise to power as President of the United States. As we will discuss in the next chapter, Donald Trump embodied some of these same principles both in belief and practice. Driscoll's crassness helped create a permission structure for many evangelicals to support his campaign and ultimately elect Donald Trump as President in 2016.

Eventually, Driscoll would go on to create an unmanageably toxic environment that was steeped in militant complementarianism. Women were not allowed certain leadership roles and when they were granted leadership roles in other areas they were not allowed to challenge their male peers. Likewise, men were often pressured and held accountable for leading their wives and ensuring their households were maintaining biblical headship standards. This was not only intrusive but required men to treat their wives and children in ways they may not have felt comfortable with. Additionally, anyone who opposed Driscoll was fired.

Despite Mars Hill's initial popularity, the 2000s would see a lot of unrest for the church and Driscoll. Much of the unrest involved in-person and online protests. Ultimately, this led Driscoll to step down from power in 2006 so that Mars Hill's leadership could reorganize the church.

However, in the summer of '07 Driscoll returned to his former leadership role. This time he created a leadership team that would support his vision and blindly follow his leadership. Driscoll and his new executive elders reworked church bylaws, which resulted in Driscoll getting even more power than he had before. Then, in 2013 formal charges were filed against Driscoll by former church elders for mistreatment. This was followed up by online protests by former leaders of Mars Hill, including co-founder Leif Moi. In 2014 Driscoll finally left Mars Hill for good.

Although he left Mars Hill, he was not finished bringing his vision for the Church to life. In 2016 Driscoll opened the doors to a new church in Scottsdale, Arizona, called Trinity Church. Despite calls for Driscoll to be completely removed from the Ministry, as of the writing of this book he is still their pastor. Mars Hill disbanded in 2014. Eleven of its thirteen churches still exist but do so independently.

The story of Mark Driscoll serves as a cautionary tale, illustrating the potential for power to corrupt individuals, irrespective of their initial intentions. Driscoll's rise and subsequent fall from fame within evangelical circles highlights the consequences of authority gone unchecked. Furthermore, his narrative provides insight into the practical implications of evangelical beliefs when manifested in real-world scenarios. By examining the practical implications of complementarianism and authoritarianism, we can see how those beliefs cause real-world harm in people's lives and are, therefore, not what Jesus intended for his Church.

The New Kind of Christians

The Emerging Church had been making waves since the mid-90s as the annoying little rebellious brother of Evangelicalism. Evangelicalism had largely ignored this small movement that was directed by a few disgruntled misfits. No doubt, evangelical leaders thought this small movement would quickly fade away as another fad. And perhaps it might have, if not for a book published by a largely unknown author in 2001. In 2001, author and pastor Brian McLaren published a little Socratic dialogue called "A New Kind of Christian." The new book detailed the journey between two fictional friends who would dialogue about various aspects of their faith such as doubt, reason, mission, and spiritual practices. It was a tale of the ages that illustrated many of the conversations that were taking place throughout Evangelicalism. Surprising evangelical leaders, A New Kind of Christian quickly became a bestseller and solidified emergent Christianity as a legitimate rival.

McLaren's name was soon being whispered in Colleges and Seminaries across the country. Evangelicals tried to dismiss him as a radical liberal. However, this failed to stifle the growing intrigue surrounding him. Perhaps it was the insightful questions that McLaren was unafraid to ask or the humility and wisdom with which he chose to try and answer those questions. The fact remained that throughout the '00s McLaren was a *tour de force* who was not going to go quietly into the night.

Soon the emerging church movement consisted of more than just displaced and ostracized evangelicals. People from all denominations and religious perspectives began participating in emerging church communities throughout the country. All of them brought to their communities their unique experiences and ideas on how to do "church."

Although difficult to pinpoint or even categorize (nor would they want such designations) these new kinds of Christians were like vagabonds within Evangelicalism. They were a rebellion against the establishment and refused to be silent about the problems in Evangelicalism. Much like with postmodernism, evangelical leaders were not equipped to speak to the issues that the Emerging Church was calling out. Evangelicalism was too intertwined with modernism, and this made it difficult for them to engage with emergent Christians.

Part of the problem was that evangelicals saw emerging Christians as an anti-evangelical movement (and in some ways they were); instead of a movement concerned with the Gospel and the mission of the Church. No doubt they existed as a corrective of Evangelicalism but that was not their primary purpose. Unfortunately, evangelical leaders were unable to see past the corrective tone to enter into constructive dialogue with them. Evangelical leaders never cared to try and understand emergent Christianity from any legitimate perspective. Instead, they just saw them as an enemy who had capitulated to liberalism.

Just as they had in the past with other factions, evangelical thought leaders believed they could outgun emergent Christians with their superior intellect and cunning debate skills. Instead of listening to the concerns of these former evangelicals and exercising compassion, they chose to pursue them as though they were traversing a dense forest in hunt for heretics.

Much of what the Emerging Church was trying to do was create safe spaces for authentic conversations about life and what it meant to proclaim the Gospel in a new age. It was not as much about evangelicals as evangelicals thought it was, which speaks to the hubris of these leaders during this time. This paranoia would become problematic moving forward as it not only affected how evangelicals were treating other Christians but the culture at large. If evangelicals were willing to treat their own this way; how would they ever relate to a culture that was much more reflective of the emerging church culture than evangelical culture? The short answer is they wouldn't. They would begin a trajectory of dissociation from culture by presenting a version of the Messiah not too different from the religious leaders of Jesus' day.

Despite what evangelicals have proclaimed, there were many positive things that the Emerging Church provided for the Church at large. One such value was access. The Emerging Church attempted to downplay or eliminate entirely the hierarchy and power structure common in many evangelical churches. This meant that lay people had access to their leaders. They were safe to ask them questions. They were safe to struggle and doubt while being mentored by competent, knowledgeable leaders. This became vitally important for a generation of skeptics who desperately wanted a place to worship God more authentically. Ultimately, the emerging church movement should be viewed as an attempt to practice Christianity in the real world based on the life of Jesus, instead of simply a belief in certain propositions about him.

Evangelicals Fight Back

Evangelicals were now taking the Emerging Church seriously. They had to, they were losing too many of their congregants to these new radical communities. Enter D.A. Carson. Carson is an overpowering intellectual who has written voluminously on the New Testament. Carson has been a longstanding professor at Trinity Evangelical Divinity School and is now the Distinguished Emeritus Professor of New Testament. In 2005 Carson wrote a book that was largely based on talks he gave at Cedarville University the previous year. The book, Becoming Conversant with the Emerging Church, was meant to educate evangelicals on what the Emerging Church was, who the key leaders were, and evaluate how "biblical" the movement was.

Carson's book was a huge success within evangelical circles and soon many of the arguments presented in the book against the emerging movement could be heard uttered in colleges throughout the United States. Despite its success in sales, its utility in presenting a clear articulation of the emergent movement was inadequate.

As was the case with most non-postmodern writers, Carson's analysis of postmodernism was significantly flawed as it misrepresented its core principles. For example, a significant premise that Carson operates within requires that one can either know truth exhaustively or they cannot.

Since Carson knows that postmodernist theory rejects the idea of *absolute* truth, he deduces that they don't believe in any truth. However, this premise is incorrect because it makes use of what is called the false dilemma fallacy.

The false dilemma fallacy creates a false binary premise where the choices given are presented as the only options when more are available. The same is true here. There are more options available than the either/or he presents. We will discuss the various ways that truth expresses itself in Part Two but for now, suffice it to say, postmodernism does believe that truth can be known, but that truth is limited by things like language, perception, and bias. It would be more accurate to state that postmodernism holds to a nuanced version of truth. Moreover, they don't reject that true knowledge can be obtained, they reject that truth can be understood in its absolute form.[10]

Although Carson has ultimately created strawman arguments due to his misarticulation of the issue, this is mostly unintentional. His mischaracterization is largely the result of his misunderstanding of the nature of postmodernism. Carson was not alone in this as he simply represented a large contingent of evangelicals who were unable to see the forest for the trees.

Evangelicalism's lack of understanding was a direct result of the philosophical and theological box that modernism had forced them to exist within. Evangelicalism's attempt to present an overly simplistic view of a movement that was highly complex was their way of trying to demonstrate an intellectual immaturity that should ultimately be dismissed.

Not only does Carson's inability to think outside of his modernist binary context make it impossible for him to truly grasp the issues that postmodernism raises, but it also demonstrates the extent to which evangelicals are trapped in their philosophical/theological perspectives. The irony of the situation shows that in Carson's attempt to box in postmodernism, he has inadvertently revealed the weaknesses within his own worldview.

Carson's venture into philosophy and theology, despite his expertise in New Testament studies, may have been overly ambitious. His lack of comprehension regarding the significant impact of modernism on Evangelicalism highlights a notable shortcoming. Moreover, his arguments lacked originality by merely echoing previous critiques of postmodernism, indicating a disconnect with his intended audience. However, his engagement does underscore the substantial influence the Emerging Church had on Evangelicalism, compelling even a scholar of the New Testament to engage in response.[11]

The Globalization of Evangelicalism: The New Christendom

It could be argued that the '00s were the culmination of something that had been in the works since at least the '90s—The globalization of Evangelicalism. Globalizing Evangelicalism was a way for evangelicals to spread their values and principles by co-opting America's political and economic globalization efforts.

According to Sarah Cline from the University of California, Santa Barbara, evangelicals intensified their missionary efforts in Latin America during this period, particularly targeting Catholics for conversion.[12] Since Catholicism is the dominant religion in Latin America, a competitive dynamic emerged between the Catholic Church and the incoming Protestant evangelical missionaries. Pastors relied on their congregations for financial support and churches struggled for influence within their communities. The utilization of Christianity in this manner was a means to legitimize, consolidate, and sanctify existing social power structures.

This wasn't just a problem in Latin America. The evangelical missional movements established political power in the Philippians as well as throughout Africa. In the written work titled Exporting the American Gospel, Steve Brouwer, Paul Gifford, and Susan Rose demonstrate the potent presence Christian fundamentalists have in these places. They underscore that evangelicals have long bundled together their cultural values along with capitalism, consumerism, and Western Modernity into a package that is irresistible to the poor in these regions. Christianity acts as a cover for a more subversive cultural and economic imperialism. The authors go on to assert that the draw for these people is not the Gospel but they convert because they feel powerless to do anything else. They are looking for practical ways to change their lives and seeking spiritual aid was their only option.[13]

The subterfuge by evangelicals in using neo-colonialism to establish a democratic Christendom throughout Africa is an all too familiar echo from the past; reminiscent of other times when Western promises were made in subversive attempts at taking away a people's culture and identity for economic gain. However, whereas before, a better life was promised in a far-off utopia to those willing to leave their home behind, this time a better life is promised right at home to those willing to leave their culture and values behind. Obtaining the rights to this false gospel only cost evangelicals 30 pieces of silver.

In 2020, Lifeway conducted research into where around the world evangelicals were located. Three in five evangelicals were located in either Asia or Africa. In fact, North America was fourth on the list, behind Asia, Africa, and South America.[14] This leaves little doubt that evangelicals' efforts to replicate themselves around the world have been hugely successful.

The evangelical agenda in these nations was not just political but also religious, as there was a growing movement to eradicate homosexuality and abortion in these nations. A report by Opendemocracy.net revealed that over 28 US organizations have collectively spent a minimum of 280 million globally to shape legislation, policies, and public sentiment against sexual and reproductive rights. Notably, The Fellowship Foundation, a clandestine group, reportedly contributed over 20 million solely to Uganda.[15] Uganda has gained notoriety for its severe measures targeting the LGBTQ+ community, often perpetrating human rights violations and justifying these violations in the name of the God that was brought to them by these modern missionaries.

There are currently three countries in Africa that have the death penalty for someone caught having consensual same-sex relations: Uganda, Nigeria, and Mauritania. There are four countries where the person would be sentenced to life in prison and at least 21 other countries that would give the individual some type of legal punishment for getting caught. This means more than half of the continent has criminalized homosexuality.

Evangelical organizations like the Family Research Council have regularly supported many of these countries, from financing to advising discriminatory legislation against the LGBTQ+ community. For example, in 2010 Zimbabwe began the process of drafting a new constitution. In response, the American Center for Law and Justice (founded by Pat Robertson), created the African Centre for Law and Justice. Joining forces with the Evangelical Fellowship of Zimbabwe they promoted constitutional language that affirmed the nation was Christian and ensured that homosexuality remained illegal.

Evangelicalism 2.0

While many evangelical political leaders were replicating their values across the globe, in America, Evangelicalism was undergoing logistical changes to its leadership. The old guard was dying out and retiring which meant that their roles were being taken over by a new generation of younger leaders. Leaders like Rick Warren (former pastor of SaddleBack Church—a megachurch of over 22,000 people) and Bill Hybels (former pastor of Willow Creek—a megachurch of over 20,000 people).

Rick Warren was widely criticized by evangelicals for not being militant enough in his political views. According to William Leonard, former Dean of Wake Forest Divinity School, Warren was theologically conservative but a little more liberal when it came to social issues. For example, he joined the fight against global warming and put money into helping those with AIDS. Additionally, Warren spoke at Barack Obama's inaugural invocation. For some, Warren was the perfect person to create a bridge between the left and the right, but for others, he lacked the machismo of his predecessors. Warren has responded to these criticisms by calling the old guard "activists too partisan and overly focused on gay marriage and abortion."[16]

Bill Hybels was considered the chief expert on church leadership within Evangelicalism. His unique approach to leadership principles meant that he was unafraid to explore new, innovative ideas when it came to leading and running a church. At one time, Hybels was the most influential leader in Evangelicalism. The Willow Creek Association is like a small denomination within itself, once containing over 12,000 sister churches. However, just like Warren, Hybels lacked the killer instinct that his predecessors had.

Both leaders were interested in pushing more centrist theologies. As the New York Times Magazine characterized them:

> [There is] a push to better this world as well as save eternal souls; a focus on the spiritual growth that follows conversion rather than the yes-or-no moment of salvation; a renewed attention to Jesus' teachings about social justice as well as about personal or sexual morality. However conceived, though, the result is a new interest in public policies that address problems of peace, health and poverty—problems, unlike abortion and same-sex marriage, where left and right compete to present the best answers.[17]

According to Pew, President Bush, who once held a strong 90% approval rating among white evangelicals, was now looking at an abysmal 45%. David Welsh, Senior pastor for one of Wichita's largest evangelical churches, Central Christian Church, stated to the New York Times that *"even in evangelical circles, we are tired of the war, tired of the body bags.'*[18] For many evangelicals, the debacle surrounding the war in Iraq created an opportunity to regroup and reassess priorities; a necessary process if they were going to have any effect on the 2008 election.

This new movement toward social justice and a generally more responsible view of society was being characterized as the new Evangelicalism - created by the influence of the Emerging Church. Scot McKnight, an evangelical theologian at North Park University in Chicago echoed these sentiments when he stated: *"It is the biggest change in the evangelical movement at the end of the 20th century, a new kind of Christian social conscience."*[19] A changing view of society meant a changing view of how evangelicals saw themselves contributing to society. John Green of Pew echoed this sentiment stating: *"...That kind of hard-edge politics no longer appeals to them."*[20]

The once nascent worldview of the Emerging Church was starting to embed itself in the fabric of Evangelicalism. For the old guard, this was viewed as weak and a capitulation on the part of evangelicals. The Emerging Church's more socially conscious worldview was not just swaying centrist evangelicals but once-conservative and even fundamentalist Christians.

Rev. Gene Carlson, a prominent conservative Christian pastor, spent 40 years growing his church to more than 7,000 members. Known for his conservative activism, even leading hundreds of conservatives to jail one summer during a pro-life protest, he stated in an interview with the New York Times regarding his activism:

> I thought in my enthusiasm, that somehow we could band together and change things politically and everything will be fine. But the closing of Dr. Tiller's clinic was fleeting. Electing Christian politicians never seemed to change much. When you mix politics and religion, you get politics.

If evangelicals continued on their current trajectory they would surely fail. If the 2008 election of Barack Obama was any indication of that failure, then something needed to change.

White Evangelicals & a Black President

In 2008, the United States made history by electing its first black President, Barack Obama. Before his political career, Obama served as a civil rights attorney in Chicago, where he established connections with prominent figures in Washington. His political journey began in 1998 when he was elected to the Illinois State Senate. Swiftly rising through the ranks, Obama was chosen by the Democratic Party as their presidential candidate for the 2008 election.

The Democrats needed a strong candidate to run against the Republican nominee, John McCain. McCain, a former war hero, was not your typical Republican. McCain strongly opposed special interest groups, and he was perceived as being soft on Republican social issues, which did not sit well with evangelicals. However, McCain was also a warrior who was unafraid to stand up to those with whom he disagreed, a virtue important to evangelicals.

The Republican Party went all in on John McCain despite potential setbacks due to his anti-special interest philosophy, which ruffled feathers among important Republican voting blocs, like evangelicals. In 2000, McCain had publicly criticized evangelical figures Pat Robertson and Jerry Falwell as "agents of intolerance". Consequently, James Dobson publicly expressed his view on McCain's nomination, asserting that McCain did not align with conservative values and failed to represent the convictions of evangelical constituents.[21] Democrats knew that McCain had a strong following among swing and independent voters. If he was able to get evangelicals too, then it was going to be an uphill battle for Democrats.

Despite McCain's remarks in 2000 and Dobson's withdrawal of support, 88% of evangelicals still voted for McCain. That was more than had come out to support George Bush in the previous election race (85%).

Barack Obama's Faith

Barack Obama had a lot in common with evangelicals. Obama is what evangelicals would call a born-again Christian.[22] Obama was not raised in a Christian home. His father was a former Muslim turned atheist and his mother was a former Christian turned agnostic.

However, it was during his work in Civil Rights that Obama began considering belief in God. He saw the faith of those in African American churches and became inspired to search his soul for spiritual truth. Obama states in his autobiography that he would routinely fast and pray in order to find God. He was eventually baptized at Trinity Church in Chicago by Rev. Jeremiah Wright Jr., who was not only a scholar but also a controversial political activist.

Despite this controversial relationship with Wright, Obama became a Christian within the greatest of evangelical environments. Although white evangelicals would consider Obama's faith as influenced by "Liberal" theologians like Paul Tillich and Reinhold Niebuhr; he was also heavily influenced by Saint Augustine. Obama's pastors emphasized doctrines like original sin and salvation through grace by faith alone, as well as the authority of Scripture.

The question that would later be asked with the rise of White Christian Nationalism was if Obama reflected many of the theological values that evangelicals held, then why were they so opposed to him becoming President? Was it only because he was pro-choice? Would evangelicals have voted for him if he was white?

Obama knew he would not be able to capture the important evangelical endorsements that traditionally go to Republicans, but he did think that evangelical youth were within his reach. Younger evangelicals did not care about special endorsements; this growing demographic, who was being heavily influenced by conversations coming out of the emerging church movement cared about authenticity. Social issues like abortion, although still important, were not at the forefront like poverty and immigration.

Despite early campaigning towards those demographics, gains were only modest. According to Barna, who surveyed evangelicals after the election, most were unsatisfied with either candidate and mainly voted party lines. That said, much of McCain's support came from those complacent voters.[23]

Church or State?

After the election, evangelicals had to regroup and strategize ways to take back the Republican party. The message to the Republican party after John McCain's loss was clear: the party needs to listen to and respect the values and opinions of the evangelical voting bloc. The Republican party needed to heed the opinions of the evangelical lobbyists if they ever wanted to staff the White House again.

Evangelicals were not used to feeling ostracized from the party they had been dedicated to for the last 25 years. Nevertheless, evangelical leaders began to work even harder to get their candidate on the ballot for the 2012 election. However, in their zeal, accusations that people like James Dobson, Pat Robertson, and Jerry Falwell were blurring the lines between Church and State began circulating - an almost sacred threshold that has allowed churches to maintain the luxury nonprofit status.

There is a fine line in the world of politics between Church and State. The line is not always clear but it is a necessary threshold that not only helps ensure fairness in elections but it also enables the Church to remain a nonprofit. Maintaining nonprofit status for the Church is its lifeblood. Losing that status could very well see the collapse of the modern Church as millions rely on its tax exemptions when they donate.

However, this did not stop evangelical leaders from pushing the boundaries of that fine line in the years leading up to the 2012 election. By using subliminal messaging like "vote your conscience" or "vote biblical values" to influence their congregations, they were implicitly endorsing candidates. While churches cannot endorse specific candidates or parties, they can define values such as being pro-life, which often aligns with a particular political party, without explicitly stating it. This approach allows churches to indirectly sway Christians to vote in a certain direction without violating campaign laws.

In the years leading up to the campaign, those approaches intensified. Making the delineation even more nebulous were the relationships between special interest groups and evangelical leaders who frequently pumped money into funding these organizations. Lobbyists act as the middlemen between the individual or group and the campaign. It's a workaround for gathering support from large groups without violating cherished campaign finance laws.

Obama went into the 2012 campaign as an incumbent with a respectable 47% approval rating, which meant that unless Republicans put forth an all-star candidate, Obama would probably see a second term.[24] In a surprising move, Republicans decided to put up Mitt Romney to challenge Obama. Romney, though far from an all-star, was a highly regarded Senator who was more moderate than his alternatives. The strategy was to appeal to the widest constituency possible.

When it was announced that Mitt Romney would be the Republican nominee, some evangelical leaders began crossing that sacred line, both from their pulpits and on the national stage. There was a significant gap that they needed to bridge for their followers—Romney was a Mormon. Although Mormons consider themselves Christian, most evangelicals disagree. Some even consider Mormonism a cult. The question that Republicans had to consider was how to sell this to one of their most influential voting blocs.

In a surprising turn of events, no sales pitch was necessary. After four years with Barack Obama at the helm, evangelical leaders were eager to support Romney. This was puzzling to pundits who knew of the tension between Mormons and evangelicals. In fact, in a PRRI/RNS poll in

2012, evangelicals stated that they preferred a candidate who shared their beliefs.[25]

The dislike evangelicals had for Obama was unusual considering that he shared most of their beliefs. Even though Obama's spiritual journey was unique from that of other presidents it was not unique for evangelicals. His faith should have made him more relatable but it seemingly had no effect. In fact, James Dobson had sent out a letter to his followers titled: *Letter from 2012 in Obama's America,* which described what America would be like if Obama was re-elected. Dobson intimated that Americans would see "terrorist strikes on American soil, gay marriage in every state, and the end of Boy Scouts," to name only a few. The 16-page piece of propaganda described a "liberal apocalypse where homeschooling is outlawed, pornography is mandated for gas stations, and Russia nukes Israel."[26]

What some saw as a desperate attempt at fear-mongering to sway a voting bloc, others saw it as just the newest in a long line of questionable methods for persuading voters. From hell-fire to an apocalyptic America, evangelical leaders have used fear to steer their people since the movement began.

On paper, there should be no reason for evangelicals to support Mitt Romney. The only commonality he had with them from a religious standpoint was being pro-life. They may have also agreed on some economic and foreign policies but that is not what evangelical leaders used to persuade their congregations. Leaders like Dobson made religious arguments stating that Christians should nominate people who hold strong biblical values. That should have been referring to born-again Christian Barack Obama, but he was playing for the wrong team. Although most evangelical leaders would never admit this publicly, there is an unspoken rule that one cannot be a Christian and vote for a Democrat. This is largely based on the issue of abortion and it haunts many independent evangelicals who might otherwise vote for a Democrat.

This forces us to ask the question, why? Why is the issue of abortion so important that it trumps Godly character and wisdom? Or is there something else that underlies everything? Is there something fundamentally flawed in the evangelical worldview that would account for such an irrational paradigm? In the next chapter, we will see how this paradox comes to a head and we will begin to connect the dots that evangelical leaders have been placing throughout history.

5

Donald Trump & White Christian Nationalism

Emphasis on "White"

In the beginning, evangelicals were not excited about Donald Trump. But just like Trump sold the Republican party on his brand of politics, so too did evangelicals fall for the same sales pitch. Republicans were not difficult to convince, as they were willing to compromise their values to prevent Hillary Clinton from becoming President. Surprisingly, so were evangelicals.

The Republican party struggled throughout the Obama years to put forth a candidate who had the same strength as former President George W. Bush; for whom evangelicals turned out in droves. Evangelicals wanted a fighter in the office who wasn't afraid to stand up for their religious and political values. The only way evangelicals were going to turn out in large numbers was to find them a cowboy. Republicans found the most unexpected cowboy—Donald Trump.

Donald Trump was not a Republican. He became a Republican to become President, which was his only goal. He did not care about Americans or their plights. He did not care about America's persona on the world stage except to the extent that it helped his personal business ventures. In an interview in 2022 with Maggie Haberman, who is the author of *Confidence Man: The Making of Donald Trump and the Breaking of America*, Trump stated his reason for running for President: he wanted to be known, he wanted to be the greatest among his kind so as to be remembered forever.[1] His ambition matched well with the Republican agenda because the party was willing to do anything to prevent Hillary Clinton from becoming President and Donald Trump's popularity among the general public was very high.

Trump and evangelicals may seem like strange bedfellows but as Kristin Du Mez points out in her book *Jesus and John Wayne,* their partnership was several decades in the making. It is Du Mez's thesis that the election of Donald Trump was simply the inevitable result of an ongoing evangelical pursuit of Christian militancy and toxic masculinity. For many evangelicals, much of the biblical narrative involves stories about the warriors of God. Even Jesus is personified this way in the book of Revelation when he comes riding in on a white horse to save believers by rescuing them from destruction.

Proof of Du Mez's thesis was demonstrated in the convergence of evangelical leaders upon Donald Trump in 2015. Would Trump be willing to support their pro-life, anti-immigration, religious freedom initiatives? Only time would tell. But one thing Trump knew for certain—he needed evangelical support if he was going to win the presidency.

By now, there was little doubt that White Christian Nationalism's ideology was in full effect within Evangelicalism and the Republican party. If congressional races were any indication, then White Christian Nationalism was becoming a significant force of influence.[2]

Conservative pundits and politicians went all in on Trump's campaign and began to spread misinformation. These tactics are not uncommon in a presidential race and have, to some extent, always been a part of the political process. However, for evangelicals who see themselves as the guardians of truth, how could the overtly unethical tactics of Trump win the support of a group that prides itself on integrity?

Plausible deniability was the key. In order to give evangelicals what they needed to stay the course, pundits and evangelical leaders began to change their rhetoric. The ultimate spin campaign was soon underway to explain why such a godless person should be supported. Arguments were bountiful. For example, in order to quell evangelical hangups over Trump's past sins, some televangelists argued that Trump had recently become a Christian.[3] Despite its obvious falsity, the argument was a brilliant move that leveraged a theology of grace within Evangelicalism, allowing those concerned to dismiss Trump's indiscretions as a thing of the past—part of his non-Christian, worldly self. That meant Trump was a new man in their eyes and deserving of a clean slate.

Hillary Hatred

The hatred that evangelicals have for Hillary Clinton runs deep, although to many it is not entirely clear why. Hillary is a lifelong Methodist who attended weekly prayer breakfasts as a Senator and even taught Sunday school. As far as spiritual qualifications went, she ranked far above her opponent.

Much of Evangelicalism's disdain for Clinton began in the '90s when her husband, Bill Clinton, was President. It was during those years that many of the present "culture wars" began. Hillary stayed with and supported her husband through the tumultuous Monica Lewinsky affair, but evangelicals still could not support her, despite the many virtuous boxes she checked on paper.

When running for office, she was questioned about her past years as a lawyer: "I suppose I could have stayed home, baked cookies, and had teas." This comment flew in the face of the traditional evangelical idea that a woman's role is to be a homemaker for her husband. Evangelicals never forgot that quote and it forever colored their impression of her. Clinton was the stereotypical feminist that evangelicals despised.

Echoing this disdain for Clinton were people like Jerry Falwell Sr. who stated in 2006 at the Values Voter Summit that he hoped for a Clinton candidacy because nothing would motivate his constituency more, not even if "Lucifer" ran. The contempt that evangelicals had for Clinton demonstrated that the seeds planted by people like Francis Schaeffer in the '70s and '80s were now in full bloom. Clinton's perceived feminism was not limited to an innocent quote. Clinton held strong stances on issues like abortion and the right to choose. Her advocacy for women was an outright rejection of evangelical ideas about femininity and masculinity. Due to their profound hatred of Clinton, evangelicals would have voted for anyone running against her. What people did not realize was just how much they would fall in love with Donald Trump. It is one thing to vote against a person; it is another entirely to vigorously advocate for her amoral opponent.

Courting Evangelicals

Donald Trump knew that in order to become president he needed to court evangelical leaders. Although evangelicals are a small percentage of Republican voters; they are a powerful bloc. Their power is in their turnout. Evangelicals vote and can be relied on to do so. Given Trump's past relationships and controversies, convincing evangelicals was not going to be easy. Trump had to find the magic bullet that could persuade evangelicals to give him their vote. Did they want power? Maybe. Did they want unfiltered access to him when he became President? Possibly. Mostly, they just wanted someone to fight for their religious values and freedoms and protect them at all costs. They needed a strong man who would put the liberals in their place.

Donald Trump's pandering in 2015 was characterized by a notable lack of boundaries. His successful presidential campaign was partly attributed to his adeptness at appealing to a wide range of individuals, regardless of the sincerity behind his promises. Despite initial reservations stemming from Trump's past behaviors, his active support of evangelical special interests swiftly assuaged any concerns. By acquiescing to the requests of evangelical leaders, Trump facilitated his acceptance among their followers, resulting in a successful promotion of his candidacy within this demographic.

Many were curious how a man who had been married three times, divorced twice, was careless with vulgar language, had no apparent principles or morals, knew little to nothing about Christianity or politics, and was a habitual liar would be the primary candidate for conservative

Christians. And yet, in 2016, Donald Trump ascended to the presidency in large part because of white evangelical Christians.

Donald Trump was unafraid to do what was necessary to ensure that Christian values remained a priority of his presidency. While past presidents had been hesitant to engage in aspects of the perceived culture war between evangelicals and society, Trump was undaunted. For evangelicals, the means justified the ends, and Trump was the mercenary they were looking for. This was a different age. The Trump evangelicals were much different than the previous Bush evangelicals, which ultimately helped to define, in large part, the Trump presidency. Donald Trump was the reckoning evangelicals needed in a post-Obama world. And evangelicals were the instrument Trump needed to gain power and renown.

The persecution narrative that Donald Trump pushed worked well with the perceived threats that white evangelicals felt within the culture. His supporters were primed for the various conspiracies that would come to define "fake news" and "misinformation."

It was at the Ritz Carlton in McLean, Virginia, where Donald Trump assembled the most unlikely of bedfellows for a fateful, top-secret meeting. The gathering included the conservative Christian leaders of the so-called Council for National Policy. Instead of walking into deafening hard rock anthems and an anticipatory, cheering crowd of onlookers, Trump's guests encountered opulent chandeliers and a small crowd of pastors worshiping with hands raised and eyes closed to "Seek ye first the Kingdom of God." It was the perfect environment for wooing conservative Christian leaders.

The Council for National Policy event was originally created in 1981 by Tim LaHaye (Co-author of the Left Behind Series and then-head of the Moral Majority) and the Christian Right. It has been a staple for Republican candidates ever since. In 2015 the event was organized by Tony Perkins of the Family Research Council, James Dobson of Focus on the Family, Bob Vander Plaats of The Family Leader, and Gary Bauer. Helping to lead the charge was conservative Christian sweetheart Mike

Huckabee, who was a former pastor and upcoming candidate for the gubernatorial race in Arkansas.

The event was meant to provide Trump with useful information about what conservative Christians wanted and it also allowed leaders to learn more about how the soon-to-be President could help them with their political agendas. Trump was superb in peppering his language with religious jargon and moral absolutism. He was upfront about his failures and chalked it up to problems of the past. These leaders had plenty of grace for Trump; they just needed to hear some form of contrition in order to justify handing it over. Trump was on the offensive, using crafty language to create narratives that leaders could get behind. Trump assured evangelical leaders that they would be his top priority because "restoring religious freedom" was of the utmost importance.

This promise was an important one for evangelicals, as many conservative Christian business owners across the nation were facing lawsuits for refusing to do business with the LGBTQ+ community. They argued that being compelled to sell products or services to this community violated their religious freedom, as they believed the Bible deemed homosexuality a sin. They claimed that selling certain items or services would imply that they endorsed the perceived sin. Therefore, forcing them to do this would violate their religious freedom.

One of the first cases, and perhaps the most famous one, involved a bakery owner in Colorado who refused to bake a cake for a same-sex couple. In 2012, Jack Philips, owner of Masterpiece Cakeshop, was commissioned by a same-sex couple to bake a celebration cake for their union. Philips declined the order, citing his religious beliefs. The couple then filed a complaint with the Colorado Civil Rights Commission, who eventually went on to represent the couple in front of the Supreme Court. Ultimately, the baker won the case.[4]

Trump demonstrated a mastery of manufacturing problems where none existed. One of his tactics involved fear-mongering, particularly when it came to religious freedom. Although religious freedom was patently not under threat, Trump played on conservative fears and used them to his advantage. He specifically targeted concerns about Church tax exemptions, assuring conservatives that they would remain intact. However, his most significant exploitation came in the form of his opponent, Hillary Clinton. Trump capitalized on conservatives' deep-seated dread of a Clinton presidency; a presidency that conservatives were willing to do almost anything to prevent.

Trump's Apostle Robert Jeffress

After Trump's election, he needed someone who could help guide him in all things evangelical. Enter, Robert Jeffress. Jeffress, a megachurch Baptist pastor in Texas, and Donald Trump fit together hand in glove. Jeffress is as smart as they come and like most megachurch pastors is well-spoken, articulate, and persuasive. Jeffress can articulate a biblical argument for practically anything and used that skill masterfully with the various conservative media outlets. Not only does Jeffress have 14,000 people that he preaches to every Sunday morning but he also has a program that airs on over 1,200 television stations in the United States and across 28 other countries. Additionally, he is heard on radio stations spanning 195 countries. In other words, Jeffress has a significant influence on evangelicals around the world.

Jeffress was able to craft biblical responses and justifications seemingly out of thin air for many of Trump's indiscretions. Many of the arguments that could be heard from evangelicals throughout the country were the brainchild of Jeffress. For example, during the campaign when the tape came out of Donald Trump with Russian prostitutes, Jeffress's response on Fox News was a Master Class in spin: "...[his words were] crude, offensive, and indefensible, but they're not enough to make me vote for Hillary Clinton." When it came to light that Trump had an affair with porn star Stormy Daniels, Jeffress was quoted as saying on Fox News "Evangelicals knew they weren't voting for an alter boy."[5] Going on news programs and providing five-minute sound bytes was a perfect way for Trump and Jeffress to plant arguments in the minds of evangelicals who watched these programs in huge numbers. Jeffress' role in helping Trump connect to evangelicals cannot be overstated.

With all of the spin and obvious subterfuge, the question still lingered, do evangelicals genuinely believe the misinformation they propagate or are they intentionally embracing plausible deniability? It is important to keep in mind that many evangelicals, perhaps even most, are unwitting victims of deception. This distinction holds significance as it determines the level of culpability for perpetuating misleading information. It is also important to understand when they are victims of indoctrination and when they are co-conspirators. While those actively involved in spreading falsehoods should be held responsible, it is equally important to educate and inform those who may have unknowingly fallen prey to deceit.

The idea that evangelicals may be victims of deceit by their leaders was picked up by the National Association of Evangelicals (NAE) which published an article titled, *Clinging to Truth*. In the article, Rich Nathan pleads with evangelicals to take the truth seriously and not to cling to false narratives because by doing so they are turning away from what the Bible teaches instead of toward it.[6] In other words, to take the Bible seriously means to take the truth seriously.

Trump knew that he needed more than just advisors. He needed to surround himself with some of the most influential leaders in Evangelicalism. Jeffress worked well for Trump as one who could spin for conservative evangelicals, but Trump needed someone who could appeal to charismatics - the other arm of Evangelicalism. Trump chose the controversial and provocative Paula White to help bring in charismatics.

From Paula White to God's Ear

Trump's relationship with televangelist Paula White, who served as his spiritual advisor, is indicative of his relationship with evangelicals in general. White, the first female to pray for the Presidential inauguration, is known for promoting the prosperity gospel. This brand of Evangelicalism is centered around the belief that God desires to bless believers with wealth and health. If ever there were a brand of Evangelicalism that worked with a billionaire businessman it was the wealth and health gospel.

For Trump, Paula White had God's ear and he would often spend hours seeking advice from her. The good news for Trump was that she was also very devoted to him—an uncompromising requirement for anyone wishing to work with Trump. The extent of her devotion was demonstrated in the time she spent talking about him from the pulpit. From speaking in intercessory tongues for him to calling out for angels to intervene on his behalf, White was a perfect vessel for Trump's ideology. She had no qualms about preaching politics from the pulpit, at one point even declaring that those supporting Trump's impeachment practiced "witchcraft and sorcery."[7]

Paula White could often be heard stating things like: *"I do believe that President Trump was God's answer to so much prayer, and he was and is appointed [by God] to lead America."*[8] White knew the language that persuaded those within her brand of Evangelicalism, and she used it masterfully.

Additionally, White was the one responsible for intimating that Trump was a Christian. Citing her continued relationship with him and his family, she could testify to his "deep convictions and faith."[9] She has even asserted that she personally led Trump to Christ.[10] White is a master at creating spin narratives and she used her platform to create those narratives which were almost always picked up by the media.

Even though White in no way represents the larger evangelical contingent—in fact, many may even consider her a charlatan—it nevertheless did not stop them from believing the ideas she peddled. White was, in part, responsible for creating the persona that evangelicals saw when they looked at Trump.

Jeffress and White were only one component of a much larger phenomenon taking place. They may have been responsible for helping shape the perception that many evangelicals had of Trump but evangelicals had to be primed first in order to see him within a larger contextual worldview. That worldview was White Christian Nationalism.

COVID-19

Whether it was bad luck or simple coincidence, the most dangerous pandemic to hit the United States since the Spanish flu was upon the country in December 2019 and would test the resolve of Donald Trump and his followers. As of the writing of this book, there have been nearly 112 million people infected with COVID-19 (COVID), which has resulted in the deaths of nearly 1.3 million Americans.[11] Although many who contracted the disease have survived, an alarming number died, and many of those deaths occurred at the beginning of the pandemic and were the direct result of Trump's lackluster efforts to implement public health and safety measures.

According to the National Library of Medicine, Evangelicals were among the greatest groups who expressed hesitancy toward social distancing and masking early on, and toward vaccines once those became available. In their conclusion, they stated that those who were most hesitant were that way for faith-based reasons, specifically religious leaders who had put up intellectual roadblocks preventing them from seeing the value of vaccinations. Of those evangelicals who were vaccinated, most of them had no problem with the vaccination because they were encouraged by their faith leaders to get them. However, in both cases, it was their faith leaders, not their doctors, who were instrumental in their decision-making.[12]

In a similar study about Christian Nationalism, the National Library of Medicine came up with almost identical conclusions. It showed that nationalist Christian conservatism was the most significant factor in their anti-vaccination attitudes. This warrants the same conclusion that their faith dictated their attitude toward the vaccine.[13]

These studies demonstrate the extent of the power and control that evangelical leaders have over their people. That is, evangelicals preferred to get advice from their faith leaders regarding significant health matters than to listen to their doctors. The same phenomenon occurred in the '80s and '90s (and to some extent still does) where congregants would often go to their pastors for issues related to mental health instead of trained therapists. The amount of control and influence evangelical leaders have over their congregations is staggering. What was once a phenomenon associated primarily with fundamentalists had now become a part of conservative and mainline branches of Evangelicalism.

The Donald 2.0

In 2019 evangelicals had their chance to repent from the disaster that was the Trump presidency. If they wanted to, they had a chance to make things right and learn from their mistakes; repentance through voting. It seemed almost a divine opportunity and the solution seemed self-evident. However, to the amazement of everyone, evangelicals doubled down and voted for Trump again, turning out in even greater numbers than they did the first time. According to Pew, Trump had a whopping 84% of evangelical votes.[14] That is more than a significant difference from the previous 77%. This meant that Trump picked up approximately 4 million more evangelicals throughout the country between 2016 and 2020.

Evangelicals approved of Trump and his performance in the four years of his presidency and the numbers proved it. This time there was no feminist running against him. Joe Biden was a centrist Democrat who would have been a perfect alternative candidate for evangelicals if they wanted to send Donald Trump a message. Any illusions that evangelicals simply voted for Trump the first time because of his opponent were obliterated when they came out en masse to support Trump's bid for a second term.

Assisting Trump with their endorsements were Wayne Grudem (co-founder of the Council on Biblical Manhood and Womanhood), Eric Metaxas (evangelical radio host, speaker, and writer), Pat Robertson Sr. (media mogul, religious broadcaster, political commentator, and former presidential candidate), Tony Perkins (former Southern Baptist pastor and former president of the Family Research Council), Ralph Reed (American political consultant, lobbyist, and the first executive director of the Christian Coalition), Robert Jeffress (Southern Baptist Pastor and Televangelist), James Dobson (founder of Focus on the Family, the Family Research Council, and "political fixer"), and a number of other influential leaders.

The focus on abortion in Trump's second campaign was prominent, resonating strongly with evangelicals and potentially solidifying their support. Despite their arguments to the contrary, it does make one wonder whether evangelicals prioritize the issue of abortion above all others when voting. The prevalence of misinformation related to abortion within the evangelical community has contributed to a steadfast allegiance to the Republican party regardless of who is running.

White Christian Nationalism

The narrative that has been presented so far in this book has had a specific trajectory. That is, to paint a picture, establish a context, and lead up to a specific moment in time. Presenting this history was necessary in order to unravel why evangelicals supported a Presidential candidate of considerable ethical compromise. How was it that evangelicals were willing to look past so many blatant lies, or to compromise their integrity by embracing them and the one who offered them on a daily basis? What was in it for them? The moment this book has been leading to is the one we're living in now. Understanding how we got to this point will help us understand this period, which will in turn be necessary to understand where things are heading.

On January 6, 2021, in Washington D.C., a group of rioters breached the United States Capitol building during a protest aimed at overturning the 2020 election results. The day, which commenced with prayer, tragically concluded with five fatalities and numerous injuries. However, these events did not occur spontaneously. They were not merely the actions of an extremist faction seeking to intimidate government officials. Nor were they the actions of any one specific entity, but of disparate individuals and groups who all rioted for the sake of a common worldview. A worldview that was not of their own making but one that had been slowly working itself into various aspects of religious and political life. As the old saying goes: "The Devil is in the details." The details of history and of the events leading up to that day reveal that Devil.

On that day, waving proudly among the rioters was a white flag emblazoned with the Ichthys symbol (AKA, the Christian Fish) that read: "Proud American Christian". These same proud Christians could also be heard exercising their right to religious expression by chanting "F-Antifa!" Antifa is a collection of radical left-wing groups similar to the White Christian Nationalist group the Proud Boys but on the other end of the political spectrum.

Between the random outbursts of chants and hymns, you could still hear the faint echo of the soon-to-be former President Donald Trump beckoning the public to: "Stop the steal!" Moments before the first group stormed the Capitol many of them had been attending Donald Trump's nearby rally where he used subliminal language to urge his followers to stop Congress from certifying the election results. He had been telling his followers for weeks that the election was "stolen" and "a fraud" and that morning he continued stoking their misguided patriotism into stopping the certification of Joe Biden's election. His speech acted like the initiation of a program; a program that had been seeded in his followers long before Donald Trump was a household name. When Trump insisted that "the election had to be challenged," and urged his faithful to "stop an illegitimate President" from being sworn in, telling them that they needed to "fight like hell or they were not going to have a country anymore," the switch was flipped and the program set in motion.

In March of 2021 on the Christianity Today Podcast, Adam Kinzinger (R-Ill.) stated: "*Had there not been some of these errant prophe-*

cies, this idea that God has ordained it to be Trump, I'm not sure January 6 would have happened like it did." It was this destructive worldview that combined faith with politics and led to the actions of those people on January 6th.

The Walls of Jericho

The day before the riot, on January 5th, another protest was held. This protest was called "the Jericho March". The march was a throwback to the biblical story of when the Israelites marched around the walls of Jericho in the Old Testament. In that story, the Jews were going to take the city of Jericho but the king shut them out of the city. Therefore, God commanded them to march around the city wall for 6 days, once every day and seven times on the seventh day, after which they were to blow the shofar (an ancient musical instrument made from a ram's horn). After blowing the horn after the seventh lap on the seventh day, the walls came tumbling down and they were able to take the city. For march organizers, the Capitol was their Jericho.

The marchers donned red, white, and blue and brandished signs that read "Donald v. Goliath." As the group marched around the Capitol building they sang the hymn: "How Great Is Our God" to the resounding sound of shofars.

Often referred to simply as the Jericho Marchers, this was not the first march they participated in. The previous December they had attacked houses of worship and torn down Black Lives Matter signs throughout the city of Washington D.C. In that march, Eric Metaxas, conspiracy theorist Alex Jones, and LT. Gen. Michael Flynn spoke to the eager crowd, stoking their outrage with angry rhetoric and conspiracy theories. Inspiring the crowd further was Donald Trump who did a fly-over with Marine One, hovering over the crowd in a show of support.[15] No doubt, the Jericho marchers of January 5th felt vindicated and that God was on their side as they watched rioters break down the walls and storm the Capitol the following day.

The events of January 6th were the culmination of a series of deliberate actions taken by evangelical political and religious figures over time. Each clandestine meeting, each intentionally provocative policy decision, every sermon vilifying members of an opposing political party, and every conspiracy theory peddled by evangelical leaders, collectively contributed to the events that transpired.

In an interview with the Religion News Service about the relationship between White Christian Nationalism and Evangelicalism, Kristin Du Mez, a history professor at the evangelical institution Calvin University and author of Jesus and John Wayne said:

> A mistake a lot of people have made over the past few years... is to suggest there is some fundamental conflict between Evangelicalism and the kind of violence or threat of violence we're seeing... For decades now, evangelical devotional life, evangelical preaching and evangelical teaching has found a space to promote this kind of militancy.[16]

It has been argued that all of this is a result of White Christian Nationalism. There seem to be a lot of misconceptions about what exactly White Christian Nationalism is and who the major players within the movement are.

By the title alone, White Christian Nationalism sounds extreme. It elicits thoughts of white hoods and burning crosses. It's an extremism that most evangelicals say they don't believe in, and yet their actions seem contrary to that claim.

Andrew Whitehead and Samuel Perry, who have conducted the largest analysis of White Christian Nationalism to date, define White Christian Nationalism (more generically Christian Nationalism) as "A cultural framework—a collection of myths, symbols, narratives, and value systems that idealizes and advocates a fusion of Christianity with American civic life."[17] They go on to clarify their definition:

> The Christianity of Christian nationalism represents something more than religion... it includes assumptions of nativism, white supremacy, patriarchy, and heteronormativity, along with divine sanction for authoritarian control and militarism. It is as ethnic and political as it is religious.[18]

Whitehead and Perry's definition of white supremacy demonstrates how the various systems are woven together into a unified tapestry. Furthermore, to freely participate in these various aspects of Evangelicalism is to participate in White Christian Nationalism.

Rebranding White Supremacy

Despite what many Americans may believe, white supremacy never went away, it simply re-branded itself. Over time it has replaced its symbols, but it has never forsaken its message. We often think of white supremacy in its 1920s extreme form of white hoods and burning crosses, but white supremacy is a worldview; it is a perspective that colors how white men and women view themselves, their religion, and their country. Most white supremacists for example didn't don hoods, burn crosses, or even resort to violence. Most imposed their ideology through government or community influence. That aspect of it has never changed.

More important is the ability to identify these new symbols that white supremacists use and identify with. In our modern world masks are replaced with subversive politics; hoodie pajamas with a suit; burning crosses with a Bible, and lynchings with public policy. White supremacy remains a strong worldview in our culture. Unfortunately, in its current iteration, it has captured the hearts and minds of some evangelicals, most of whom are unaware that they are caught in its snares.

As much as evangelicals may try or want to deny it, and as much as white evangelical leaders might want to obscure it, white supremacy is built into American Evangelicalism. Ignoring it or wishing it away will never change that. Only recognizing it for what it is and actively rooting out its manifestation will be able to render it powerless.

Most religious Americans don't realize how integrated this worldview has become with Christianity. Fundamentalists like Billy Sunday, who influenced thousands of Americans in the early part of the 20th century, were known to take bribes characterized as donations from the Ku Klux Klan to promote their agenda. Other evangelists like Bob Jones, Charlie Taylor, and Alma White spoke freely in their promotion of the Klan's values at their rallies. These evangelists spread the gospel of white supremacy throughout the country in speech and song.[19]

While not solely responsible for spreading white supremacy, the active participation of these fundamentalist preachers in its spread demonstrates the extent to which that worldview had begun to influence Evangelicalism on a larger scale. Though this does not supply a reason for why so many evangelicals voted for a white supremacist like Donald Trump, it does show us how that worldview might not be as foreign to them as one might think.

Just the Facts Ma'am: Denialism

Many evangelicals take issue with the idea of White Christian Nationalism. Some even deny outright that it exists. These individuals are called denialists. They believe that denying something that is verifiably true creates in and of itself another truth. As long as people believe the premise of the denial, then it paradoxically asserts a positive truth of its own.

Donald Trump popularized denialism through his rhetoric about fake news. Instead of arguing the logic of a claim, denialists outright reject the legitimacy of the claim. This ensures that the truth of the claim can never be substantiated because the premise is outrightly rejected. Denialism should be differentiated from ignorance. Some people will deny an axiom simply because they lack the knowledge that could substantiate it for them. A denialist is one who outright rejects a premise after being faced with irrefutable evidence to the contrary.

This requires us to consider that perhaps our connection between Evangelicalism and White Christian Nationalism is inaccurate. Is there verifiable, irrefutable evidence to the contrary? Luckily, the aforementioned Whitehead and Perry study has provided us with those facts. The study the authors conducted contained the following statements which the respondents answered using an agreeable scale:

1. "The federal government should declare the United States a Christian nation."
2. "The federal government should advocate Christian values."
3. "The federal government should enforce strict separation of church and state."
4. "The federal government should allow the display of religious symbols in public spaces."
5. "The success of the United States is part of God's plan."
6. "The federal government should allow prayer in public schools."

One of the conclusions of their study was that 52% of all Americans agree with the major tenets of Christian Nationalism. Of those Americans, 88% were white evangelical.[20] The study broke those respondents who affirmed White Christian Nationalism at least to some extent into two categories: those who strongly agree with the tenets (AKA, Ambassadors), and those who partially agreed (AKA, Accommodators). Of those pertaining to these groups, 55% were Ambassadors (half living in the South and one-third living in rural areas) and one-third were Accommodators (mostly living in suburbs and small towns, one-third lived in the South, one-third lived in the Midwest, and the rest were in rural areas).[21]

Additionally, theologies that White Christian Nationalists hold also corresponded to those who were surveyed. Although most of the beliefs could just as easily be held by people outside of Evangelicalism, one was particularly noteworthy. Over two-thirds of White Christian Nationalists hold to a literal interpretation of the Bible. Although there are varying perspectives on literalism, 85% believe that the Bible is the inspired Word of God.[22]

The paradox of White Christian Nationalism is how little theology plays in its ethical policies. For this group, theology informs the foundation and purpose behind their ideology (Dispensationalism) but not their policies (Constructivism). This in part, is also true of Evangelicalism. Although evangelicals are more inconsistent (using theology when it helps their agenda), they mostly adhere to a similar separation.

The Sum of Its Parts

Like any human being, evangelicals are the sum of their parts. They are the inevitable result of their forefather's agenda and their movements' beliefs. Many of their beliefs have been forged in the fire of their political ambitions. And like any thinking human being, they have presuppositions and biases that go into what they think and how they behave. There is no avoiding these aspects of human nature. But there is a significant difference between those who simply accept this premise as true and those who are self-reflective; between those who are critical thinkers and those who accept the status quo. Until white evangelicals begin to use these evaluative tools, they will continue in their struggle to understand what is right from what is wrong; between what is true and untrue.

As of this writing (2024), 1 in 10 white evangelicals still believe that Trump's election was stolen in 2020.[23] This provokes an interesting question, are evangelicals more prone than other Christians to believe in conspiracy theories? Is there a way to understand their psychology? Or, is there something inherent within Evangelicalism that makes them more prone to be convinced of outlandish theories? The answer to each of those questions is yes. Those within Evangelicalism have been bred and programmed to adhere to the status quo—to toe the party line. They have been convinced by the idea that their inability to do these things will damn their soul.

From a hypermasculine theology that has been preached by evangelicals for the last 40 years; to the intentional cultivation of fear through Dispensationalism, it should not be surprising that an angry mob of Christians stormed the Capitol building on January 6th, 2021. In an interview in February 2021 with Religion News Service, Andrew Whitehead associate professor of sociology at Purdue University and co-author of the book "Taking America Back for God" stated that the riots were perpetuated by a "cultural framework" bolstered by "mutually reinforcing" elements.[24]

Although the majority of people who attended the rally that day were peaceful, they were anything but well-intentioned. Most were there to pray that God would overturn the election. Despite its irrationality, many believed they would see divine intervention. So convinced were they of the lies that Trump had peddled to them, that many traveled from all over the country to participate in this rally—to play their part in God's work. And for the thousands that did not show up, they still participated through prayer from the comfort of their living rooms as they watched gates being torn down, and people being trampled.

The blind faith and dedication necessary for someone to believe that God would reinstate a man to the most powerful office in the world who was morally bankrupt, a pathological liar, narcissistic, incompetent, and racist, is profound. Despite the fact that nothing about Donald Trump represented Jesus Christ, on that day, Donald Trump was their Messiah.

On May 30th, 2024, Donald Trump was convicted on 34 counts of trying to influence the 2016 election through hush money. Despite this felony conviction, support for Trump for the 2024 election remains high.

6
THE AMERICAN PRECIPICE

THROUGHOUT OUR SURVEY, WE have noted the evolution of Evangelicalism from its relationship with early Fundamentalism to becoming a distinct movement that emphasized cultural engagement. In recent years, however, Evangelicalism has faced criticism for its perceived lack of positive influence on American culture. Critics argue that instead of fostering constructive dialogue and collaboration with those of differing beliefs, evangelicals have been seen as imposing their values on others. Perhaps, evangelicals have been overly concerned with the spec in the other's eye while ignoring the plank in their own.

In this chapter, we conclude Part One. We will cover the remaining years that bring us to where we are today. We will see that much of what we have discussed has contributed to the overall perception of Evangelicalism in our current American culture. We will also see the value of certain humanistic movements, often labeled "liberal" under the banner of "political correctness" by evangelicals. Evangelicals tend to see these ideas and movements as anti-evangelical because they shine a light on the corruption and abuse within their ranks. Moreover, this chapter will begin connecting the pieces we have scattered throughout Part One.

Where Did the Emerging Church Go?

A once robust phenomenon impacting Evangelicalism in profound ways had all but vanished from the picture by the late '00s. Where did it go? Many evangelical leaders would tout that they were the reason for its disappearance, claiming victory over this fringe movement. A movement they deemed dangerous because it threatened their power and influence. The movement encouraged evangelical laity to question their leaders and to challenge deeply held views. The conspicuous absence of emerging church leaders from the publishing world and blogosphere helped to stoke these rumors.

However, the Emerging Church never left. In fact, just the opposite—it grew. Its apparent silence was not a sign of defeat but of victory. The Emerging Church no longer needed to publish because all had been said. The critique had been made and now this group was no longer the type of ecclesiastical fringe movement that it once was. Emerging churches began to disappear because they were no longer needed. Their ideas had become a worldview—a worldview that is now known as Progressive Christianity.

Progressive Christianity

Progressive Christianity is not to be confused with progressive liberalism. Progressive liberalism is a political leftist movement whereas progressive Christianity is a religious worldview. Progress in this sense means moving forward in Christian understanding one step at a time in a process that would become known as deconstruction.

Deconstruction is a process of theological reevaluation and reform that an individual goes through. Many people who go through this process are victims of some kind of Church trauma and have decided to reevaluate their beliefs. Although many of these traumas were experienced in Evangelicalism, there is a significant contingent of former Catholics as well. Overall, progressive Christianity contains people from across the spectrum, politically and theologically.

Unfortunately, in the beginning, most people only deconstructed, which left many feeling hopeless and turning towards atheism. As a result, the process of reconstruction became an important next step. It is the process that reconstructs new beliefs based on the individual developing their own conclusions instead of relying on those that were given to them by their church. This process has helped to make the progressive Christian worldview more than just a gateway to atheism but a holistic process of self-discovery.

As stated before, progressive Christianity is not a church or denomination. Although there are progressive Christian churches, progressive Christianity is a perspective. Many of these Christians are integrated into traditional denomination-based and mainline churches. However, there is also a significant contingent that has stopped going to Church (AKA, The Nones). People who share the progressive Christian worldview do not hold a joint space on the political spectrum (e.g., they're not only liberal or conservative). Instead, this perspective fosters debate and learning in order to help individuals gain a better understanding of who they are in light of who God is.

In stereotypical fashion, Evangelicalism has come out strongly against this worldview. As is the case with any movement that challenges its authority, Evangelicalism has attempted to dissuade its people from investigating progressive Christianity out of fear that their questioning will result in them leaving Evangelicalism. Therefore, evangelical leaders like John Piper, Wayne Grudem, Alisa Childers, Sean McDowell, D.A. Carson, and Timothy Keller's Gospel Coalition, have come out strongly opposed to this worldview. Their aversion towards the Emerging Church pales in comparison to their abhorrence of progressive Christianity. This is largely because evangelical leaders have picked voices on the fringes to critique instead of the majority of progressives who just want to worship God without political intervention.

These evangelical leaders often label the movement as shallow, unbiblical, and ultimately heretical. As experts in subliminalism, they pump their critiques full of jargon and cliches meant to scare their congregants away from investigating or participating in progressive conversations. In reality, however, Evangelicalism's anger is a result of what can be observed when the light of truth exposes their indiscretions. Progressives are the object of their wrath simply for holding the flashlight.

Certainly, progressive Christianity has its own problems that it must address in order to remain vibrant and healthy, but such is true of any new movement. It has to evolve to remain dynamic and learn from its mistakes. It must remain flexible enough to constantly be reinventing itself. *Ecclesia reformata, semper reformanda,* "The Church reformed, always reforming!"

#SilenceIsNotSpiritual & the Hashtag Movements

#SilenceIsNotSpiritual is a movement formed in the wake of #MeToo by evangelical women and other faith leaders from across the world to help combat sexual violence and abuse. As Time magazine reported, within just a few hours of the hashtag's appearance it garnered over 3,000 signatures including prominent leaders like Jenn Hatmaker, Amena Brown, and Lynne Hybels.[1]

In a world where evangelical women oftentimes operate in the various subcultures of music, writing, and teaching, their voices were starting to be heard by their male counterparts. It has been primarily complementarianism that has relegated women to these less influential and sometimes less glamorous ministries. However, inspired by brave women who came forward in the wake of the #MeToo movement, some evangelical women were no longer remaining silent.

When it comes to violence against women there exists a cognitive dissonance not just in Evangelicalism but among Protestant churches in general. In a survey conducted by Lifeway Research, 87% of pastors believe that their church is a safe haven for domestic violence. With that said, only 52% of those surveyed have a specific policy or plan in place to address these issues. Additionally, almost half of all of the pastors surveyed (47%) said they were unsure if anyone in their congregation had been a victim of domestic violence.[2]

Ignorance is never an excuse to allow predators to operate freely within an organization. However, when an organization does not find it necessary to address issues like this within its congregation or denomination, then they are being complicit in its crime. The response that some evangelical leaders had to movements like #MeToo is just one example of how evangelical leaders manipulate their people through political activism. In the same way that early American Christians deemed slavery a political and not a religious issue in order to justify it, modern American Christians continue to apply similar methods to other civil rights movements today. To be clear, not all evangelical leaders oppose the #MeToo movement. Although initially, most of those who supported it were evangelical women like Beth Moore and Megan Lively, through the years some evangelical men have also supported the movement.

When it comes to understanding civil rights movements there are important distinctions that must be made—especially for Christians. This is a distinction that many evangelical leaders fail to make when they speak out about the issue. There are two ways to look at a movement like #MeToo. The first is to see it as a political movement—which is often the go-to approach for evangelicals.

The second is to see it as a conceptual movement. What astute evangelical leaders understand is that behind every politically motivated movement, there is a truth. They understand that despite whatever political agenda a movement might have, it is ultimately based on some injustice. For example, instead of acknowledging and addressing the various ways that systemic racism still exists in America, many conservative leaders chose to disarm the call for justice by calling out the political liberal agenda behind the #BlackLivesMatter movement instead. They then went on to come out in support of movements like #AllLivesMatter and #BlueLivesMatter. In doing this they not only dismissed the legitimate concerns that African Americans were raising, but they also created a permission structure for their congregants to dismiss the problem of injustice clearly evidenced throughout the country. Instead of being reactionary to movements that call out injustice, evangelicals should be leading the charge for justice, just as Jesus did. If evangelical leaders dedicated a mere fraction of the efforts they give to issues like abortion towards calling out systemic racism, movements like #BlackLivesMatter would not be needed. Ironically, it is because of their indifference and inaction that social justice movements develop. Their acceptance of the status quo sets the bar for the rest of the country.

The Evangelical Spin Doctors

There is an algorithm that toxic leaders often employ in order to convince their people to come out against these important social movements. It is a formula that has been used since the dawn of Evangelicalism.

First, they label the movement "political." They may even offer examples of liberals who support the movement in order to evoke negative emotions in their followers. Second, they spin the political aspect to argue that its real purpose is to subvert their Christian faith. This will often fall into the culture war rhetoric. Finally, they appeal to the Bible to make a religious argument that supports their premise, oftentimes cherry-picking verses to create a false narrative.

An example of this was the roll-out of the vaccine during the COVID-19 pandemic. In general, apart from perhaps a small fringe, evangelicals are not opposed to inoculation. American children are required to be vaccinated before starting school. There are millions of evangelical children in the school systems who have all been vaccinated. But a handful of evangelical leaders were able to convince a large contingent of evangelicals not to get vaccinated for a virus that was killing millions around the world, simply by using the aforementioned formula. The first arguments that were made fostered political conspiracies aimed at Doctor Anthony Fauci and the medical establishment (The National Institutes of Health and the World Health Organization). Undermining medicine generally in the process of discrediting one vaccine may have led many evangelicals to seek healthcare advice from their religious leaders instead of medical professionals, not only during the pandemic but also in the years since.

From the Jewish prophets to the book of Revelations, apocalyptic literature was always born out of crisis. The same is true when invoking those prophecies. Capitalizing on the COVID crisis and using dispensationalism as their guide, some religious leaders began claiming that the vaccine was "the mark of the beast." They spread the false narrative that there existed an international plot to infect the world so that they would be required to take a vaccine that contained something akin to nanotechnology, which would make it possible to track Americans.[3]

The same formula was applied to the #MeToo movement. Some leaders believed that the movement was a product of the feminist agenda, which as we have discussed is a political buzzword for evangelicals meant to stir negative emotions. Take John MacArthur's statement when addressing his Master's Seminary student body in 2019:

> There seems to be less and less willingness to fight these days among many evangelical leaders. They seem to be capitulating to whatever the whims of the culture happen to be. And that is because we now are into about the fourth decade of pragmatism and it has sucked all the masculinity out of so many men who are unwilling to take a strong stand when it may be unpopular.
>
> Caught up in the feminist agenda are evangelicals who don't want to offend people because they're pragmatic and they've sold their souls to pragmatism in ministry so they become part of the #MeToo or #YouToo, or this race or that race, or this identity or that identity. They lose the fierceness that is required in defending the faith.

MacArthur goes on further to rehash the same argument in different ways, but in this excerpt alone, one can observe the aforementioned formula. The buzzwords are aplenty. First, MacArthur uses phrases like "capitulating to culture," which is based on the fear that Christians are not to be "of the world." He then cites the philosophy of pragmatism as the first enemy. Pragmatism is a view of truth that says the meaning of a theory or its truthfulness should be judged on how practical it is in the real world. Although this is a valid theory of truth, he is using it in a way that communicates that affirming the theory's validity is akin to denying those truths in scripture that might not be practical. The logical next step is to deny the truth of Scripture. However, he is also equivocating "practical" with "easy" and, in so doing, he misrepresents what Pragmatism means by creating a false dichotomy.

Next, he employs another political enemy: feminism. MacArthur does this by making the connection between the political philosophy of feminism and the #MeToo movement. Finally, he brings in the individual's faith and implies that in going along with these movements one is compromising their faith, or choosing the easy faith instead of the faith demanded by Scripture.

Despite the millions of people around the world who heed the words of people like MacArthur, nothing he stated was actually true. He, like many evangelical leaders of the same ilk, creates narratives whereby issues of culture are made into issues of spiritual warfare. They make people believe that there exists a deep conspiracy that is meant to specifically undermine Christianity and that this is all a part of the end times; it is all a part of how Satan will deceive Christians.

However, in reality, the subversiveness is not only based on the cultural issue itself but is often an attempt at misdirection in order to take attention away from whatever special interest they themselves might be promoting. In the case of the #MeToo movement, it was to redirect evangelicals away from the abuse happening in their own communities. The #MeToo movement may be political but the courage it gave women throughout the country exposed the underbelly of Evangelicalism and put in motion an era defined by uncovering sexual and spiritual abuse.

Furthermore, this goes deeper than conspiracies and misdirection. It goes to the heart of Evangelicalism's pattern of dehumanizing others through political and theological agendas. The disdain towards movements like #MeToo is often an attempt at getting rid of the light they shine on Evangelicalism itself.

The Secret Sins of Evangelical Men

In 2019 the Houston Chronicle published an expose on the Southern Baptist Convention (SBC) which showed that hundreds (later thousands) of people—particularly women—were sexually abused over the course of 20 years. Not only did it document the abuse but it also demonstrated that the SBC had been complicit in covering up the abuse and propagating it by reassigning predators to other churches.[4]

Even though this was not news to the SBC, the fact that their sins had been made public meant that they needed to address the issue. Only then did the SBC decide to commission a study to understand the extent of the abuse. The Chronicle found that the SBC spent years covering up sexual assaults of parishioners. The primary reason for the cover-up had to do with liability. The abuse was not just limited to local pastors but was committed by those higher up in the SBC leadership as well.

For years the SBC had been asked to construct a database of those clergy who had been convicted of sexual abuse. In 2008 the SBC explained: "We cannot tell our churches who they can or cannot hire." This resulted in many sexual offenders continuing to prey on congregations.

According to the Chronicle's investigation, there were over 700 victims from 2000-2019, abused by over 380 leaders. However, since sexual assaults are one of the most underreported crimes, those numbers are probably much higher.

Despite the fact that complementarians believe that women are equal in worth, they just perform a different role than men, the SBC situation reveals the extent to which this is not practiced. Complementarian theology has dehumanized women by limiting their rights and viewing them as inferior. The theological milieu of complementarianism provides men the implicit right to take advantage of others through the power granted to them. At the end of the day, women are seen as the enemy if they come forward. They are viewed as the ones destroying the family. Furthermore, the continuation of this form of patriarchy is enabled by the indoctrination of conservative women who not only buy into it as a biblical mandate but are also convinced of their own inferiority.

If the trauma associated with the sexual abuse that these women faced in the SBC was not bad enough, many of them also suffered spiritual trauma. From victim blaming to patriarchal preaching, spiritual abuse runs the gamut. Some of these women were even humiliated publicly. The SBC in particular made it a priority to protect their political interests by fostering a culture of plausible deniability and asserting that they "don't have the right to tell churches who they should or should not hire." However, in 2023 they disfellowshipped several churches for hiring women as pastors. For whatever reason it was okay for them to get involved when it meant that women would gain power, but when the power of abusers was threatened, there was nothing they could do. The clear double standard illustrates the lengths to which the SBC is willing to go, in order to protect the power of the men who lead that organization.

In May of 2024, Matt Queen, pastor and former vice president at Southwestern Seminary (the SBC's seminary), was indicted for obstruction of justice during the ongoing investigation by the Department of Justice regarding these assaults. It is claimed that Queen "knowingly altered, destroyed, mutilated, concealed, covered up, falsified and made false entries in a record, document and tangible object with the intent to impede, obstruct, and influence the investigation."[5] Despite promises of transparency and reform, the SBC is still trying to cover up their indiscretions. This type of cover-up is not new to the seminary. In 2018 a federal lawsuit revealed that the seminary had fired former president, Paige Patterson, who was accused of covering up a rape and intimidating the victim.

Sexual abuse is not limited to the SBC or their seminaries. Throughout the last 15 years and largely because of movements like #MeToo, many trusted leaders throughout Evangelicalism have been exposed for abusing women. According to the Associated Press, a study by 3 of the largest Protestant clergy insurance companies found that from 1987 to 2007, 7,095 out of 160,000 churches reported sexual abuse. The study claimed that between those years there were on average 260 claims per year.[6]

Mike Bickle

Unless you are a part of Pentecostalism you may not be familiar with Mike Bickle. However, Bickle is a well-known charismatic Preacher and founder of the megachurch the International House of Prayer Kansas City. Bickle has been a leader and important voice in charismatic circles for 40 years. He was the leader of a Bible school and is an accomplished author.

Bickle became a Christian after an encounter with the group Fellowship for Christian Athletes at the age of 15. That fateful encounter set Bickle up in subsequent years to build a significant ministry, including serving at several megachurches and founding his own megachurch consisting of over 2,500 staff members. His church was also responsible for creating the annual OneThing conference which was focused on worship and eschatology for young people.[7]

The OneThing conference was created from the vision of a former staffer and friend of Bickle's by the name of Paul Cain. You might call Cain the Billy Graham of the neo-charismatic and charismatic movements of the '40s and '50s. His early success saw tents full of 30,000 to 40,000 people throughout Europe. However, just as quickly as he arrived on the scene he vanished.

Cain did not reappear in the public eye until the '80s, during the Jesus People movement, to work with Mike Bickle and others in various leadership roles. Throughout the years Cain amassed a significant resume serving as advisor to three Presidents, including being special ambassador to the Middle East for Bill Clinton. As liaison for Bill Clinton, he helped broker talks between the United States and Saddam Hussein as well as with Benjamin Netanyahu. Cain also served as a consultant for the CIA and FBI.

In 2005, Cain admitted to sexual misconduct or, as he stated, he participated in an "immoral lifestyle" by being a practicing homosexual while married.[8] Cain also admitted to being an alcoholic and officially resigned from his ministry.

Enter Bob Jones (not associated with Bob Jones University), another player in this saga and one of the founders along with Bickle and Cain of what was called the Kansas City Fellowship (later Metro Vineyard of Kansas City). All three encountered one another in the late '80s. Jones is credited for his prophecy to Bickle about the formation of the aforementioned conference, OneThing. However, in 1991 Jones was disfellowshipped from Vineyard Christian Fellowship (VCF) for sexual and spiritual misconduct. According to VCF, Jones was preying on spiritually vulnerable women and used his spiritual authority to manipulate them into misconduct. The women explained that they did not want to come forward due to their respect for Jones, but after confronting him they had no choice but to appeal to church leadership. Although Jones admitted to the misconduct when confronted by leadership, he has always downplayed the incidents by emphasizing that the misconduct did not include intercourse.[9]

The three men known as the Kansas City Prophets were active participants in the "Latter Rain" movement, which emerged from the neo-Pentecostalism movement discussed in chapter 1. Despite being viewed as controversial within Pentecostal circles, they managed to amass a considerable following over time. Their prophecies, preaching, books, conferences, and churches all emphasized the importance of being prepared for the end times, and their teachings had a profound influence on millions of people.

In 2023, Mike Bickle was accused of sexual misconduct spanning decades. Adding to the irony, Bickle not only severed ties with his two former friends for their misconduct but also served on the board that judged and terminated Jones for his own sexual misconduct, while simultaneously engaging in the same behavior.

It is worth noting that in each of these instances, the organizations that employed these men demonstrated a serious commitment to addressing the allegations brought against them. If there is anything positive that came out of this situation, it was that none of the victims were marginalized or silenced in an effort to shield these well-regarded pastors.

America's Apologist

Ravi Zacharias was arguably Evangelicalism's most successful apologist. Born in 1946 to Indian parents, Zacharias' life was mostly mundane until he attempted suicide at the age of 17. It was at that time where he met a local Christian worker who introduced him to John 14, which convinced him that only a life lived for Christ was worth living.[10] The rest was history.

For the next 50 years, Zacharias dedicated himself to the defense of the Christian faith. He published more than 30 books dedicated to his cause and was the founder of the Ravi Zacharias International Ministries (RZIM), an organization dedicated to apologetics. A product of Trinity Evangelical Divinity School, Zacharias spent time teaching at various universities including Cambridge.

Then, in 2017 the first indications that something might be amiss came to light. A woman by the name of Lori Anne Thompson filed a lawsuit stating that Zacharias had exchanged inappropriate texts that included nude pictures. Although the case was settled out of court and Zacharias claimed he was innocent, the damage had been done. It would only be a matter of time before investigators would find more people with stories to tell.

In 2020 Zacharias died of cancer. Four months after his death an investigation was launched and what they discovered shocked the evangelical world. According to a report by Christianity Today, three women had come forward and claimed that Zacharias had sexually harassed them, which included masturbating more than 50 times in front of them.[11]

Ultimately, it was discovered that Zacharias leveraged his reputation as a famous apologist both in the United States and overseas to abuse massage therapists. He used his international travel as a smokescreen for these abuses. He not only used funds from his organization but preyed on his victim's spiritual problems to lure them into his grasp.

An investigation conducted by the RZIM organization found that not only were the claims by these victims true but there were also additional victims—perhaps as many as 200 throughout the world. Interviews with these victims were truly disturbing as some even indicated that he would pray with them after raping them, thanking God for what had happened. During the investigation, hundreds of photographs of his victims were found on his phone which sealed his fate as a predator.

As is common among powerful evangelical men, it was discovered that Zacharias had created an environment within his organization where he acted like a dictator. He had developed an atmosphere of fear where he had no accountability. It is believed that the world may never know to what extent Zacharias abused others, as many are bound by non-disclosure agreements.[12]

The Godfather of Fundamentalism

Bill Gothard was the Godfather of fundamentalism. Gothard's organization, the Institute in Basic Life Principles (IBLP), was an independent fundamentalist organization meant to teach extreme complementarianism and other fundamentalist doctrines. Although the organization had been around since 1961, it gained popularity in 2008 by being featured on TLC's The Duggar Family, a program in which the family had participated. In 2015 the eldest son Josh Duggar would be convicted and sent to prison for molesting five girls.

In 2014 IBLP placed Gothard on indefinite leave while he was being investigated for sexually harassing around 34 female employees and volunteers throughout the years. Although no criminal charges were brought against him, in 2016 another lawsuit was filed claiming sexual harassment and assault.

In the documentary Shiny Happy People it was revealed that Gothard's organization helped to cover up the assaults. IBLP was the most prominent homeschooling association in Evangelicalism and it was a front for Gothard and others to abuse women and girls. It was a way for Gothard to pass on his extreme patriarchal teachings to other men as well. Despite all of the allegations made against Gothard, he was never convicted because the statute of limitations had run out for most of the cases.

According to reports, Gothard would target women who were already sex abuse victims, believing them to be easier prey. He would offer them counseling services. He would often blame the victim for their assault based on things like the clothes they wore. Additionally, one victim stated that the organization sold her into sex slavery and other girls were locked in rooms to force compliance. Although never corroborated, it is believed that Gothard's sexual exploits extended beyond his own into other organizations and churches creating a network of sexual abuse and cover.

Bickle, Jones, Zacharias, the SBC, and Gothard are just a few examples meant to represent the multitudes of cases where evangelical men have used their positions of power and complementarian theology to justify sexual and spiritual abuse. These are not just fringe cases but have affected thousands of evangelical women and are based on a theology interwoven into the fabric of Evangelicalism.

The disenfranchisement of women within Evangelicalism is part of a long history of not just subjugation but a view that women are intellectually inferior to men. For example, women did not get the right to vote until 1920. For almost 150 years of this country's history, women were viewed by white men as inferior at making important decisions. Even after being given the right to vote, many women were prevented from voting due to race, which was not included in the 19th Amendment. Native American women, for example, were not allowed complete freedom to vote until 1962.[13] This demonstrates that white men have been actively involved in discriminating against women voicing their opinions.

Is it possible that white men had good reason to prevent women from voting? Are women intellectually inferior to men? William T. Sedgwick, a biologist, professor at the Massachusetts Institute of Technology, and a health consultant to the United States stated in 1914 to *The New York Times*:

> It [the right to vote] would mean a degeneration and a degradation of human fiber which would turn back the hands of time a thousand years... Hence it will probably never come, for mankind will not lightly abandon at the call of a few fanatics the hard-earned achievements of the ages.

For Sedgwick, the evolution that had fostered the hierarchical establishment for most of human history happened for a reason. Humans should not mess with the natural order because doing so could cause the collapse of society. Sedgwick was not a fringe scientist espousing urban legends but a highly educated and well-respected biologist. He represented the majority opinion in the United States during that time. Another theory, developed in the field of medicine, asserted that it was not good for women's reproductive health to vote since it would cause them too much mental strength.

In addition to these mainstream academic theories, there existed cultural stigmas that contributed to the overall cultural antipathy towards the idea that women were competent to vote. Given that we are currently only a couple of generations removed from those ignorant days we cannot think that it is of no consequence to us today. These ideas did not just disappear when legislation changed, they were and still are a part of our subconsciousness—the same aspect of our mind that makes decisions and acts out beliefs.

Unfortunately, this is just one of many ways that the idealism of evangelical theology dehumanizes people. Over the past 10+ years, the #BlackLivesMatter movement has played a significant role in modern civil rights and its mission is to bring to light the various ways African Americans continue to suffer violence and inequality.

The American Dream?

What do you want to be when you grow up? That is a question that permeates the lives of American children. From princesses to astronauts, the idea that you can be anything you want to be is based upon what Americans call, "The American Dream." It is the idea that in America the future is open, and as long as you are willing to work hard and persevere through difficulty, an individual can achieve upward mobility in society.

The American dream is based on *The Declaration of Independence*, which states that "all men are created equal" and have the inalienable right to "life, liberty and the pursuit of happiness." The problem with ideals is they are not real. And when boys of color grew up they realized that the American dream was not intended for them. This was echoed in the words of the great American poet Langston Hughes who wrote, in part:

Let America be America again
Let it be the dream it used to be.
Let it be the pioneer on the plain
Seeking a home where he himself is free.

(America never was America to me.)

Let America be the dream the dreamers dreamed—
Let it be that great strong land of love
Where never kings connive nor tyrants scheme
That any man be crushed by one above.

(It never was America to me.)

O, let my land be a land where Liberty
Is crowned with no false patriotic wreath,
But opportunity is real, and life is free,
Equality is in the air we breathe.

(There's never been equality for me,
Nor freedom in this "homeland of the free.")[14]

For people of color (and women), the American dream has been something only attainable for white men. Many have even argued that the lack of upward mobility says more about the collective consciousness of these groups than it does any conspiracy. However, history seems to demonstrate something entirely different.

Symbolic Racism

Part of the reason that many white people have difficulty accepting the fact that they might be racist is that they don't practice overt forms of racism. That is, they don't use the "N-word" or they don't actively oppress black folks in the traditional sense. Unfortunately, many white people believe that is what constitutes racism. And although it is true that overt racism was the most significant form throughout the post-Civil War era, it has changed in modern times. In today's age, the most significant form is symbolic racism.

Symbolic Racism is a newer term meant to describe an old reality. It refers to the coherent belief that reflects a one-dimensional prejudice and stereotype towards people of color.[15] According to David Sears and P.J. Henry, there are four stereotypes that often accompany this form of racism.

- Black people no longer face much prejudice or discrimination.
- The failure of black people to progress results from their unwillingness to work hard enough.
- Black people are demanding too much, too fast.
- Black people have gotten more than they deserve.[16]

This form of racism can often be more dangerous than its more explicit version because those who possess this type of racism are rarely able to see it. As a result, it can go long periods without accountability—just as it has in the United States. It could be argued that conservative Evangelicalism, not just White Christian Nationalism, contains a certain level of implicit racism.

For years evangelicals have remained firm in their belief that accusations of racism toward them are a Trojan Horse created by their rivals and are not a reflection of reality. Part of the reason for this has to do with their misunderstanding of racism. For many white evangelicals, their idea of racism is overt and they don't see how evangelicalism's' historical actions played a role in developing their subtle racist tendencies today.

Protecting them from this awareness are their leaders who oftentimes "white-wash" the history that has contributed to all forms of racism. Despite these denials, there is ample evidence suggesting that not only have evangelicals been complicit through their silence, but also participated in its proliferation.

There is a wide-spread belief held by white Americans that systemic racism is simply a political ideology and has no real manifestation in the real world. For many white people, systemic racism doesn't exist because they cannot imagine how people in our contemporary world would act in a way that normalizes prejudice. For them that was part of the past, not the present.

For example, for many white people, the police are seen as those who protect and serve. In their worldview, police would never *intentionally* harm another person. And yet in many black communities the police have been viewed just as dangerous as gangs. In white communities, children are taught that they can trust the police. Even in school, these children learn that when they are in danger they can go to a police officer to ask for help. Police routinely do talks in schools to reiterate this message. However, it is not the same reality in black communities. Boys of color are routinely given "the talk" by their fathers and mothers, about the dangers police pose and how to prevent a life-threatening encounter.

Brianna is a successful African American journalist. She is a single parent and very proud of her two older boys who are active in sports and great students. Brianna has just had her third child—another boy. As she is feeding her newborn she can't help but stare into his big brown eyes. Then suddenly her eyes begin to well up with tears. She thinks again about George Floyd (an African American man who was profiled and murdered by a Minneapolis police officer in May of 2020).

The tears represent the fears that Brianna has. Each tear that races down her cheek reminds her of the many talks she has had with her other two sons. Each talk she has with them is different but the same. When they were younger it was how they should act when they played at the park: "Keep your hoodie off"; "Keep your hands out of your pockets"; "Don't do anything to draw attention to yourself." But she knows that boys will be boys and that terrifies her. As they got older it was: "If you see a police officer, put your hands up, don't make any sudden moves, don't run, and be respectful." And as they got even older it became: "if you get pulled over, keep your hands on the wheel, do exactly what the officer says, don't make any sudden movements, say 'yes sir,' don't look into their eyes, and don't argue with them."

Brianna could not help but think that every time she let her sons go out to play, it could be their last. The anxiety of raising black boys in modern America is overwhelming at times as she exists in an almost constant state of worry. She sees in her newborn's eyes a beautiful boy who she hopes will make it to be a productive black man in American society. But she knows that it's not entirely up to her and that terrifies her.

Brianna's story is not unique and it certainly isn't invented fluff meant to tug at one's heartstrings. This is a reality that occurs over and over in African American homes throughout the country. It is the reality of being black in America. However, this reality is so distant for white Americans that it seems like a myth. White people do not experience anything remotely similar—especially from civil servants.

Moreover, even when confronted with incontrovertible evidence such as witnessing police brutality over and over again on television, white conservative people are more inclined to doubt what they are seeing than that there is something wrong with policing in America. They immediately consider the more implausible theories than what is right in front of them. This is because their idealism blinds them to reality.

Additionally, many of these same people have little to no engagement within the black community, so they never see the reality of their situation; they are stuck in their idealism and have intellectualized and abstracted the problem. Part of this is not their fault. It is, for example, not their fault that they have white privilege. But what separates the racist from the non-racist is their approach to that privilege. The refusal to recognize one's privilege will almost always result in a predisposition toward racism. That doesn't mean recognizing it will result in the opposite effect, but it does take one step in the right direction.

Much of the racism that exists today, even within Evangelicalism, manifests through unconscious bias. This problem extends beyond white evangelicals and conservatives but is particularly notable within these groups. Addressing this challenge becomes complex when individuals within these communities deny the existence of such biases. The pertinent question arises: how can one effectively demonstrate to those who do not perceive themselves as racist that certain behaviors they exhibit, are indeed, racist? One way is to stop teaching a white-washed history in favor of one that more accurately reflects reality regardless of who it may villainize.

Evangelicalism and Racism: A Brief History

As discussed in the previous section, there are degrees of overtness when it comes to racism. Subtle racism is often practiced at a subconscious level and takes the form of unconscious bias and microaggressions. It is often practiced unwittingly by well-meaning people but felt painfully all the same by people of color. This form of racism is perhaps the most dangerous because of a lack of awareness and thus a lack of accountability and course-correction.

There are also varying levels of institutional and structural racism that exist across large-scale systems, including in government, in business, and in organizations. These forms of racism were often implemented intentionally at some point in history when racism was practiced overtly and considered socially acceptable. Though much change may have taken place since these policies were put into place, not much has been done to proactively change the policies themselves, or their long-lasting consequences. As a result, structural racism continues to limit equal access to opportunities and justice for people of color. The Church, particularly the white, evangelical, and conservative sector of it is just one example of this.

Evangelicalism has a history of both overt and subtle racism, which was practiced so heavily early on that remnants of it continue to exist today. That does not mean people are helpless to do anything about it. Acknowledging it has to be the first step. To continue denying its existence results in its perpetuation.

Although it would be naive to think that the Church did not have a role in the staging and persistence of slavery, many would be surprised to learn just how active some evangelical leaders were in its perpetuation.

At the outset, there are two misconceptions that should be addressed. First, not all conservatives and not all evangelicals were pro-slavery. As is often the case, even today, their voices were simply not as loud or influential as those they disagreed with.

The second has to do with the nature of race. Race is a cultural and sociological construct designed to distinguish groups of humans primarily by physical attributes (i.e. skin color, hair, etc.) and social factors. (i.e. social status, familial ancestry, etc.).[17] Despite minor biological differences between genders, humans are fundamentally the same. The concept of race is rooted in societal ideologies such as social status and familial lineage, leading to the diverse racial classifications observed today.

Although the idea of race has always existed in the sense that humans have always made delineations between groups of people, it was not a prevalent issue in the early days of colonial America—at least not in the way we understand it today. That leaves us with the unsettling fact that colonial Americans created the modern idea of racism through the practice of slavery. According to Jemar Tibsy, author of the New York Times Bestseller, The Color of Compromise, between 1500 and 1700 CE most men were on equal ground regardless of skin color or station. That doesn't mean racism did not exist, but it was not a predominant aspect of life at that time.[18] People were largely concerned with survival, which meant that cooperation, not division, was the most important aspect of that period.

However, two things changed that brought race to the forefront. Population booms helped to establish a more stable economy and advancements in the agriculture and textile industries helped settlers maintain the economy. It was these two primary factors that created the slave industry in the American colonies.

While the growing economy and various industries in the colonies, along with changes that were taking place in Europe, created the colonial slave industry, early slavery was very different from its later version. Early slavery was akin to indentured servitude. That is, after a person served their time (i.e. paid for their voyage to the colonies), they were freed from their obligations. This meant that in the early days of slavery, Africans were becoming integrated into society and establishing a permanence that made them Americans.

Eventually, it was no longer cost-effective to free indentured servants. Over time indentured servitude became slavery. With the establishment of the Middle Passage—the trade route between the colonies and Africa, slavery became a full-blown industry.

Up to this point churches served two purposes in regards to slavery. The first was using Christianity as a means to strip a slave's identity away. By forcing Christianity upon a slave, their owners were stripping the slave of any prior religious affiliation or practice. The owner wanted their slaves to be fully dedicated to their work. This also served as a way to spread ideology and was ultimately used to "Americanize" Africans.

Second, church buildings were used to wrangle slaves. Although most owners preferred slaves not to worship alongside them (or in a segregated section), it was safer than allowing them to worship in their own buildings where gathering could lead to an uprising. However, what these Christians could not foresee was that the Jesus they introduced Africans to was not just the great Redeemer, but one who proclaimed: "Take my burden, for it is light."[19] He was a suffering servant[20] and the great liberator for those who were enslaved.[21] This resonated with Africans and as a result many welcomed Christianity and its message.

Evangelicalism and Slavery

Even though the term "evangelical" was not coined until the mid to late 19th Century, its ideals can be traced back to the earliest colonists. If we were to draw a historical parallel, we might consider Puritans akin to modern fundamentalists, and most other religiously conservative Christians as similar to modern evangelicals, with a few exceptions: Quakers and Anglicans.

It was the first Great Awakening of 1720 that helped establish religious boundaries across doctrinal lines instead of geographical ones which resulted in what we see today as denominationalism. Pointing to those delineations is the only way to create a modern equivalency with Evangelicalism.

Religion did not create American slavery. Slavery was first and foremost developed for economic reasons and represents an early display of Capitalism. With that said, religion played a significant role in cementing slavery into the fabric of early America. Since most colonists were associated with Christianity in some way, their public lives would eventually intersect with their spiritual ones. As lines began to be drawn by Christians between the ethics and the economics of slavery, the Church faced its first significant debate—and it was a big one.

Ever since Africans began coming to the colonies, the devout used it as an evangelistic opportunity. Although many Africans had already been exposed to either Christianity or Islam by this time, the colonists largely thought of them as pagan. This was mainly due to their dark skin and misinformation about their Continent. Most European settlers in the colonies thought of Christianity as a religion practiced by light-skinned European people because those were the only ones they ever saw practicing it. Today, we label that as "Western" thinking, or "Western" Christianity. However, largely unknown to them was the fact that not only had Christianity spread throughout Northern Africa as early as the 1st Century, but places like Ethiopia had a storied Christian tradition that was older than most European ones. Jewish roots in Africa go back even further.

The issue of debate was whether or not baptized Christian slaves were entitled to freedom. The idea was that since these individuals became Christians they were now brothers and sisters and to be treated with equality. This debate had far-reaching implications. If the Churches said yes, they deserved freedom, then that could upend the entire country's economy since much of its wealth was established and maintained on the backs of slaves. This would not only destroy most of the country but it would inevitably destroy most churches.

In order to "protect" their churches and way of life, most churches made the unfortunate declaration that conversion was not a means of freedom for slaves. Their reasoning was simple: *slavery is not a religious issue, but a political one.* This is a rationale that still reverberates throughout our society today, often touted by political Christians To justify making questionable ethical decisions.

This separation more or less solidified the stance of most Southern churches on slavery for the next few hundred years. Churches in the North were often split on the issue. This led Southern pastors and academics to begin creating "segregationist theology"; a theology meant to embolden slaveholders and justify slavery.

Reconstruction & Stereotyping

They were wrong! Those who believed that the country would crumble if Christian slaves were freed believed in a myth. Today, we might call this misinformation or a conspiracy theory. But, ultimately they were wrong. They were wrong because the country did not fall apart once slavery was abolished. The South's economy did suffer greatly and many in the South were forced into poverty as a result, but they were sleeping in the bed they had made.

After the Civil War and the abolishment of slavery, the country went through a phase known as Reconstruction. The idea of Reconstruction was to create ways to integrate slaves into society. In retrospect, the reconstruction era is largely considered a failure. The death of Abraham Lincoln meant that his successor, Andrew Johnson (1808-1875) was responsible for properly integrating blacks into society. Johnson, a Southern sympathizer, was ill-equipped to handle a country that needed him to help them heal from the brutalities of war. Johnson wanted the country to be restored as quickly as possible. In his haste, he made several errors of judgment (intentional or not we will never know). One of those errors was failing to provide any protection for African Americans. Ultimately, this is what led to his impeachment hearings in Congress (he later was acquitted by one vote in the Senate).

In many respects, white Americans had more disdain towards blacks than they did before emancipation. Southerners held them responsible for their blight. Northerners were angry because they sent their sons and husbands to die in a war that they felt had no connection to them. Consternation towards blacks during Reconstruction was at a fever pitch. This fostered the development of groups whose sole purpose was to target blacks and other minorities. At first, much of this was accomplished through public policy, both at a national and local level.

The lack of proper integration by President Johnson resulted in legal chaos and helped to establish Jim Crow laws. Jim Crow, a derogatory term toward African Americans, was a system of formal and informal laws meant to suppress African Americans' freedoms and segregate them from white society. Although Jim Crow laws were formalized in the South, they were also informally adhered to in the North.

The first phase of Jim Crow acted as the preamble for what was still to come. It sought to prevent African Americans from voting. Voter suppression measures included a polling tax which was meant to charge for the right to vote. In other cases there were literacy tests which quizzed African Americans about the constitution and in some cases required them to read certain texts. There was also a grandfather clause that granted only those who voted or had family that voted prior to 1867 the right to vote. Since the right to vote is a hallmark of American civil action, finding ways to suppress African Americans suffrage helped to prevent them from assimilating.[22] Jim Crow lasted until the Civil Rights Act and the Voting Rights Act of 1964 and 1965.

The Ku Klux Klan & White Supremacy

White Christian Nationalism is built on the foundation of the Ku Klux Klan (KKK) and White Supremacy. The KKK had three iterations - each of which built upon the previous one. The first iteration was a short stint but helped to establish the group as a significant movement. In the early 20th century the second iteration emerged with the goal of fusing Christianity with nationalism. Kelly Baker argues in her book, The Gospel of the Klan, that the KKK "*was not just an order to defend America but also a campaign to protect and celebrate Protestantism. It was a religious order.*"[23]

The third iteration of the KKK was accomplished by Thomas Dixon Jr., the son of a Baptist preacher and a pastor himself. Although Baker was a preacher, he was also a writer who was responsible for creating propaganda for the KKK. In fact, one of his books, *The Clansman,* was adapted as a silent film and became the blockbuster called: *The Birth of a Nation*. This film was meant to portray the invading Yankees and Blacks in a way that would make the Klan appear heroic as they defend their southern way of life.

Woodrow Wilson even viewed it in 1915 and reportedly stated: "*It's like writing history with lightning. My only regret is that it is all so terribly true.*"[24] He went on to host special White House viewings of the movie for hundreds of guests. Inspired by the movie, Clansmen gathered on Thanksgiving of that year at Stone Mountain where they practiced an old Scotch-Irish ritual of burning a cross and built an altar where they placed a Bible and the American flag. This was the birth of what we now view as the modern KKK.

Much of the KKK's agenda was a response to the significant increase of immigrants. The KKK believed their ideology would protect their white Christian heritage. In fact, the KKK was so infused into Christian culture that it would not be uncommon for a man to be violent on a Saturday night and then preach with conviction from the pulpit the next morning. Throughout the early 20th Century, White Supremacy gradually became infused in mostly Southern but also Northern denominations.

It is important to understand that this ideology is often not practiced overtly. It does not necessarily manifest itself by pastors pounding pulpits preaching "white power," but can be much more subversive. It is an ideal that can exist in someone's subconscious without them even knowing, simply because it has been infused into the fabric of their belief system. Regardless, its existence is evidenced through one's behaviors and is further corroborated through the significant number of denominations that, for better or worse, have denounced the sins of their past. Denominations like the Southern Baptist Convention (the largest evangelical denomination in the United States), the Episcopalian Diocese, and the Presbyterian Church of the United States to name a few.

However, perhaps the greatest observable evidence exists in the segregation that is present in pews every Sunday morning around the United States. 87% of Christian churches in the United States are completely made up of only white or black parishioners.[25] Despite its diverse racial profile (according to the Public Religion Research Institute (PRRI), 1 out of every 3 evangelicals is a person of color.[26]) Evangelicalism is one of the most segregated groups within Christianity.

This segregation was not a cultural phenomenon that occurred organically over time, but a product of the atrocities that accompanied the Jim Crow era. A single volume could not contain all of the brutality that African Americans experienced under these laws. We could discuss lynchings and random acts of violence. We could talk about how blacks could not worship, eat, or drink with whites—not even in mutual celebration. Most people are or should be aware of how various politicians and legislators contributed to the segregation of African Americans from the development of the highway system to the establishment of suburbs. It is not our purpose to rehash that sordid history here but it would be irresponsible to ignore it.

Instead, it has been our purpose to lay a foundation in order to demonstrate the various ways that White Nationalism has become a part of Evangelicalism's subconscious through its various sub-cultural exploits. Despite what some may think, issues like these were complicated and heavily embedded in the fabric of American culture. They did not simply vanish with the establishment of new legislation or the Civil Rights Movement, as some may wish, and simply ignoring them doesn't make them go away.

Instead, issues like these will always exist until they are confronted in such a way that substantive change results. The lack of awareness and the willful ignorance associated with the white man's role, past and present, is profound. The lack of attention and value given these issues within White America is why much of it persists—affecting everything from theology to public policy.

The Church is not immune to the problems of culture. Unfortunately for evangelicals, instead of trying to get out in front of the influence of White Christian Nationalism, many have done their best to avoid the problem altogether. From proclaiming that White Christian Nationalism does not exist (denialism) to writing it off as another fringe movement, evangelicals have done everything except confront it for what it is—a blight. A blight brought about by the same indifference that has defined much of their social action. A blight largely accepted in exchange for power and influence. An evil considered worth participating in as long as it brings about the "Kingdom of God." Instead, what it brings is an agenda meant to transform America into a powerful, rich, white, theocratic nation—a kingdom for men.

As stated earlier, our purpose has not been to survey the history of all the ways African Americans have been treated, but to make observations on how evangelicals have interacted with that history. Did they serve as a beacon of hope and love to those who were considered less than them by society? Do they now? Some certainly did and do but many did not. Our purpose was to show how certain ideologies have influenced Evangelicalism's worldview. It is important to recognize the complicity many in Christianity had whether they were aware of it or not because ultimately, those influences created a heritage of dehumanization that in many cases still exists today.

To Be or Not to Be Human

In general, dehumanization is a way to control people. Sometimes it is overt and intentional such as in the Holocaust. Most of the time it is subversive and subconscious. Through the collective treatment of women and African Americans, evangelicals have put their stamp of approval on various forms of dehumanization all in the name of God.

In today's world, this dehumanization reaches beyond race and gender to include issues like abortion, immigration, LGBTQ+, poverty, etc. These are all issues related to basic human rights and dignity. Instead of spreading the hope of Jesus, many evangelical leaders have used these issues to gain more power and control over the country. Their rhetoric around politically charged phrases like "family values', helps to convince their followers that they must accept certain forms of dehumanization. For example, even though allowing a gay couple to marry presents no infringement on the evangelical's right to marry or carry out their faith, they still *aggressively* and *actively* oppose it. As we will discuss in part two, this type of dehumanization is a result of the idealism that is built into its worldview and until that changes, Evangelicalism will continue to destroy others and itself.

One might wonder why it is so difficult for evangelicals to see themselves reflected in White Christian Nationalism. There are a couple of reasons for this. The first has to do with the fact that evangelicals have been trained for years by their leaders to participate in or fight against certain ideals. The second has to do with the art of misdirection that has been used to blind evangelicals to the reality that their belief system creates.

This sleight of hand has been most prominent in their support for Donald Trump. Much of the support from evangelical leaders can be attributed to the perceived similarities between his behaviors and their own actions and beliefs. Through our historical survey, it has become evident that Trump's behaviors, such as involvement in misconduct and preservation of patriarchal power dynamics, resonate with these leaders. This alignment likely explains their vocal advocacy for Trump, as they recognize elements of themselves reflected in his actions and values.

However, the lack of awareness among the laity can be attributed to the pervasive subliminal messaging they are exposed to through various media channels and religious teachings. Interestingly, these individuals frequently contend that those who depart from Evangelicalism are also influenced by similar subconscious messaging, despite not recognizing their own participation in it. This paradox underscores the intricate nature of the influences and perceptions that have shaped evangelical beliefs and ideologies.

In Part Two we jump into some of these intricacies and show how the evangelical worldview has fused together the various aspects of personal and civil life in such a way that they have become indistinguishable.

PART TWO

The Two Kingdoms

7

Theology & Politics in the Fundamentalist-Evangelical Imagination

Evangelical and fundamentalist theology plays a significant role in the justification of certain actions performed by each group. In order to properly understand how theology plays a role in this justification it is necessary to explore the various theological frameworks utilized by evangelical and fundamentalist groups. Specifically, we will look at how Dispensationalism works and show how that theological perspective is responsible for creating the distortions that we see in the conservative Christian political worldview. Doing this will shed light on the complex relationship between theology and ideology, and the ways in which religious beliefs can be used to justify certain actions and political positions.

The Evangelical Worldview: The Three Spheres

Before we can understand the theological perspective we must first have an understanding of the evangelical worldview—a worldview that is complex and at times paradoxical. Having a clear understanding of the presuppositions that evangelicals have will better help us understand the convoluted relationship they have with religion and politics.

The evangelical worldview can be a confounding world of mystery. Attempting to understand how evangelical beliefs don't stand in contradiction to their political ideologies can be difficult. In order to better understand this phenomenon, I have created an analogy that I am referring to as the Three Spheres.

A healthy, well-rounded worldview has three spheres that inform, influence, and support one another. Those spheres consist of: the individual's *beliefs*, their *culture*, and their *society*. When functioning properly, a worldview has a balance between external input and internal evaluation. This allows the individual to learn, grow, and change in a healthy and balanced way. The external information acts as nourishment for a worldview and considering various perspectives helps a person develop their own. Taking in unhealthy information without evaluating it will result in an unhealthy worldview.[1]

In an unhealthy worldview the individual is single-minded; taking in only that information that confirms their bias. When this happens the individual aspects of belief, culture, and society move closer together until they become entangled. This entanglement is a result of the echo chamber that the individual has created within their thinking. This closed system results in circular thinking as the individual becomes more reliant on unhealthy information.

As mental atrophy sets in, the individual's various spheres become fused to the point that they lose any meaningful distinction between them. The lack of definition between the various spheres means an inability to properly separate the information the individual takes in through each sphere. This fusion is extreme and unhealthy and eventually leads to the destruction of the individual and their connection to the world around them. [2]

As we have surveyed Evangelicalism through history, we have seen how each piece of their worldview was crafted and maintained. We have also observed that through the passage of time, all three spheres have become intertwined. As time went on and evangelicals failed to course-correct, the spheres have since become completely entangled. More recently, we have seen these spheres become fused. This is what we are witnessing today. What once were three separate aspects have fused together to become a single, convoluted whole, leading to confusion and contradiction for evangelicals. As a result of this fusion, there exists an inability to receive and evaluate new information; to prioritize, synthesize, and interpret it in a healthy way.

Sphere One: Beliefs

The first sphere consists of the individual's beliefs, which serve as the foundation from which the other two spheres are built (though as we will see, all of the spheres continually inform one another). For evangelicals, this aspect is the most important. Their belief system comprises two major components. The first is the preservation and protection of orthodoxy. Second, the relevance and authority of Scripture. Identifying them for now will suffice as we will discuss them in more detail in subsequent sections.

Additionally, morality plays a significant role in the evangelical worldview. A product of a particular way of viewing the Bible, evangelicals have made morality the centerpiece for many of their beliefs. However, as we have already seen, the distinction between the belief sphere and the societal sphere quickly became entangled during its first few decades of the 20th century, making any form of meaningful distinction between them difficult if not impossible throughout most of evangelicalism's history.

There are several examples that one could use to demonstrate this entanglement; whether the continual battle in various states (particularly southern states like Texas, Alabama and Louisiana) to display the Ten Commandments in the public square, or the "battle for prayer" in public school systems throughout the country. Even the act of legislating biblical morality demonstrates the extent to which these boundaries have become entangled.

Sphere Two: Culture

The cultural sphere of the evangelical worldview also consists of several components, namely, relationships to people and ethnicity. Within Evangelicalism, distinct subcultures have been formed that have their own way of looking at things. For example, the sub-culture of white Evangelicalism is influenced by the parent culture of Christian Nationalism. And although it is true that Christian Nationalism has also affected black evangelicals, they have experienced its influence in radically different ways, thus creating an important distinction between the two subgroups. This distinction helps explain why two subgroups that share the same parent culture can have radically different ideas as to how their common worldview is to be applied in society. Culture, along with beliefs, determines how input is received, processed, and interpreted.

The cultural sphere also includes aspects of ethnicity. Ethnicity plays a crucial role in how the worldview is applied in society. An example of this can be observed in how black and white evangelicals interpreted the George Floyd murder (as well as all cases of racial or police violence before and after). There were radically different responses from each group. African American evangelicals treat situations like these more personally - because for them it is. Many black evangelicals can relate to the positions that these boys and men found themselves in because they have had similar experiences. It is a social cause that demands their involvement. For many black evangelicals this issue was interpreted through their cultural lens.

Seeing these murders was drastically different for white evangelicals. Many of them interpreted these murders through their societal lens, oftentimes viewing them as political spin from the far left. For white evangelicals, their understanding was political and informed by an ideological perspective that was a result of their white nationalistic influence.

Sphere Three: Society

The societal sphere is about time and place and how that position creates one's perspective. One's location in the world and time in history acts as the contextual milieu for their overall worldview. The societal aspect synthesizes the other two into something communicable to the world. Political engagement is an example of something expressed through this sphere, as is legislation and other aspects that make up our political institutions. The key components that influence this sphere are based on elements of the individual's identity as an American, the individual's personal and familial history, and is often exhibited through patriotism or in white Evangelicalism's case, nationalism.

Worldview Formation

When these three spheres are working as they are supposed to, they act in harmony with one another. They are constantly informing one another without compromising or having their distinct identities consumed by one of the other spheres. Beliefs, culture, and political engagement can function separately and new information encountered in one sphere can be processed relatively independently of the others. Once the information is synthesized it is shared with the other spheres as a new but complete thought that can be adapted appropriately in each new context. This allows an individual or group to maintain flexibility and mobility in their thinking.

However, when the spheres are not maintained properly through the lens of introspection and evaluation, they eventually become intertwined. The first warning sign that the individual or group is moving in the wrong direction is when they become inflexible and incapable of processing information independently. The more ideas begin to lose distinction, the more degraded they become. The more rigid individuals or groups become in their worldview, the more divided society becomes. Nuance is lost.

Eventually, if the intertwinement continues, the spheres become entangled. Entanglement is not easily undone and takes time and intentionality to repair. It is important to carefully observe each component in order to put it back in the right place. As we discussed in Part One, one way this can happen is through a process called deconstruction. Deconstruction allows the individual to isolate certain beliefs and reevaluate them based on changing context or additional information.

Oftentimes evangelicals resist deconstructing because they falsely believe that a changing context should not alter the content of one's belief, especially if that belief is universally true. However, what they are failing to understand is that these two things are not mutually exclusive. Context can and does change, which alters one's perspective on information - including factual or universal information. In other words, new information has dictated that one's interpretation of the information has changed, even if the content remains the same.

Finally, if left unchecked, the spheres become fused into a single whole. This fusion doesn't allow for any meaningful distinction between aspects. All information that comes in is processed through a single fused worldview. New information lacks introspection and reasoning because it has no sphere delineation to process new information with. This results in actions in the world that are unharmonious and harmful.

Prior to the Protestant Reformation, much of Western Medieval Christianity lacked distinction between politics and faith, which led to a corrupt institution and by extension, society. The fusion within the Roman Catholic worldview at the time was so strong that they were unable to see the need for differentiation. That is until Martin Luther began a process of deconstruction and ushered in the Protestant Reformation, followed by the Counter-Reformation.

The rigidity of the Catholic Church that Martin Luther knew and rebelled against was the inevitable result of Constantine making Christianity legal in 313 AD and the Edict of Thessalonica which made Christianity the official religion of the Roman empire in 380 AD. Prior to these major events, sporadic persecution kept the Christian worldview grounded and centered. It was easy to distinguish between Caesar ("render unto Caesar") and God ("render unto God") when Caesar was hunting Christians for his Colosseum. However, when Christians gained the political upper hand, their beliefs began to inform the culture and the social order. The Church's urgency toward distinction diminished in light of its new freedom and power and these, in turn, gave way to apathy and rigidity, the enemies of truth and transformation. Eventually, all three spheres fused, the Pope became the most powerful religious and political figure in Europe, and the Church dictated every aspect of life in the Middle Ages, for better or for worse.

The Reformation helped to disrupt the corrupt system and infuse new life and truth into their faith but at a significant cost - their identity as Catholics. At the time, people did not make the distinction between Catholic and Christian (even despite the existence of the Eastern tradition) so you could not be a Christian without also being Catholic. When the Reformers lost their identity, they took upon themselves the idiom Protestant (or protestors). This new identity helped them to create a new worldview that was rooted in a historical orthodoxy (at least their interpretation of it) and distinct creedal convictions.

Much of the experiment we call the Reformation was not that dissimilar to what existed in the first Century when Christianity was trying to become distinct from Judaism. Just as early Christianity had to wrestle with Jewish theology, so too did the Reformers have to understand their faith in light of their former Catholicism.

Additionally, the First and Second Great Awakenings in the United States might also be considered as times where priorities and perspectives needed to change. These movements were akin to a spiritual deconstruction which helped them to refocus. The Great Awakenings sought to disrupt the Christian's movement, which, at the time, was headed toward fusion.

A worldview is something that one rarely takes conscious notice of. After all, a worldview is simply the perspective an individual uses to make meaning of the world around them. However, the lack of critical thinking and introspection among Americans has resulted in a need to reflect on one's beliefs and re-evaluate priorities.

Our natural tendency as humans is to be selfish. Paradoxically, being selfish results in movement towards our own destruction. Being in harmony as we exist in a world of other people requires at times relinquishing selfish tendencies to focus on the "other." Unfortunately, we live in a society that is heavily individualistic and focuses on one's own good above and beyond the well-being of others. America's entire economy is built on this premise. Businesses, for example, have to create models of sustainability in order to survive the market. That means, their focus is often on self-preservation, which can come, and often does, at the expense of the other.

Toward the end of his life, Jesus stated to his disciples that "I am the way, the truth, and the life." We often view this verse in the context of heaven. However, this limited interpretation misunderstands what Jesus was trying to teach his disciples. Above all, Jesus is saying that belief in him is where true life exists (on earth), and that through him, people can experience their humanity the way it was intended. As Christ demonstrated through his life, that "way" is through service to others.[3] To do anything else is to move towards our own destruction.

Until evangelicals stop justifying their actions in order to save face and begin to practice introspection and self-awareness they will continue on a path that will lead them towards destruction. They must "clean up their own house" before worrying about the transgressions of others. Instead of avoiding their humanity they must turn and run towards it. They must embrace it instead of denying it.

The remainder of the book will focus on the evangelical worldview in light of its various spheres. We will discuss many of the issues Part One raised and offer answers that help clarify a worldview that currently exists in a perpetual state of idealism. We will demonstrate how a worldview firmly grounded in realism will offer individuals the needed distinctions that will lead them into life instead of destruction; into hope instead of despair.

Dispensationalism

We have talked a lot in this book about Dispensationalism and its effects on Evangelicalism, giving only pithy explanations along the way. In this section we will do a deeper dive into some of the core beliefs as well as show how these beliefs inform Evangelicalism's worldview.

At the core of the religious discourse surrounding the evangelical and fundamentalist movements lies the concept of the second coming of Jesus Christ. This belief, which has been a central tenet for these groups, has been shaped by the theological work of John Nelson Darby (1800-1882). Darby, a prominent figure in the early days of these movements, developed the theological framework that has allowed evangelicals and fundamentalists to make their ideological claims. His work has been instrumental in shaping the beliefs and practices of these groups and continues to be a significant influence on their thinking to this day.

In 1827, Darby, a minister, experienced a horse-riding accident in Ireland, which led him to embark on a journey of self-discovery. Taking time off from his ministry, as he recuperated, he began to question some of the Church's teachings, (today we might say he was deconstructing). A matter that had long been troubling him during his tenure as a minister was the purpose of the Church. Through his rigorous research, Darby concluded that the Church was in a state of total ruin, a realization that eventually led him to abandon his role as a minister. This period of deconstruction marked the beginning of a new life for Darby as he set out to create a language around the ideas he was thinking about.

After Darby's period of deconstruction, he decided to begin meeting with a few gentlemen in his home as a replacement for church. Slowly the group began to grow until they were no longer able to meet in his home.

It was during this time that Darby began to publish small pamphlets that reflected some of his theological reconstruction.[4]

Darby's interest in prophecy was heavily influenced by the cultural impact of Napoleon on his society. Many in Darby's culture believed Napoleon to be the antichrist, leading to a cultural anxiety that spurred Darby's curiosity in prophecy.[5] As a result, Darby began attending prophecy meetings and conferences, which ultimately acted as the foundation for his theology known as "Dispensationalism." This belief system is characterized by the division of history into different "dispensations" or periods, each with its own unique set of rules and requirements for salvation.

Dispensationalism was a theology for the Church about the Church. It placed higher importance on the role of the Church, making it a key player in the larger narrative that was taking place. This emphasis on the Church meant that Darby also believed in Replacement Theology. This is the idea that the Church, not Israel, are heirs to the covenant promises, which stopped applying to Israel once the New Covenant was established through the death and resurrection of Jesus.

Darby's ideas were widely disseminated through his travels and numerous publications and had a significant impact on Christian thought in Ireland, England, and North America. In addition to his theological writings, Darby also undertook the task of translating the Bible into multiple languages and produced a substantial commentary on Scripture. Although some of the rudimentary ideas of Dispensationalism can be seen as far back as Justin Martyr (110-165), it was Darby who organized these ideas into a prophetic system.

The Return of Christ and the Rapture

The return of Jesus Christ is a central doctrine for most protestant and Catholic churches. There are many Bible passages that dispensationalists believe clearly predict this event, such as 1 Thessalonians 5:23:

> Now may the God of peace Himself sanctify you entirely; and may your spirit and soul and body be preserved complete, without blame at the coming of our Lord Jesus Christ.

And Acts 1:9-11:

> And after He had said these things, He was lifted up while they were looking on, and a cloud received Him out of their sight. And as they were gazing intently into the sky while He was going, behold, two men in white clothing stood beside them. They also said, "Men of Galilee, why do you stand looking into the sky? This Jesus, who has been taken up from you into heaven, will come in just the same way as you have watched Him go into heaven.

And other passages such as: Matthew 42:24; James 5:7; Revelation 1:7; Revelation 22:12 and many more...

However, what is not as clear is what the return of Jesus will look like. That is the gap that Dispensationalism attempts to fill. One of the key components of Dispensationalism is the idea of a future tribulation period, which is believed to be a time of intense suffering and upheaval before the return of Jesus Christ. This concept is based on a variety of prophetic works, primarily from the Hebrew Scriptures and the book of Revelation. While the exact details of the tribulation period remain somewhat nebulous, dispensationalists believe that it will be a time of great testing for believers and non-believers alike. One of the most quoted passages regarding this period comes from 2 Timothy 3:1-5:

> But mark this: There will be terrible times in the last days. People will be lovers of themselves, lovers of money, boastful, proud, abusive, disobedient to their parents, ungrateful, unholy, without love, unforgiving, slanderous, without self-control, brutal, not lovers of the good, treacherous, rash, conceited, lovers of pleasure rather than lovers of God—having a form of godliness but denying its power. Have nothing to do with such people.

Based upon cryptic passages like Daniel 9:27, dispensationalists believe humanity is given the length of this period as seven years.

> He will confirm a covenant with many for one 'seven.' In the middle of the 'seven' he will put an end to sacrifice and offering. And at the temple he will set up an abomination that causes desolation, until the end that is decreed is poured out on him.

For Darby and his followers, the Church will not go through this period but rather will experience what is known as the rapture. In fact, it could be argued that this divine event is what kicks off the tumult that these passages seem to talk about. In Darby's words:

> ...by His coming to receive them to Himself where He is; His introducing them into His Father's house, and in the kingdom placing them in the heavenly seat of government with Himself. This is effectuated by His coming, and causing them, raised or changed, to come up to meet Him in the air. This is the rapture of the saints, preceding their and Christ's appearing: at that they appear with Him. So that at their rapture He has not appeared yet. Such

> is the general doctrine of the rapture of the church—a doctrine of the last importance; because it is immediately connected with the relationship of the church to Christ, its entire separation from the world and its portion. It is the act which crowns its perfect justification. This rapture before the appearing of Christ is a matter of expressed revelation

The idea that the Church will be raptured before the seven years of tumult is known as pretribulationism, which is based upon passages like Revelation 7:13-14:

> Then one of the elders asked me, "These in white robes—who are they, and where did they come from?"
>
> I answered, "Sir, you know."
>
> And he said, "These are they who have come out of the great tribulation; they have washed their robes and made them white in the blood of the Lamb."

However, some read this passage as demonstrating that the Church will go through the tribulation as indicated by the phrase "*they who have* ***come out of*** *the great tribulation*". Those who believe that Christians will go through part of the tribulation are known as *Midtribulationists.* Finally, there are others who believe the Church will go through the entire tribulation and are known as *Posttribulationists.* These three views are what mostly comprise Evangelicalism's eschatology.

The second connecting point between Dispensationalism and conservative Christianity can be observed in the creation of the Scofield Reference Bible. This influential work was authored/edited by Cyrus Scofield (1843-1921), an American theologian and minister who was born in Michigan in 1843. After moving to St. Louis to study law, Scofield found himself serving a brief jail sentence in 1879, during which time he underwent a religious conversion. It was while studying theology under James H. Brookes, a prominent figure in the development of Dispensationalism, that Scofield became deeply involved in this theological framework. In 1909, Scofield published the first edition of the Scofield Reference Bible, which included extensive notes and cross-references that aimed to provide readers with a comprehensive understanding of the biblical text as well as Dispensationalism.

The Scofield Bible quickly gained popularity among fundamentalists and evangelicals and served as their primary reference source. With the creation of the Jewish State of Israel in 1948, sales skyrocketed to more than 2 million copies in the years after World War II and helped to solidify Darby as a prophet for the ages.[6]

The Scofield Bible also contained one of the first systematic treatments of creationism. Scofield even postulated a date for the creation as 4004 BC. Additionally, he presented a strong argument for the "Gap Theory," which argued that each day of creation was not a 24-hour period of time but contained gaps in between each "day." The creationism advocated for in the Scofield Bible kicked off fresh debates at a time when science was trying to promote evolution within the public school system.

Ultimately, what set the Scofield Bible apart was its comprehensive documentation of dispensational theology, as well as its built-in reference system for cross-referencing passages. It is safe to say that without the Scofield Bible, the popularity of Dispensationalism would not have been as widespread as it became. The Scofield Bible played a pivotal role in shaping the theological landscape of the early 20th Century and is still used today.

The End Times & Xenophobia

Christians have long proclaimed the imminent arrival of the end times, a belief rooted in the teachings of the New Testament. Throughout these texts, we find numerous declarations regarding the return of Jesus, suggesting that the writers themselves anticipated the end to be near. This sense of urgency may have been further fueled by the rise of anti-Christ figures such as Nero and Domitian, who subjected Christians to persecution and suffering. Additionally, significant events like the destruction of the temple in 70 AD likely contributed to this prevailing mindset. The combination of these factors created an atmosphere in which belief regarding the imminent end of the world became deeply ingrained within the Christian consciousness.

Throughout Church history, there have been instances where certain events and individuals have led church leaders to proclaim the impending end. Examples of such events include the Bubonic Plague, the Crusades, the Reformation, the rise of evolution, and the Starbucks annual holiday mug. However, it can be argued that no event has convinced Christians of the end times as much as the rise of Adolf Hitler and World War II.

World War II marked a significant turning point, as it was the first time that fundamentalists and many evangelicals actively declared that the end was near. The eventual involvement of America in the war further solidified the idea that Christians could actively participate in the end times.

Although initially reluctant to enter the war, religious conservatives swiftly changed their mind after the bombing of Pearl Harbor. That was not surprising as the changing political tide simply reflected the nation on the whole. What became more difficult to justify was the mass slaughter of innocent people through the use of atomic weapons. Harry S. Truman, who assumed the presidency after the sudden death of Franklin Roosevelt understood how to get his conservative Christian nation on board with using atomic weapons. Truman addressed the nation over the radio to talk about the "Potsdam Conference' and towards the end mentioned the Atomic Bomb saying in part "...we thank God that it has come to us, instead of to our enemies; and we pray that He may guide us to use it in His ways and for His purposes."

Evangelicals by and large believed (at least during the second part of the war) that this was not a battle of political ideology but a battle between God and atheism, which was often equated to God against socialism and/or communism. Moreover, by the time the Atomic Bomb was deployed, there were very few qualms about its use. This was bolstered by the newsletter, the King's Business, which said about the bomb that it was "...a work of God."[7]

It is worth noting that there was some minor dissent from Moody Bible Institute, which was expressed through its *Moody Monthly* newsletter in posing the question: "where do we go from here?" This was in no way a condemnation of the action or a questioning of the humanitarian consequences. Instead, it was a political posturing regarding the fallout of using such a weapon.

It was also during this period that xenophobia was on the rise. One of its more significant expressions targeted the Japanese. Although most evangelicals and fundamentalists did not actively promote encampments, they did not defend the Japanese either. Evangelicals and fundamentalists did not even help their Japanese brothers and sisters as they were being rounded up. This refusal to assist in the release of Japanese Christians served as a clear demonstration of the deeply ingrained xenophobia within their beliefs.

There were some who wanted to make their opinion on the matter known. One well-known evangelist at the time was Aimee McPherson (1890-1944). McPherson, a Pentecostal evangelist and founder of Angelus Temple (one of the first megachurches in America), was the most popular evangelist and media figure of her generation—surpassing even Billy Sunday. In 1943, McPherson addressed the issue of Japanese internment and responded in a telegram to state leaders with the following:

> We know positively that these Japs will carry on extensive and organized sabotage... We know the treachery of the Japanese... The greatest possible mistake that could be

> made at this time by our Government would be to force these Japs back upon the people of the Pacific Coast. It will incense the people and create riots and even bloodshed. We earnestly pray that they will not be freed.[8]

Despite the fact that some of the events regarding the internment of the Japanese, which she proclaimed during her life, were exaggerated or proven later to be false, McPherson is still looked at today as one of early Evangelicalism's most respected leaders.

Xenophobia and racism within the church are not just bound to history. In recent times we have witnessed the same attitude toward Muslims—especially after the events of 9/11. Referred to as Islamophobia, the disdain many Christians have towards Muslims is not new but has become much more prevalent since the events of 9/11. In fact, Islamophobia runs so deep in many Christian communities that it even affects public policy at the highest levels of our government.

In addition to Islamophobia, conservatives and fundamentalists have lauded attempts at rounding up Latinos, who are in the country illegally, by detaining them and subjecting them to squalid living conditions until their deportation. Making a terrible situation exponentially worse, many families were also separated due to a Trump administration policy, resulting in children being displaced and alone—a fact that many evangelicals ignore or plead ignorance to.

The evangelical xenophobia prevalent in American culture can be traced back to the xenophobic themes found in the Bible, particularly the Old Testament. The animosity depicted between Israel and other nations in the Hebrew Scriptures has the potential to influence modern perceptions, despite the original text's intentions. Stories portraying cultural violence and even genocide, seemingly condoned by God, can perpetuate a sense of justification for xenophobic beliefs. This historical context, though rooted in ancient beliefs, can still resonate with some evangelicals today, leading to discriminatory attitudes justified under the guise of divine approval.

Additionally, the interpretation and interpolation of prophetic imagery and the nations mentioned to fit modern contexts exacerbates this issue. This unfortunate consequence arises from the adoption of an eschatological-centric theology.

Ironically, Dispensationalism is also inherently anti-Semitic. This may seem like a contradiction since evangelicals defend Israel with intense zeal. However, that zeal is for their own benefit. Their defense of Israel has nothing to do with the well-being of Israel but is related to prophecy that places Israel at the center of the world stage for the "Gog-Magog" war (Ezekiel 38-39). Although the New Testament uses these names metaphorically, many evangelicals take the events associated with them literally (again, devoid of context). In other words, the only reason to support Israel is so that they can be destroyed as a result of the apocalypse.

In fact, as recently as April 2024, John Hagee, one of Evangelicalism's most influential lobbyists and a megachurch pastor, made a declaration that the current war taking place in Palestine was a precursor to Gog and Magog who he asserts is Iran.[9] Hagee is the founder of the largest pro-Israel lobbying organization in the country, Christians United For Israel (CUFI), which boasts over 8 million members and dwarfs the competition by comparison.

Finally, Dispensationalism also promotes something called Replacement Theology. This is the belief that God's covenant with Israel was nullified upon the establishment of the New Covenant. The New Covenant was accomplished after the death and resurrection of Jesus. The Church essentially became the new Israel. However, this theology fails to take into consideration context (again). Covenants did not void one another out in ancient times. In fact, this is evidenced in the covenants that we see in the Hebrew Scriptures. Instead, they build upon one another—or tangentially supplement. They never replace. What's more, we have no indication in the New Testament that the traditional rules of covenants have been broken or changed. Moreover, Replacement Theology seems more interested in being anti-Semitic than it does in being faithful to the biblical text.

Dispensationalism & Evangelicalism: A Match Made in Heaven

Evangelicalism works well with dispensational theology because it quenches their thirst for the militancy that seems built into it. Dispensationalism allows a narrative to be created that is participatory and nationalistic. It tells a story that puts America and its people at the center of an ever-evolving cosmic plot where the decisions made by the participants will result in either good or evil triumphing.

For example, U.S. Representative Lauren Boebert, who often gives a voice to White Christian Nationalists, stated at the Truth and Liberty Conference on September 9, 2022:

> It's time for us to position ourselves and rise up and take our place in Christ and influence this nation as we were called to do… We know that we are in the last of the last days, but it's not a time to complain about it. It's not a time to get upset about it. It's a time to know that you were called to be a part of these last days. You get to have a role in ushering in the second coming of Jesus.

This is not uncommon rhetoric for the congresswoman who can often be heard uttering words related to the end times or making the U.S. a Christian nation. She is certainly not alone in this line of thinking. We often hear White Christian Nationalists use their congressional pulpits to spread misinformation to the public.

However, as we have already demonstrated, the narratives that are advanced by politicians are the result of a particular theological posture developed by their religious leaders. It is important to recognize that even though they are congressional leaders, most of them are not theologically trained. They are lay people who are leaders in their industry of politics. They, like many lay people, simply reiterate the arguments they hear their pastors and religious leaders make.

Dispensationalism also feeds into the propositional nature of evangelical theology, allowing evangelicals to understand and defend its tenets through reading and repeating verses that seem to support their position. Perhaps no one has ever exemplified this in action better than Jack Van Impe. Van Impe, along with his wife Rexella, hosted a popular television show nestled in the affluent community of Rochester Hills, Michigan, called Jack Van Impe Presents, which could be seen across 25,000 cities. Van Impe's show was unique in that it used news from around the world to connect listeners to the impending end times. Van Impe could often be heard quoting an enormous amount of bible verses as proof texts for the articles he was sharing. These articles, and sometimes video clips, of strife in Russia and the Middle East were the backdrop for much of Van Impe's presentation. It is said that he had ⅔ of the Bible memorized.

Van Impe also had an impressive resume as he worked with some renowned evangelicals and fundamentalists through the years.[10] He has also influenced some of today's most famous dispensationalist preachers such as John Hagee and David Jeremiah.

Van Impe's ability to convince people that they existed in the end times (ironically for 40 years) is an example of the power that propositional theology has in Evangelicalism. Propositionalism is a word that most lay people may not be familiar with. It presupposes that language can arrange itself in such a way that propositions retain their meaning despite the surrounding context to the contrary. So far in this chapter we have demonstrated several cases where Dispensationalism will oftentimes ignore context in order to promote its particular belief. The idea that propositional content can be extracted from the Bible apart from its context is related to the doctrine of biblical inerrancy, which we discuss in the next section.

The use of propositions does not entail that verses are being used irresponsibly, but many propositionalists do use them that way. In fact, much of the book of Revelation is used in this way. Even though the book was written to specific churches regarding very specific situations, modern dispensationalists re-interpret those passages to be for modern times. Even in some cases when verses are being quoted properly in context, they still may be incorrectly applied, which often results in people using biblical verses to support nefarious agendas. It is also the reason that many evangelical lay persons are so easily convinced of strange and even contradictory ideas related to the end times.

Dispensationalism lends itself to be a propositional-based theology because at its core it's about how certain biblical texts are used and abused in order to convince the public of their veracity for today's world. One such workaround has been for theologians to argue that prophecy always has a double purpose. One purpose is within its immediate or surrounding context and one purpose is for the future. Even if this is true, much of the prophecy contained in the Hebrew scriptures was fulfilled through Jesus.

This way of interpreting the Bible is dangerous for people as they often come up with erroneous conclusions and make impulsive, uninformed decisions as a result. Additionally, the misinformation can result in Christian politicians making misguided decisions at the highest level of government—affecting the lives and well-being of millions.

Biblical Inerrancy

Dispensationalism has no power apart from the doctrine of biblical inerrancy. In fact, no evangelical theology has authority apart from this doctrine. According to the Chicago Statement on Biblical Inerrancy, inerrancy is defined as: *"Scripture in its entirety is inerrant, being free from all falsehood, fraud, or deceit."*[11]

The definition set forth by the council is problematic on many levels. Although this definition is usually followed by the attempted clarification of: "Scripture in its entirety is inerrant, being free from all falsehood, fraud, or deceit *in the original manuscripts,*" this is a difference without distinction since what is contained in modern Bibles is believed to be somewhere around 95% accurate to the originals. In other words, the caveat is a misnomer because what we have is as close to accurate as possible for documents that are over 2000 years old. In fact, the Bible's provenance far surpasses any of its contemporary writings that exist today.

However, the definition is unhelpful in other ways notwithstanding the caveat. The terms falsehood, fraud, or deceit are all qualifiers that deal with the intention of the author. If those are the real qualifications then most people could probably agree to some version of inerrancy. The problem is that most people don't understand what those qualifiers mean and as a result proclaim the more generic idiom "the Bible is without error." Moreover, what is usually meant by this is that there are no mistakes in the Bible, which is untrue.[12]

By all accounts, the authors of the Bible made sincere efforts to convey accurate information and did not *intend* to deceive their readers. In other words, they were not lying. It is widely recognized that though at times the authors may have mistaken certain details, there was no benefit for the authors of Scripture to intentionally mislead their audience. What's more, particularly in the New Testament, the writers did not believe they were writing something equivalent to the Torah. They wrote honest letters and biographies that represented what they remembered to the best of their ability.

Although the doctrine of biblical inerrancy as it is currently articulated is problematic; there are two things in particular that make it *dangerous*. First, it provides a *false sense of security*. That is, it does not provide the methodological certainty that one expects when basing a belief on it.

For example, using scientific methodology we can reasonably conclude that something is true or false (albeit, scientifically true or false) because we know that the formula for coming up with that conclusion is based on a tested logical approach. The same is not true for using inerrancy as a basis for theological ideas. Inerrancy is a theory that is untestable and is in essence a doctrine no different from any other doctrine - perhaps even a lesser doctrine since there is no theological evidence for it.

Evangelicals use what is known as circular reasoning to justify their belief in inerrancy. For example, 2 Timothy 3:16-17 is a cornerstone passage for those defending inerrancy:

> All Scripture is God-breathed and is useful for teaching, rebuking, correcting and training in righteousness, so that the servant of God may be thoroughly equipped for every good work.

Many cite this passage as proof of the inerrancy of Scripture. And, if you were a propositionalist you might be inclined to believe them .[13] It plainly says all Scripture is God-breathed (meaning, from God). However, a proper interpretation of this passage within its *context* tells us that this is not referring to the "Bible" as God-breathed. We know this because the Bible had not been compiled yet, so it could not possibly be referring to itself. Instead, it is referring to the Hebrew scriptures also referred to as the *Tanakh,* consisting of the Torah, the Writings, and the books of the Prophets. There are also pseudepigraphical writings and the Mishna which are often used alongside the Tanakh. Propositionalists leave out that context and simply quote the verse in order to justify an unbiblical belief.[14]

Making this even more problematic is that most theologians begin with the doctrine of inerrancy as the foundation for the rest of their theology. The logic behind this is, since the Bible is God's primary revelatory source to humanity, then it should be the foundation for theological inquiry. This is not unreasonable per se. However, evangelical theology is much more nuanced and contains two additional requirements (at least in its current form).

First, it requires systematic consistency. This is a methodological aspect. Creating a systematic theology is based upon an impractical premise; namely, that 66 ancient religious documents spanning two thousand years can agree in all aspects. This would be an irrational premise if not for inerrancy. Inerrancy helps to answer the question, how is this possible? Inerrancy allows the possibility because ultimately God is the author (God-breathed) and therefore makes the impossible plausible. It is based on God's standard instead of a human standard of plausibility.

Second, if ultimately God is the author, then that means we cannot use conventional hermeneutical methods of interpretation which are based on how humans construct literature. This gives the theologian permission to interpret the Bible propositionally because the entirety of the text is constructed by God and therefore doesn't necessitate human context.

With that said, there are varying views of inerrancy. The "soft" view of inerrancy would see the bible as dynamically inerrant. That is, God did not dictate Scripture but inspired the writers on what to write. There are varying views on what it means to inspire a writer. These various dimensions are related to the degree to which God communicated to the authors. Did God dictate to humans? Did he whisper in their ear? Or, did he just bring to memory events or ideas that the individual then recorded? Regardless, what is missing in all of these scenarios is the human element. And, as we have stated numerous times, humans cannot operate outside of context, whether that be writing, interpreting that writing, or even general communication.

Ultimately, this means much of the theology that evangelicals create is built upon a false premise and leads to further theological problems later in the process. *The false doctrine of inerrancy is the theological foundation through which all of Evangelicalism and Fundamentalism are built, which is why evangelical theology must be held accountable and re-evaluated.*

The doctrine of inerrancy is also what dispensationalists rely heavily upon in order to render their ideas about the end times. They provide their followers with lists of verses that seem to prove their theories and as a result, the reader has no choice but to believe in their arguments even if those arguments are circular.

In psychology, this phenomenon is referred to as "confirmation bias." Confirmation bias is when someone wants to believe something to be true so badly that they only surround themselves with information that confirms their belief. Since much of this happens subconsciously, it is very difficult for the individual to see themselves as being biased. Moreover, this is why the idea of theological certainty is so dangerous—it gives the believer a *false sense of security*. It is vital that anytime individuals participate in the task of information processing they approach that endeavor with humility. That means understanding our presuppositions and limiting them as we evaluate new information. Ultimately, *if we begin with the idea that what we already think we know is true, then we can never know when we are wrong because we are never open to the possibility of being wrong*. That is not only intellectually irresponsible but dangerous.

In addition to creating a false sense of security, inerrancy also creates a *false sense of authority*. This authority is derived from the false sense of certainty that is part of inerrancy. In other words, because individuals believe they have some form of revelation directly from God they believe their theology or beliefs carry the same authority. This false sense of authority gives people the courage to spread beliefs that might be misinformed because they infer they have been given that authority by God himself. Further complicating things is when this false sense of authority is paired with what they believe to be their mission in life (e.g. spreading the gospel), resulting in a misguided and dangerous zeal.

A false sense of authority is also dangerous when it is used to galvanize people into missional action. This has been a part of evangelical culture since its formation and is not only a part of the Church but is used in political leadership as well. Inerrancy has formed the backbone for the evangelical bias.

Our Inherent Biases

It is said that history is written by the victors. Likewise, much of theology and doctrine has been composed by Western (philosophically) men. Many of whom are also husbands and fathers. Men who are also responsible for the establishment and maintenance of most of the world's power structures, like governments. In modern times, most of those men have also been white.

These statements are not meant to be disparaging, they are just truisms. These are inescapable biases that have influenced thinking for generations. Biases are inescapable, but they are not impossible to overcome. For example, there is a difference between a person who accepts and works to understand their bias versus the one who denies or ignores it. The one who does not accept this fact has no choice but to continue thinking only in terms of what they have been programmed to think. On the other hand, the one who does accept this fact is one who has the ability to understand their thinking in light of their bias and is able to render a more accurate conclusion as a result—if they choose to. This is a small but important distinction. Despite the fact that understanding one's biases doesn't necessitate that what the individual says is true, it starts them in the right direction.

Understanding our biases is a relatively modern phenomenon. It is not that historical thinkers did not understand that they had biases, they just did not care. In fact, many of them thought their biases were not hindrances but strengths. They believed their education and privilege, for example, were useful biases that gave them an advantage against those who did not have the same experiences. However, they did not understand that they could only be right if their biases were also right, which they could not have known because those who came before them had the same biases.

Modern thinkers inherit this history of bias. That is why it has become necessary to understand our biases and, at the very least, be skeptical of them. If biases are inevitable, then we should take the time to understand how they influence our thinking. Perhaps no theology has been more influenced by bias than that regarding the role of women in the home and society.

Why the Role of Women is No Complement

Although it would be easy to go through and refute complementarian arguments point by point, it is better to begin with the core reason for why the role of women has been so misunderstood. It has been the case that the restrictions placed upon women have persisted throughout most of Church history. If this belief is presumably orthodox, then why question it now? Additionally, is it not presumptuous for us to think that we know better than those theologians throughout history who have upheld these doctrines?

In most cases, it would probably be presumptuous. However, this situation is different for two reasons. And the fact that theologians have not recognized this major difference is a testimony to the misogyny behind the theology.

The first problem is in hermeneutics (how we interpret the Bible). Historically, theologians have been inconsistent with how they attempt to differentiate between what is contextual and what is universal for application. Sometimes, getting lost in their academic rigor has alienated them from common sense, which in this case, is all that is necessary for understanding some of these passages.

In general, when people read the Bible it can be understood in one of two ways: prescriptive or descriptive. Prescription is when an author writes statements that should be understood in terms of commands. Description refers to a writing that is describing something for their reader (like a historical event). Outside of the Bible's creative writing (poetry, songs, etc.), most of the Bible can be understood within one of these two aspects.

Traditionally, the role of women has been understood prescriptively, which is the way it should be understood. However, there is an additional requirement when deeming something to be prescriptive. One must determine whether the prescription is contextual (something specific for that time) or whether its application is universal (for all times). This is where the disagreement often lies. Complementarianism argues the commands for women are universal. In the context of the role of women in church and home we will use the complementarian justification as a framework for evaluation, as it represents the majority view in Evangelicalism.

A Study in Complementarianism

Complementarianism is based on the premise that men and women were created by God to serve different functions both in the home and society. Their presupposition is their belief that this command is found all throughout Scripture, spanning all the way back to creation. Therefore, since the creation argument acts as the foundation for their overall argument this is where we should begin.

There exists this idea that because Adam was created first and given a mandate before Eve was on the scene, that this gives man a role distinct from that of his future wife. This idea is largely based on 1 Timothy 2:13 which explicitly argues this. Although it is difficult to understand why the author of 1 Timothy (often presumed to be Paul, but almost certainly was not)[15] stated this, the conclusion the author makes is not warranted based on the context of the creation narrative. This is a difficult thing for evangelicals to ignore given their view of inerrancy, which places all scripture on equal footing regarding its truthfulness.

In its current form, the overall argument is as follows: God could have created Adam and Eve at the same time. Instead, he chose to create them at different times and with distinct characteristics. Therefore, there must have been a purpose for him to do so.

The first assumption this argument makes is that the intent of the author of Genesis was to provide a "blow-by-blow" account of how God created. This overly literalistic view of the creation account is a profound misunderstanding of how ancient authors communicated through narratives. This lack of contextual awareness means that the view also misunderstands the purpose of the story.

Although it is true that God could have created them together, the bottom line is that the author is taking creative liberty to poetically communicate the beauty of the created order, the pinnacle of which was humanity. The author is isolating both man and woman in order to describe their intricacies. The communication style is artistic, poetic and beautiful.

However, beyond the contextual misunderstanding, the theological implications of this argument are problematic because it must also infer that God is incompetent and imperfect since he created man without a partner. It was Adam who brought that fact to God's attention. Why could God not do it right the first time? One could also ask why did God create every individual aspect of creation instead of just making it appear all at once? Was he impotent?

Of course a complementarian would never argue this, but it goes to the theological double standard that is often employed by evangelicals in order to justify certain beliefs. A double standard that, as we will see, is applied every chance they get when arguing for the subordination of women.

Additionally, Adam himself did not view Eve as someone subordinate to him but as an equal. This is illustrated in the short poem in Genesis 2:23:

> This is now bone of my bones
> and flesh of my flesh;

> she shall be called "woman,"
> for she was taken out of man.

When Adam equates Eve to his bones and flesh, he is specifically stating that she is equal to him because she is of him. This statement is in the context of Adam looking among the subordinate animals to find a "helper." Moreover, when Eve came on the scene it was not that she was simply "suitable" but she was more than that, she was just like Adam. Adam's poem symbolizes the awe he felt in seeing her.

Ultimately, the creation story is a poetic expression of God and serves as the preamble to the story of the Hebrews that follows. It is important to understand this story as it was intended, which is that God cares so deeply for his creation that he took the time to fashion it. Just as an artist forms beautiful pottery from clay, so too does God take the time to show his own artistic expression through his creation. That is why theologians also say that God is revealed through creation—because his fingerprints are all over it. And, his signature can be found every time we look into the eyes of another human being.

Since both men and women were created in the image of God, then this also means that there can be no inequality or subordination among them. Gender-based hierarchy is inequality. Even complementarians agree on this point.

For complementarians, the creation account acts as the justification for why passages like Ephesians 5:22-23 should be taken literally.

> Wives, submit yourselves to your own husbands as you do to the Lord. For the husband is the head of the wife as Christ is the head of the church, his body, of which he is the Savior. Now as the church submits to Christ, so also wives should submit to their husbands in everything.

As well as passages like 1 Timothy 2:11-12

> A woman should learn in quietness and full submission. I do not permit a woman to teach or to assume authority over a man; she must be quiet.

For literalists and propositionalists they see passages like these as obvious prescriptive commands regarding the strict adherence to gender roles within the family as well as the Church. The failure in such interpretations is not in the delineation between prescription and description but in the application of prescription. What the complementarian does is take passages like these and give them universal application when they were not meant to be understood that way. Moreover, if one reads the context of the passage, they will quickly discern that it should be understood culturally and not universally.

Take the 1 Timothy passage as an example. Verses 11-12 do seem to justify the complementarian perspective. However, if you read the verses directly preceding that passage you will read the following:

> ...I also want the women to dress modestly, with decency and propriety, adorning themselves, not with elaborate hairstyles or gold or pearls or expensive clothes, but with good deeds, appropriate for women who profess to worship God.

If it is true that this should be applied universally, then why don't most complementarian churches forbid women to wear nice clothes or jewelry? In fact, it is usually just the opposite - women in these churches are oftentimes dressed very nicely and adorned with all sorts of jewelry. It is because they interpret that part of the passage as cultural. How can it be that one part of a passage is cultural while the rest of it is conveniently universal? It can't.[16]

Although the complementarian is correct in asserting that this text is prescriptive, they are incorrect in saying that it should be applied universally. This is the convenient double standard we mentioned above. This seemingly biased interpretation is clearly based on an anachronistic reading of the text, which may or may not be fueled by inherent misogyny.

With the creation of Adam and Eve understood within its proper poetical context and the commands in the New Testament understood in light of their context, there is no apparent argument that can justify the continuation of preventing women from ministering within the Church and helping to provide for their family.[17]

There is also the practical aspect of what the complementarian chooses to ignore. In general, we can look to our not-so-distant past to see how this theology has played out in the real world. This particular theology has resulted in both physical and spiritual abuse by men towards women. Although many complementarians would say that this argument is a Trojan Horse and not the intent behind the theology, the fact still remains that it happens. One's intent always takes a back seat to the truth that is contained through one's actions. This is the root of the idealist problem that we will address in the next chapter.

With that said, complementarians know very well that this belief can manifest in abuse. One need not look any further than the following statement from the Council of Biblical Manhood and Womanhood (CBMW), the creators of this view:[18]

> In the family, husbands should forsake harsh or selfish leadership and grow in love and care for their wives; wives should forsake resistance to their husbands' authority and grow in willing, joyful submission to their husbands' lea dership.[19]

The only reason for a statement like this is due to the awareness of existing or potential abuse. This clarifies for us that the founders of this movement knew how plausible abuse was. More than likely, they looked to their recent history and saw how these beliefs triggered domestic and spiritual abuse. But, what they had not considered was just how much power their perspective would give clergy over their congregations. They probably could never have imagined to what extent that power would be used by evangelical leaders to violate their sisters in Christ.

You may wonder how a belief that seems obviously false could have persisted so long in the Church. The answer is quite simple. The Early Church Fathers simply continued in the cultural traditions that were reflected within their society. The perpetuation of this belief led to it becoming a part of orthodoxy, which forced later theologians to attempt justification in order to preserve their orthodox tradition.

The language that CBMW uses is not that uncommon among evangelicals. Evangelical leaders have perfected the use of language to invoke certain messages using perceived authority - which they are also responsible for planting. Using terms like "biblical" or phrases like "family values' is a type of subliminal messaging that buries itself in the individual's subconscious and convinces them without needing to investigate the claim themselves.

The Subversiveness of Subliminalism

Evangelical leaders and pastors have perfected the art of subliminal messaging. Subliminal messaging is typically used in advertising to promote products subconsciously. For example, in movies, you will often see product placements. The McDonalds in the background was no accident but placed there intentionally to appeal to your desire for a Big Mac. That is a form of subliminal messaging. But there are other ways to appeal to people's subconscious, such as how we use language.

Linguistic subliminalism has been used for years within the Church. This is in no way exclusive to evangelicals but they have certainly perfected the art over the years. Using terms like "biblical," "inspired," and phrases like "It's God's Will," "God's Word," or "God told me," are examples of loaded language meant to appeal to an individual's subconscious.

Terms like these are pseudo-authoritative. That is, when partnered with other ideas, they give the false impression that they have authority. This subliminal messaging often happens so quickly people may not recognize when it occurs. Consider these two phrases as answers to the question, what is your view of the role of the wife within the family?

> **Person 1**: I believe in the biblical view that a wife has to submit to her husband.
>
> **Person 2**: I believe that a wife has to submit to her husband.

Person 1 is firm but has softened and legitimized their position by using the term "biblical." Person 2 seems crass and much more misogynistic than the first person. By using the term "biblical." the person making the statement has not only legitimized their statement in the minds of the hearers but has made the harsh statement easier to digest. For the listener, the first person's perspective is a directive from God, whereas the second answer is the close-minded view of a misogynist.

Once the individual is convinced that something is biblical, they rarely change their opinion, regardless of its irrationality. The problem is that when someone uses the term biblical they oftentimes conflate it with their belief in the idea they are justifying. When the individual uses the term biblical they are saying that at some point they encountered a verse or passage in the Bible *they believe* justifies their position. The doctrine of inerrancy bolsters that authority in its assertion that what they read was a directive from God which makes its veracity unimpeachable.

But there are additional problems in using idioms like this so liberally. Not only does this do damage to Christians, but it ruins the Church's reputation among non-Christians as well. Oftentimes Christians will hide behind this type of superfluous language to protect themselves from being judged or to justify beliefs they would be otherwise uncomfortable sharing. However, doing this has significantly harmed how non-believers view God.

Those unfamiliar with God see him as misogynistic, homophobic, and intolerable. This has been proven through research by the Barna Research Group. According to Dave Kinnaman, President of the Barna Research Group, the top non-Christian perceptions of Christianity are as follows: 87% view Christianity as judgemental, 85% hypocritical, 78% old-fashioned, and 75% view Christianity as too political.[20]

This perception is worrisome because while this is the public's view of Christianity, by extension it is also their view of the God that Christianity represents. If evangelicals care about culture as they have historically claimed, then this should be problematic for them.

Why so Many Evangelical Women Support Complementarianism

It is indeed complex to explore the reasons behind the continued presence of evangelical women in churches despite doubts about the biblical foundation of complementarianism. One significant factor contributing to this phenomenon is the deeply ingrained societal and familial expectations placed upon women within these religious communities—largely due to subliminal messaging. Over generations, women have been taught to believe that their primary duty is to serve their husbands, a notion passed down from their mothers and grandmothers. The weight of tradition and the fear of challenging established beliefs can create a sense of obligation to conform, even in the face of doubt. The upheaval that would accompany the rejection of these long-held beliefs can be emotionally and spiritually overwhelming, as evidenced by the testimonies of women who have questioned complementarianism. The realization that the sacrifices made in the name of God were not divinely ordained can shatter core beliefs about faith, family, and identity.

The primary reason for this is that both men and women have been hammered with authoritative language for so long that they are convinced that going against the tradition would be akin to succumbing to temptation. To be labeled a "feminist," or "worldly," or "liberal," or worst of all not a Christian is a deep-seated fear. There is a realization that occurs for many women that the things they were attempting to sacrifice for God—their self, being, and even at times their worth, was nothing more than a capitulation to misogyny. And what they have viewed as their greatest strength within this belief system has turned into their greatest weakness - their undoing. For many it is better to stay within this tradition than to rebel against it because they believe it allows them to keep their worth and dignity.

Complementarianism is a good example of how idealism has real-world consequences despite its ideals not existing in the world. Take Sue for example. Sue is a 55-year-old fraud investigator for a large credit union. As you can imagine, she is highly competent and has a high degree of emotional and spiritual intelligence. Sue is one of those people that women would often seek out for spiritual advice. She is one of the few people in the Church who possess the gift of wisdom. In an attempt to find a volunteer to help lead some classes in their church, a leader approached Sue to see if she would be willing to teach a class. Sue smiled and reluctantly said "no, I probably shouldn't."

The leader was surprised at her response and followed up to find out why. Sue explained that many years prior she was attending a small evangelical church when through a myriad of circumstances she found herself teaching a Sunday school class. As she began to give her remarks, a young pre-teen boy stood up and told her she was not allowed to teach. He then walked out of the classroom and refused to return until she was replaced.

Later that week, Sue spoke to the Pastor about the situation. He informed her that it was probably not a good idea for her to teach Sunday school anymore. Although he disagreed with the young man's approach, the boy was correct in his assertion. The pastor explained to Sue that their church/denomination believed that the Bible clearly forbade women to teach men. He then went on to show Sue the biblical passages for this reasoning. Despite her intelligence and spiritual prowess, Sue believed the pastor and as a result had not shared her wisdom within any class since.

Stories like Sue's are a refrain throughout the history of Evangelicalism and demonstrate the extent to which evangelical churches suppress strong female minds from engaging in the Church. This is another example of how the misunderstood authority of the Bible coupled with idealism stands in the way of spreading the Gospel.

A question that is rarely considered is, why would God put rules in place that suppress the Gospel instead of spreading it? It makes more sense to think that perhaps we have misunderstood those passages than to believe they restrict women in ministry. The only explanation seems to be that theologians have had an agenda to keep women oppressed. In fact, this agenda will become clearer as we consider one of the main reasons that Fundamentalism was established.

As I pointed out in Chapter One, one of the reasons for the establishment of Fundamentalism was in protest to feminist propaganda. There may exist a subconscious fear that women will be influenced to become liberal or buy into feminist propaganda. If Kristin Du Mez's thesis is true, namely that evangelicals have spent most of their history trying to establish a masculine patriarchal belief system aimed at establishing power throughout the nation, then it would seem reasonable to conclude that the suppression of women is part of that agenda.

The fusion of the evangelical worldview seems almost obvious at this point. It seems that because evangelicalism and politics have been so intertwined through the years, and given that there has always existed a toxic masculinity within Christianity, that white men have subconsciously equated the highest positions in the Church to the highest positions in government.

With that said, there is a fundamental misunderstanding about the nature of power. Power is often equated to brashness, popularity, and wealth; but the two are quite different. True power is the result of reasoned intelligence in decision making. Cliches like "money is power" produce "status" not power. Although some power may accompany attributes like status, true power has to be equated to decision-making and evaluated pragmatically.

Jesus may be the greatest example in history of how power works. When looking at his interactions with the leadership of his time (both religious and political), there was an intentionality and wisdom that often accompanied how he chose to respond to criticism. Jesus, who was not even formally educated as a Rabbi, was the greatest of them all, not just because he was the Son of God but because as the Son of God he understood humanity.

The only one who has true power over others is the one who can, at a moment's notice, choose to relinquish that power—to give it all up and become nothing. True power comes in the realization that power is ultimately an illusion of the elite in society. True power is in the ability to change minds not because people are forced to but because they are convinced to. That makes the ability to use wisdom to influence others the chief constituent of power.

The Subtle (Or Not So Subtle) Psychology of Racism

Within the evangelical culture, a subtle form of racism persists, often overlooked or denied by its leaders. This racism is distinct within evangelicalism due to its dual origins. Firstly, it stems from the historical involvement of evangelical and mainline Christians in propagating racist ideologies through theological discussions. Secondly, it is influenced by the societal norms of the times. However, rather than seeking a middle ground, many evangelical churches opted for exclusion over inclusion, perpetuating this issue within their communities to this day.

Within evangelicalism, systemic racist attitudes persist, intertwined with their political affiliations. These attitudes, ranging from subtle to overt, draw parallels to historical justifications for slavery. A common defense used is the assertion that issues related to race are political, not religious. Consequently, when initiatives emerge to confront racial disparities, evangelicals and conservative Christians often dismiss them as left-wing political propaganda, rather than engaging in meaningful dialogue. This is indicative of evangelical leaders' attitudes toward critique and re-evaluation—an attitude that must be reconsidered.

Perhaps this can be illustrated best through the reaction evangelicals had towards the #BlackLivesMatter movement. Although originating from left-leaning Democrats, it nevertheless still carried significant validity irrespective of its political origins. It is crucial for white evangelicals to recognize that the movement is not centered around them, rendering their opinions inconsequential in this context. The discomfort experienced by white men in not being central to the conversation can be attributed to historical power dynamics. There may also exist a latent fear among some individuals that a shift in power dynamics could occur if African Americans gain more influence in society.

The response that many white evangelicals had to #BlackLivesMatter was straight out of their conservative Republican playbook. They argued that by isolating black lives, people were making it an issue of race and therefore perpetuating the problem instead of solving it. With that said, those making this argument have done little to actively engage in the issue, making their argument largely a part of their idealism and of no practical consequence. Their response has been to support movements like #AllLivesMatter because it seems more inclusive; or even worse, #BlueLivesMatter, in direct opposition to the problem of police violence, believes that it is really the police who are at risk, rather than people of color. However, statements like these have embedded within them subtleties that betray the ignorance of white men and women toward this issue. Consider the following observations:

1. White men have always been in power and have intentionally kept African Americans from achieving equality in society. In fact, there have been so many times where white men have said "trust us" and gone back on promises or simply lied to African Americans that there is no foundation of trust that exists. Why trust white men now? What has changed?

2. It's not just white men but also the laws that white men have created, which have endured as legacies of racism. These laws exist in a somewhat eternal state to ensure racism persists in some form even if white men's opinions change.

3. And, it's not just the laws that exist but the systems that were built around racist worldviews. These attitudes don't simply vanish because of a change in policy. Like laws, unless they are specifically addressed, they always remain a part of the system.

But these are just some of the subtle ways that white men perpetuate racism. There also exists plenty of overt racism as well. For example, on February 24th, 2024, at John MacArthur's Grace Community Church, during a question and answer session, MacArthur made the statement that Martin Luther King Jr. was "not a Christian" and that he was also an "immoral man." MacArthur was commenting on how the Together for the Gospel (T4G) organization the year before did a "wonderful" conference honoring the late R.C. Sproul, which over 12,000 people attended. The following year they chose Martin Luther King Jr. For MacArthur, this demonstrated how the organization had become beholden to the liberal woke[21] movement.

On the surface one might wonder how this is racist? There is little doubt that MacArthur is a fundamentalist who is prone to judging the spiritual worth of others, which makes one wonder how this is different from any other type of judgment he might render? In fact, supporters for MacArthur could argue that MacAruthur spent much of his career as a young minister, ministering in black communities during the tumultuous '50s, demonstrating his affection for this culture.

And yet, in 2012 he did an interview with the Grace to You preaching ministry touting slavery. MacArthur argued that just because some abused slavery doesn't make the institution of slavery wrong. His distasteful minimization of what blacks experienced as akin to abuse in a marriage or a business who abuses their employees, demonstrates the existing ignorance that fuels a subtle but effective racism. If those statements weren't enough, MacArthur went on to state that for uneducated people who lacked opportunity, slavery was the best possible option for them.[22]

Finally, MacArthur states that "If you ask me to be a slave, I will simply ask you one question: who is my master... I would not be able to sign up fast enough to be a slave."

MacArthur is not alone in having perspectives like this. MacArthur is a highly educated individual; if he thinks this way, what does that indicate for those who lack higher education? This is not only an example of the type of ideas that fuel subtle and systematic racism but also demonstrates the extent to which African American history has been whitewashed both in public and private schools.

Other influential evangelicals share MacArthur's views. Well-known pastor and theologian Douglas Wilson co-authored a pamphlet titled "Southern Slavery: As It Was". In the pamphlet, Wilson provides an argument defending the large number of Christians who had been responsible for defending and perpetuating slavery in the South.[23] A simple Google or Amazon search under this topic will give you an enormous amount of books (some even bestsellers), blogs, and other literature that demonstrate the extent to which these revisionist historians are influencing American culture.

Additionally, According to an investigation by the Roys Report in 2022 a culture long been established in MacArthur's church of shaming and punishment for women who divorce their husbands—even in situations of domestic violence. The Report cites former church member Eileen Gray who had been excommunicated from MacArthur's church in 2002 because she refused to stay with her child abusing husband.[24]

Most recently, the church publically disciplined Lorraine Zielinski in July 2024 for leaving her abusive husband. The church sided with her husband who denied accusations and as a result began a campaign of bullying and ostricization which ultimately lead to her excommunicat ion.[25]

At the core of the evangelical consciousness there exists a disconnect between their beliefs and the world in which those beliefs are to be lived out. This is because evangelical beliefs are stuck in the realm of imagination where they have little to no import in the real world. This idealism puts forth the highest imaginable standards by which those outside of the Church are evaluated. If Part One demonstrated anything it was the fact that not even evangelicals can live up to the standard they put forth for others. It is this problem of idealism that we will cover in the next chapter.

8

CHRISTIAN IDEALISM

SINNERS IN THE HANDS OF AN ANGRY EVANGELICAL

THROUGHOUT OUR EXPLORATION OF evangelical Christianity, we have extensively examined its various dimensions. We have diligently differentiated between Fundamentalism and Evangelicalism when possible and we have highlighted instances where these two ideologies have overlapped or encountered challenges in defining their distinct identities. This is ultimately where Evangelicalism finds itself today.

In this chapter, I will address what I believe to be the primary issue within Evangelicalism and highlight how some influential church leaders have embraced a form of idealism that not only shaped Evangelicalism's direction but is also responsible for the overall fusion of their worldview.

In our day and age, there is a crisis within Evangelicalism; a crisis where convictions and politics collide in a battle for supremacy. This battle has resulted in a loss of identity that has impacted how evangelicals minister within their local congregations. The perceived culture war has created an "us against them" mentality that has harmed Evangelicalism's relationship with culture. Any attempt to repair this relationship is futile as evangelicals have already destroyed the trust that is necessary to lead people into new life. If culture is one's enemy, then who is there to save?

Fundamentalism & Evangelicalism: What's the Difference?

Throughout most of their history, Fundamentalism and Evangelicalism have had clear boundaries. Despite sharing many beliefs, their differences are important. Evangelicalism's distinction was in their engagement with American culture—the same culture that fundamentalists forsook. This was exemplified through the ministry of Billy Graham.

However, as Evangelicalism began to change and their worldview became more entangled with culture and politics, they pulled away from those they were commissioned to serve. Once the primary aspect of their identity, evangelicals quickly lost their perspective and the people that made their ministry valuable were now their enemy. This new anti-cultural perspective brought about an identity crisis. The only rationale that evangelical leaders had was to see themselves as the victims instead of the perpetrators. There was a new narrative created to support the idea that evangelicals were under a type of cultural persecution because of their beliefs. Despite the fact that Evangelicalism was simply reaping the natural consequences of the kind of abuse they dealt to culture, the laity have largely bought into the idea of persecution.

Thus, we are faced with a question. If cultural engagement was the key factor in differentiating fundamentalists and evangelicals, then what is to distinguish them now? It cannot be beliefs because there are not enough differences for distinction there. It cannot be behavior since we have seen many evangelicals exercising the same intolerant, hateful rhetoric that fundamentalists have become known for. Perhaps, Evangelicalism is the new Fundamentalism.

Due to Evangelicalism's significant cultural changes, its identity has evolved. Its new identity allows evangelicals to continue with a worldview that lacks proper distinctions. White Christian Nationalism is a structure that allows evangelicals to continue operating within a fused worldview while at the same time not forsaking their perceived purpose. So comfortable have evangelicals become with White Christian Nationalism that they have largely failed to see the change or even been able to identify any meaningful distinction. To many of them, it has just been a part of who they are.

The End is Here (Again)

COVID-19 brought to the public's attention just how intertwined evangelical theology is with political ideology and how much evangelicals are influenced by this relationship. Similar to how evangelical leaders created messages revolving around abortion in the '70s and '80s, the message in 2020 was simple: "there is no place for fear in the community of believers." This message attempted to obfuscate the pressing concern around social distancing and quarantining by creating a "biblical" argument for church attendance. This message naturally led people to protest against lockdown policies and mask mandates.

Harkening the days when soapbox preachers would preach hell, fire, and brimstone; modern preachers were creating a new narrative. The vaccine was the new mark of the beast. This warning was just the most recent in a long line of end times warnings that evangelicals—particularly fundamentalists and Pentecostals—were responsible for perpetuating throughout the years.

The sad fact was that even though these communities were known for their end times fervor, their interpretation of what theologians say the mark of the beast should be was significantly inaccurate. The mark of the beast, if real, is meant to be a choice made willingly over Jesus, not through deceit or coercion. This fundamental misunderstanding highlights the importance of individuals taking responsibility for their own faith development. It is evident that some leaders discourage independent thinking because the consequences will illuminate their mistakes.

Some of these accusations may seem absurd, perhaps even like a strawman argument, because some of these beliefs seem so outlandish and likely to be perpetuated only by the fringe. However, there is no strawman—this is the new Evangelicalism. Consider Emily Smith, an epidemiologist at Baylor University and the wife of a Baptist Pastor who also runs a Facebook page on the benefits of the vaccine:

> I have been met with hostility and threats... In the summertime, I thought, these were just fringe beliefs. But the further we got into the pandemic, I realized, these are very widely held, and I was surprised by how many Christians and churches subscribe to this... It's one of the scariest and most disheartening parts of this, that so many people think that when you put on a mask, it is the mark of the beast or signals that you don't have faith or God isn't in control.[1]

Additionally, videos like "Plandemic," by Judy Mikovits, which became an internet sensation with over 1.8 million Facebook views and 150,000 shares, attempted to argue how certain billionaires along with Anthony Fauci (director of the National Institute of Allergy and Infectious Diseases) conspired to spread the disease.

This inability to distinguish between the two dimensions of religion and politics is not the root of the problem. Instead, the root is something deeper—more fundamental. Namely, Evangelicalism suffers from a philosophical idealism that colors everything they do, from their theological perspectives to their political ideologies. This presents a significant paradox as it both affirms certain beliefs about itself while at the same time denying those same beliefs in action. This is the hallmark of idealism. In order to understand why Evangelicals have fallen prey to idealism we must do a deeper dive into its development.

German Idealism & Hegel

Although German Idealism encapsulates several prominent philosophers, the only one that we are concerned with is a man by the name of Georg Wilhelm Friedrich Hegel (1770-1831). Hegel was a philosophical powerhouse, the likes of which have rarely been duplicated throughout history. His contribution and influence within Western thinking is incalculable. In fact, much of contemporary Western thinking is the sole result of Hegel.

Among his many achievements, Hegel has been the most influential contributor to the philosophical framework used for the scientific method. The core of Hegel's dialectic has also been influential in fields like psychology and theology. What's more, Hegel's establishment of certainty in the field of epistemology (the study of justifiable knowledge) laid the foundation for Modernism. His impact on the development of these principles and perspectives is significant and enduring.

Although German Idealism begins with Kant (and includes a host of others) we are going to primarily focus on Hegel. Hegel's part in German Idealism was to bring both German Idealism and philosophy to a close by providing a path to certainty. This is what he believed his "scientific philosophy" accomplished. Hegel believed that nature had a formula—a logic to it that if one could understand it, they could utilize that formula to understand the nature of all things. Not only could they know but they could do so with certainty.

Hegel understood that since humans are inherently flawed, any system they developed would also be inherently flawed. Since humans can never escape their own biases and presuppositions, they are never in a position to understand things the way they are. Hegel's method was to use logic, the mathematics of nature, to understand this natural algorithm. This led Hegel to create (or more accurately, rearticulate) a natural formula called dialectic.

Dialectic consists of three parts: thesis, antithesis, and synthesis. In very basic terms, if one posits an idea (thesis) one must first consider what lies in opposition to that idea (antithesis). This consideration allows the thinker to weed out alternative explanations at the outset. Finally, one finds the middle ground (synthesis). This synthesis produces an answer. This answer is then resubmitted to the process. This pattern repeats until the core idea is found—its natural constituent.

Here is a real-world example of what this could look like. Consider a school board meeting to discuss structural issues with the local school:

Thesis: The school needs structural changes.

Antithesis: We should tear down the school.

Synthesis: Let's propose some renovations instead.

As the dialectic works itself out during this conversation we learn that too many structural changes are needed which won't allow for simple renovations. In the end it is more expensive but safer to tear down the school and build a new one.

In essence, Hegel's scientific philosophy aims to subsume all philosophical thought and, by extension, annihilate anything speculative and subjective. Consequently, that includes metaphysics. No doubt, this method seems like a reasonable and logical approach in discerning ideas.

However, one issue that dialectic failed to address were false positives. For example, what if there is some unknown anomaly in the data that is submitted? Hegel assumes that the anomaly is forced out through its submission to the system. But what if the anomaly is disguised in such a way that even the system can't identify it? Eventually, that idea makes its way into various foundations of knowledge and becomes a false premise which other ideas become evaluated against or dependent on. Let's use our school example to understand this.

What if the school did not actually need structural changes? What if the person the school board hired simply said it did as a way of making more money, but in reality the school was perfectly safe. The school board went into their conversation with a false premise and arrived at a false conclusion because of it. In fact, any conclusion they would have arrived at would have been false because their information was flawed.

Let us consider what this looks like on a larger scale. Hegelianism is built into the scientific method. That means all science that is performed does so utilizing these principles. All modern physics is based on Einstein's Theory of Relativity. That means all of the information we have about the origins and behavior of particles is based on Einstein's principles being true (and all of the minds who came after him as well). Although Relativity has been tested over and over again and always comes out on top, as good thinkers we must consider the possibility that it is either in part or whole not true. What would that mean for physics? That would mean almost everything we think we know about the world and universe is untrue (with the possibility of a few lucky guesses thrown in there).

These are the anomalies that can exist in Hegel's method. It is important to understand that these anomalies can exist because Hegel promises certainty with his method. Certainty always eliminates the idea of possibility because it has no need for it. But possibility is in itself a form of logic, which is also derived from nature. Both cannot be true.

A More Enlightened Jesus: Protestantism

Although most don't consider philosophy important enough to participate in, Hegel's ideas had a profound effect not just in the academic world but across seemingly disparate disciplines and all areas of life—including the Church. At the same time Hegel was making waves with his philosophy, the Church was struggling to find its voice in culture. For most of church history, the Church had been the power broker of knowledge. That is, until its authority was challenged on two fronts.

First, it was challenged by its own people in what became known as the Protestant Reformation. Second, and almost simultaneously, it was challenged by the Scientific Revolution (Copernican Revolution). Science was suddenly developing answers to questions that the Church had traditionally answered through theology. The Church's traditional answers were being questioned, and so was its authority over society.

Furthermore, this new knowledge was quickly revealing the corruption that permeated the Church. The fact that it misled people in order to maintain its power and wealth meant that many started distrusting the Church. The Reformation just added to that distrust and confusion. For the next 200-300 years, the Church underwent a makeover and attempted to regain the trust of its people. It was this time of newly emerging knowledge that is commonly referred to as the Age of Enlightenment.

Not one to ever take a backseat, the Church desired to regain its intellectual status and become reintegrated into intellectual life. This period was an incredible time of intellectual discovery both for Western culture as well as the Church. The Church began producing theological powerhouses in the 19th century alongside the other disciplines. Many of these religious academics began to see value in Hegelianism. Hegelianism could provide the certainty that the Church longed to give its people. As the Church began growing again, Protestant churches began falling into some of the same practices that they had formed in rebellion against.

Ever since the Reformation split the once unified Catholic Church, the Reformation had gained an enormous following. And just like Constantine had helped to usher in Christianity as the official religion of Rome, many of these Protestant churches were becoming "state sanctioned" churches. Since Germany was the intellectual capital of the West in the 18th-19th Century, Protestantism became easily infused into its culture. Lutheranism dominated parts of Germany, Denmark, and central Europe. The north was largely dominated by Reformed churches and the south was largely Catholic.

The fusion of religious institutions and the state meant that the Church was in charge of dictating national morality and law. This also meant that pastors were more political in nature, as they were often appointed by the state. In those days, being a minister was a fine way to make a living, especially for a second son. But like the post-Constantine Catholic Church, Protestantism was growing in political power which also meant corruption. The State would often use the Church as its eyes and ears and could use that both positively and negatively as it became more intrusive in people's lives. This created an awkward relationship between the Church and its people. Ultimately, these state churches became an activity for the social elite and not the commoner.[2]

The Thorn in the Side of Protestantism: Søren Kierkegaard

It could be argued that Protestantism was like a thorn in the side of Catholicism. Its mere existence became a source of constant consternation for Catholics. But just as Protestants were a distraction for Catholics, so too did Protestants have their own thorn to deal with—Søren Kierkegaard (1813-1855). Kierkegaard was not just a thorn in the side of Protestantism but of philosophy as well. Kierkegaard was a slender, frail man from the outskirts of Copenhagen. But what Kierkegaard lacked in stature he more than made up for with his towering intellect and commitment to his cause. A gadfly in every sense of the word, he dedicated his life to writing and critique. Kierkegaard firmly believed that like Jesus and Socrates, he was meant to live out his philosophy in the real world. And, like the prophets of old, he also knew that he would face the same type of death that Socrates and Jesus had faced for their beliefs. In an irony only fit for an ironist, he was persecuted by mockery and disdain for his writings and he suffered immense pain later in life from a debilitating back condition. He suffered intensely until his death in 1855 at the age of 42.

Kierkegaard's writings can be categorized into two distinct phases: the early pseudonymous works and the late religious works. These phases are characterized by different themes and approaches, reflecting Kierkegaard's passion and creativity for writing and cultural influence during this time. Throughout both phases, Kierkegaard also contributed articles to local newspapers such as the Fatherland and the Moment, which served to contextualize his writings within the cultural debates of his time. These articles provide valuable insights into the intellectual and social milieu in which Kierkegaard was immersed. And, as we will see, the issues he was addressing were not much different from our own.

As are most people who have the ability to think outside the box, Kierkegaard was heavily underappreciated in his time and to some extent still is. Part of the reason for this was that his outlook for the future lacked the optimism that people needed to motivate them into a greater existence. He was a cultural corrective for the Church and no one likes being told what they are doing is wrong—especially religious people. The other reason was that much of what he said was not understood by his contemporaries. In fact, so little was thought of him that his writings did not become widely available in the United States until the 1940s. It was then that people began to understand just how significant his thinking was. It wasn't until the emergence of postmodernism in the 1970s that Kierkegaard reemerged as an important and dominant philosophical figure.

Kierkegaard's critique of Hegel is found throughout his ironic pseudonymous works. Most of the time he does not directly address Hegel, requiring the reader to read between the lines as well as to understand his ironic kind of humor. With that said, you don't have to read too deeply to see the connections he makes in his works regarding Hegel. For example, in Concluding Unscientific Postscript (note the irony of the title); Kierkegaard states:

> Furthermore, if our generation has any task at all, it must be to translate the achievement of scientific scholarship into personal life, to appropriate it personally.[3]

In other words, Kierkegaard is saying (knowing that it is not possible in Hegel's system) that his approach to knowledge doesn't just ignore the individual but completely takes the individual out of the equation. Kierkegaard would go on to further argue that Hegel was blinded by his intellectual arrogance in thinking that he could devise a system so complete that it would put an end to the need for any other system. And in this blind arrogance, Hegel was completely oblivious to the fact that it was his subjectivity that devised such a system to begin with. If Hegel truly intended to develop something completely objective he is betrayed by the fact that it was he, the individual, who was its creator.

Hegel and his contemporaries deny metaphysics (phenomena that exist outside of the physical world) altogether. They deny it only because they have no need for it. However, not having a need for something does not necessitate its lack of existence. Despite Hegel's denial of metaphysics and his adherence to scientism, his ideas surprisingly did not deter religious leaders of the day.

Kierkegaard, always a dedicated Lutheran, hated the idea of a State Church. He had a term for this which he called "Christendom." For Kierkegaard, a Church governed by the state takes the restlessness out of being a Christian—the struggle; and instead prefers a comfortable chair in its place.

It was this inauthentic nature of the Church coupled with conservative theologians who seemed to blindly accept Hegelianism—the whole time unable (or perhaps incapable) of recognizing the irony of accepting such philosophies—that drove Kierkegaard's angst. If one were to summarize what Kierkegaard was attempting to teach the Church of his day, and consequently ours, it would be *"Christianity is not a doctrine to be taught, but rather a life to be lived."* In other words, when you take the individual out of the equation you are left with a Christianity that is simply something to know or figure out, not something that must be lived.

Kierkegaard's fear for the Church of his day and what it would become still resonates. Kierkegaard foresaw a church influenced by

Hegelianism to be one that searches for only the necessary answers, but is never equipped to know how to ask the right questions. The Church would be filled with people who were automatons, blindly following their tradition while never really taking stock in their own faith. Their introspection, if any existed at all, would be colored by their Hegelian presuppositions. They would be more like herds of cattle instead of one walking against the flow of the crowd. They would be more like the religious leaders of Jesus' day, than Jesus.

The Idealistic Hegelian Church: Evangelicalism

Not surprisingly, aspects of Hegelianism fit conservative theology nicely. Ultimately, it provided a foundation for Fundamentalism (and later Neo-Evangelicalism) which arose just half a century later. The absolutism of Hegelianism supplied the certainty that the Church longed for. It gave the Church a scientific approach to theology, thereby eliminating the subjectivity that accompanied illumination by the Holy Spirit.

Most conservative pastors and some theologians may not be familiar with the term "theological Hegelianism" largely because they are not trained in philosophy and therefore cannot grasp to what extent Hegelianism has affected how they think. This lack of philosophical knowledge can be attributed to factors such as limited philosophical education and insufficient critical thinking skills. This lack of training leads to a knowledge gap that is not entirely their fault. The emphasis in their training has traditionally been placed on other aspects of theology rather than philosophy, contributing to their lack of familiarity with philosophical concepts like theological Hegelianism.

This is not true of all intellectuals who also adhere to Evangelicalism. Conservative evangelicals like Gordon Clark and Francis Schaeffer are two notable examples who created bridges between philosophy and theology. But even in these cases one cannot escape the fact that their religious tradition heavily informed their theological methods, and their conclusions ultimately informed their understanding of philosophy.

As our survey in Part One pointed out, many of the problems in Evangelicalism begin with the indoctrination of pastors. The first major groups of seminaries were developed on the heels of the second great awakening right in the middle of German Idealism's popularity (and for what it's worth in the middle of slavery as well). The second major wave of religious schools that were developed came just after Fundamentalism began making waves. This was after German Idealism had already created what we now call Modernism and was the predominant worldview of the time.

Modernism cares much more about the answers and far too little about the questions that preempt those answers. Certainly, this is in part a failure to realize that the only way to get good answers is by asking the right questions. It is this flawed philosophy of education that permeates religious education in America.

For example, most conservative pastors, especially those associated with denominational schools are not encouraged to think critically (or, if they are, then it is within certain boundaries). Instead, they are taught to memorize, regurgitate, and capitulate to a type of indoctrination that can be easily passed on to the churches they will eventually serve. This makes sense in an environment that was created by or for specific denominations within Evangelicalism. You would not, for example, want Lutheranism being taught in Reformed churches.

However, the assumptions this model of education contains should be unbearable for anyone who desires to learn and teach the truth. This model assumes that each denomination believes that their version of Christianity is the truth. This certainty is one of the consequences of the modernist worldview and ironically also stands in contradiction with itself.

Additionally, this model acts like a cascading waterfall of information where knowledge comes from the top and trickles down to eventually reach the layperson. It's a generational phenomenon as well which means that it's cyclical; being passed down from generation to generation. This intellectual recycling leaves no room for critique or alteration to one's beliefs. There are no mechanisms for evaluating bad beliefs without compromising the whole system.

We have said this throughout but it bears repeating here: *if one begins with the premise of their own certainty, then the individual can never know when they are wrong because coming to that realization invalidates the individual's initial certainty, which results in the destruction of the entire system.*

It is for this reason that in the 1970s a new wave of thinking emerged which was dubbed Postmodernism. Postmodernism was built upon skepticism; but not of truth as many will claim. Instead, it is skeptical of how one obtains that truth. Evangelicalism has largely opposed this way of thinking and finds it not only offensive but considers it an epistemology that should not be held by anyone claiming to be a Christian. This was demonstrated in how many within the Emerging Church were treated by evangelical leaders in the '90s and '00s, which we covered in chapters 3 and 4.

If Modernism is characterized by the answers it produces, then Postmodernism can be characterized by the questions it asks. For people who are concerned about the answers, one can imagine how infuriating Postmodernism was to modernists. The primary reason that many evangelicals ostracized postmodern thinkers was due in large part to the fact that evangelicals never understood what Postmodernism was trying to do. Instead, in traditional evangelical fashion, they simply reacted to what they saw as an infringement on their ways of doing things and created an "us against them" mentality.

This mentality is not all the evangelicals' fault but is something that was taught to them through the idealism of their beliefs. Certainty is always at odds with questioning and introspection because it is threatened by the possibility of different answers. For evangelicals, questioning is the first move away from certainty, and for many, is tied to disbelief. In other words, if one's beliefs are certain then challenging those beliefs means not only challenging the certainty behind them but also the one who provides that certainty - God.

This directly correlates to Evangelicalism's emphasis on orthodoxy within the beliefs sphere of their worldview. Their protection of orthodoxy (or at least their version of it) is related to their belief in being the heirs of that tradition. However, in reality, their heritage is built on the work of the Reformers and not historic Christianity. Despite their reasoning that the Reformation was built from a more accurate understanding of orthodoxy; their inability to distinguish between the two creates an entanglement within their belief sphere.

The Never Ending Cycle of Power & Politics

First it was Judaism. Then it was the Catholic Church. Now it is Evangelicalism. Evangelicalism has fallen victim to the same misgivings and misunderstandings that these other groups and movements did. That is, inauthentic piety that is created out of arrogant idealism resulting from a complete collapse of its worldview.

It starts with Judaism. The story of the Jews in the Old Testament should act like a parable for us to learn from. It's a story about how idealism clouds one's ability to appreciate God's will for humanity. The story of how their idealism took shape looks like this:

God lived up to the promise he gave Abraham and established a new kingdom for the Hebrews to dwell within. God told the Jews they didn't need a king because he wanted to be their king and they were to be his people. It was to be the Kingdom of God.

However, the Jews desired the approval of the surrounding nations over and above that of their God. So they asked God again for a king. Heartbroken over their decision, God gave them what they desired but with the caveat that if they obeyed his commands he would ensure their flourishing, but if they abandoned them destruction would ensue. Over time the Jews saw other nations growing in power and wealth and wanted to achieve the same success. Ultimately, they abandoned God's will and created one of the most powerful nations in the region, which further alienated them from God and his presence.

God gave them another chance by sending his prophets. The prophets were the messengers of God's will to the people. Israel's faithfulness towards God ebbed and flowed but, ultimately, they decided to go their own way much like their foreparents, Adam and Eve. Throughout this period, God communicated through the prophets to warn the Jews that their behavior would result in their destruction. But they did not heed the warnings that he sent them. Since they did not obey God, the prophecies came true and they were exiled and lost their land.

God became silent for hundreds of years in order to build anticipation for his greatest act of redemption yet. It was during this time that a revival broke out among the Jews. It was an intellectual revival that produced some of the most important religious writings in human history. It was also during this time that Rabbis found a remarkable message hidden in the writings of the prophets. Among the prophets' messages of doom and gloom, God had planted a small seed of hope. That seed would come in the form of the Messiah. The Messiah would come and rescue them out of exile and restore them to their land where he would be their God and they would be his people. The Jews' faith in God was revived and there existed hope while they awaited their rescue from their Messiah.

Then God spoke. He spoke in the flesh through Jesus of Nazareth. Jesus, the physical manifestation of God himself, was present to proclaim God's will to humanity. The Messiah that was promised had finally arrived.

However, the Jews rejected Jesus because he was not what they expected the Messiah to be. Over the years they had created an idealization of what the Messiah would look and act like and, as a result, did not recognize him when he arrived. They believed, for example, that the Messiah would be a military leader—like the Judges of old. They created this image of a Messiah that was so far removed from reality that their idealization betrayed them with the incarnation of Jesus. Their idealization was a faith based in their own abilities of perception. Every conversation and argument Jesus had with the religious leaders of his day was an attempt at showing them what they misunderstood. He was the realist combating their idealism. What's more, they were so lost in their idealism that they were never able to grasp the extent to which God was present with them.

The Medieval Church

The followers of God did not learn from Israel's mistakes and Christians, the heirs of Jesus, fell into the same cycle. Out of their desire to acquire power and approval from those around them, the Church fell victim to its own intellectual arrogance and used Scripture as a means of power and control over the people they were supposed to care for.

The Church's worldview had become so entangled that it ultimately became fused and they had no choice but to embrace the idealism that almost always accompanies fusion. It is just a fact that belief in a God who exists only in the mind of its beholder will always succumb to the temptation of power if given the chance. This is a distinctly different perspective from the realism of God's existence that always demands humility because the understanding that you are in God's presence always results in falling upon the ground.

The source of their idealistic power was the Bible—specifically, access to it. The Church reserved the privilege of possessing a copy of the Bible for the elite clergy, thereby limiting the individual's access to Scripture. Consequently, the only way the layperson could learn about the teachings of the Bible was through the interpretation of the pope as delivered by the bishops and priests. This lack of access was exacerbated by the fact that the Bible existed only in the academic language of Latin. This made it impossible for lay people to understand the Bible's teachings for themselves. Ultimately, the people had to trust that their leaders were being honest.

Many believed that whoever had control of the Bible also had the ability to speak on God's behalf. Since there was little accountability within the Church, it could manipulate truth for its own gain. And, during this time, whoever spoke for God controlled not just parishioners but society. Not only was this what precipitated the Church's manipulation of its people, but because they allegedly had direct access to God, they could also decide who was "in" and who was "out" of heaven/purgatory. This held extreme importance for lay people and leaders within society.

However, as time went on and disciplines like science and philosophy began to separate themselves from the grasp of the Church, the authority of the Church was weakened. In desperate attempts to salvage their power, they began persecuting their own. The most significant threat to power came in the form of a new invention—the printing press.

John Wycliffe took the brunt of this persecution as it was his goal to translate the Bible into the common language and to make copies of it available to the public. However, the Church knew that if the Bible became accessible to everyone, its widespread corruption and abuse would be uncovered. In its first attempt at a campaign of misinformation, the Church began arguing that translating the Bible into a different language would make the Bible inferior to its original Latin form (echoes of this argument would later be used by King James Only evangelical fundamentalists throughout the 20th Century.) Since most of their constituents were uneducated it became quite easy to persuade them of this misinformation.[4] Despite this, Wycliffe's followers completed the first translation into Middle English, which today is known as the Wycliffe Bible.

The final blow came in the form of Martin Luther who had a keen understanding of Scripture and language. In a friendly gesture to warn the pope of important misinterpretations and abuses, Luther nailed his 95 complaints to the door of Castle Church in Wittenberg, Germany. The theses criticized various doctrines of the church with a heavy emphasis on indulgences, which was one of the primary means of revenue for the Church and one of their abuses. It was not Luther's purpose to reform the Church, but to protect the pope. Little did he know that the pope was not just a part but the author of the whole corruption.

Evangelicalism

Much of Part One is dedicated to telling the story of how Evangelicalism came to establish the worldview it has today, so there is no need to rehash it here. With that said, a few connecting points are important.

Modernism allowed Evangelicalism to assume a position similar to that of the Catholic Church in medieval Europe, where the Church held authority over biblical interpretation. The adage *"whoever controls the Bible speaks for God and whoever speaks for God controls the people"* has become a hidden concept within the evangelical theological consciousness. The preceding chapters offered context for the central idea that both Fundamentalism and Evangelicalism have maintained control over their beliefs through their control of the Bible.

The approach that was taken by the Catholic Church was to control the interpretation of the Bible. In Evangelicalism, it is to control the authority of the Bible. As we mentioned at the start of this chapter, within the belief sphere of Evangelicalism's worldview there are two main components: the protection of orthodoxy and biblical authority. Like the Catholic Church, evangelicals use these two aspects to control both the information about them as well as the information that is taught to their people.

By all accounts, evangelical leaders have not heeded the lessons from historical idealistic movements within Judaism and the Catholic Church, despite the Reformation's origins in opposition to such ideals. The evangelical anticipation of the antichrist and the end times mirrors Israel's expectations of the Messiah, with both groups envisioning specific outcomes. However, there seems to be a significant disparity between these idealized notions and the actual unfolding of events. If evangelicals fail to draw insights from past errors, they risk perpetuating a cycle that could result in similar outcomes as those experienced by Judaism and the Catholic Church.

The Power Brokers of Knowledge

There is more to the evangelical worldview than beliefs. Evangelicalism was born out of a need for the Church to relate to culture. This responsibility that evangelicals have traditionally felt for culture has changed in recent years. Despite living in an age of technology and not having limitations on the attainment of knowledge, somehow conservative evangelical leaders still maintain a strong intellectual hold over their congregants. This is largely because evangelicals themselves have given authority to their leaders to be the power brokers of knowledge. That means, like the laity of Medieval Europe, evangelical lay people are beholden to their leaders and inherently trust them despite all of the times they have abused that trust.

In the Middle Ages, controlling the Bible equated to power and wealth. The money they were able to scam their congregants out of was used to finance their beautiful cathedrals. In modern times there exists the same agenda within Evangelicalism, and just as it was then, corruption continues to be obscured by piety now. *You can hide a multitude of sins with piety*. Today, the money often comes in the form of donations to special interest groups or in exchange for nominations to political parties and positions, resulting in a culture of *quid quo pro*. It is from this position of corruption that the evangelicals' power is exercised; power that is meant to induce the return of Jesus.

Let us consider, for a moment, where this power comes from. The origins of evangelical influence lie within its theological framework, which has gradually filtered down to impact the everyday lives of laypeople. As discussed previously, evangelicals have crafted a theology that serves to fortify their authority over their followers. One key aspect of this is their use of history, whereby many conservative evangelical theologians assert the orthodoxy of their beliefs. By positioning themselves as the bearers of theological authority, they effectively communicate to their followers their doctrinal soundness. Thus, the power of Evangelicalism ultimately stems from its ability to shape an enduring narrative that bolsters its authority and influence within the faith community.

Another method evangelicals often employ involves utilizing subliminal messaging to instill ideas in followers by repetitively incorporating specific phrases in sermons. This practice leads to the illusory truth effect, where cognitive ease is manipulated to influence beliefs. While cognitive ease is essential for everyday safety measures, such as avoiding physical harm or accidents, its misuse can result in a biased perception of reality.

Much of the cognitive bias is performed on a subconscious level. Most teachers, pastors, and other leaders are unaware that they do this, largely because it has become a part of the overall culture that continually recycles false beliefs. Additional danger arises when certain people understand this bias and take advantage of it. Eventually this bias becomes ingrained and is simply recycled from generation to generation.

This bias is part of a larger phenomenon called tribalism. Tribalism describes the social context through which groups of people band together. Tribalism is strong in Evangelicalism and can be observed through the various ways that evangelicals come together during times of crisis—particularly during times of political unrest.

Tribalism

Tribalism is conscious loyalty to an organized group of people who share a belief system and/or ideology. Tribalism was the standard way of life for those in hunting and gathering communities. Groups formed to share the workload and for mutual protection, and tribalism was necessary for survival. However, in modern times, tribalism manifests itself differently. It often occurs as a result of some significant crisis or uncertainty. Fear drives people into groups and sparks the ancient instinct of tribalism.

In today's culture, tribalism is rarely a positive expression of group dynamics and often acts as a conduit for the "us against them" mentality. COVID was one such crisis that sent many Americans into tribal mode. Once the initial panic over the crisis subsided, people began to take sides on issues like vaccines and church attendance. Even within churches themselves, tribal groups began forming and in some cases, churches split over minor issues like whether or not to wear masks. The unwavering support that existed within various tribes was, at times, extreme.

The infusion of tribalism into the evangelical consciousness has become so deeply ingrained that it is an inseparable part of their identity. This collective support can be observed through their active engagement in evangelism's political efforts. Ultimately, tribalism becomes reinforced through the ongoing efforts of their leaders and, as a consequence, also creates greater dependence for the average evangelical upon their leaders and the beliefs they are espousing. Overall, the prevalence of tribalism within the evangelical community is a significant factor in shaping their beliefs and practices.

Evangelicalism is only one group of many that suffers to some extent from tribalism. Political parties, for example, often do as well. While not all evangelicals are part of this tribalism, a significant portion of those discussed in this book are. Regrettably, this tribal mentality contributes to the escalating polarization in the United States. Decision-making based on self-interest and tribal allegiances rather than the common good perpetuates this division, indicating that change in the near future is unlikely.

Perhaps one of the more significant problems with Tribalism is that it subsumes a person's individuality. The individual becomes simply another body among the group, never distinguishing itself from the group. Their personal identity becomes merged with that of the group to such an extent that they become dependent upon the group for their information and perspective. Intellectual laziness and complacency are the inevitable result of a person who relies too heavily upon others for their own identity. In this sense, tribalism has always been a part of Evangelicalism.

The primary manifestation of tribalism within Evangelicalism currently is White Christian Nationalism. Although most evangelicals dislike this designation and many refuse to accept it, White Christian Nationalism reflects a set of behaviors (discussed in chapter 5). In other words, most people don't wake up one day and decide to become a White Christian Nationalist. Instead, it represents a worldview that has become fused to such an extent that white (cultural sphere) evangelicals (beliefs sphere) cannot separate themselves from their own nationalistic pride (societal sphere). The sooner evangelicals realize they are not Israel and not central to the end times as touted by dispensationalists, the sooner they will be able to start unraveling their various entanglements.

However, White Christian Nationalism is not the only manifestation of tribalism within Evangelicalism. An aspect of tribalism that has been going on for years was recently unveiled to the public in the scandals surrounding the Southern Baptist Convention (SBC). To be fair, what has happened in the SBC is not unique to them or even Evangelicalism, but is a phenomenon that takes place in many organizations across the country, both religious and secular. What makes tribalism devastating in Evangelicalism is how it directly negates its mission.

For example, the SBC had cultivated a culture of concealment for clergymen and ecclesiastical officials who were found guilty of mistreating their parishioners. No matter where certain allegations landed within the SBC, they kept these crimes under wraps. Many times these coverups are contrived under the guise of "handling the situation internally." This, of course, is not meant to protect the individual making the claim but the organization that is being accused. When organizations do this, they are not just potentially covering up a crime, they have become complicit in the crime.

The SBC used tribalism to protect themselves against legal action. Instead of thinking about the victims, the SBC retreated out of fear, to their tribal safety net, making it about self-preservation rather than justice. This is just one example, but there have been many evangelical organizations and churches that have followed the same path. This tribal protectionism is so entrenched in many of these organizations that even the people mistreated by them are afraid to come forward, not wanting to challenge the power of the tribal leaders.

The various aspects of tribalism have affected the mission that has been paramount within Evangelicalism. Instead of looking for opportunities to serve (e.g. COVID, helping abuse victims, etc.), evangelicals caught in the snare of tribalism have retreated to the comfort of their groups. Instead of helping to lead out of crisis, evangelicals change the narrative and make it about themselves. Instead of braving the terrain by looking for ways to change, they resort to shouting loudly in condemnation and warning from the security of their tribe. This has damaged their people and ultimately perverted the name of Christ in order to preserve power.

The most significant reason why evangelicals are so easily convinced of movements like White Christian Nationalism is the type of thinking they have been taught through their churches. One consequence of accepting the modernist Worldview has been the impact of binary thinking on the development and maintenance of evangelical beliefs. It is also the primary reason that evangelical leaders have such difficulty understanding the postmodern cause. That is, they cannot imagine how any truth can be constructed apart from binary thinking.

Critical Thinking & the Binary Problem

The specific manifestation of tribalism within Evangelicalism is founded upon a binary mentality and impacts all aspects of their theological and political beliefs. Each tribe generally constructs a certain agenda and purpose for the group. In the context of Evangelicalism, there exists a prevalent culture of indoctrination, which is initiated through the education of future evangelical pastors by theologians in seminaries.[5] Within these seminaries, there is a pervasive culture of indoctrination that prioritizes adherence to denominational doctrine over critical thinking. While it is certainly important for seminaries to produce pastors who are well-versed in their denomination's history and doctrinal beliefs, this should not come at the expense of critically evaluating one's denomination's beliefs. Unfortunately, future pastors are often immersed solely in their denomination's doctrines and rarely venture beyond them. This is largely due to the fact that seminaries typically do not hire theologians from outside their own denomination, for various reasons, and thus fail to recognize the value of providing a broader range of education for their students.

The outcome of pastors receiving education in this manner is that they transmit the same indoctrination to their congregations. While it may seem reasonable to educate individuals within the framework of their denomination, exclusive doctrinal education can become perilous indoctrination. This approach restricts one's perspective and makes it challenging to broaden one's understanding. Congregants are inclined to accept what they are taught as the ultimate truth, without critical examination, and to view it as superior to all other denominations. This does not lead to truth, but only the possibility of truth.

But there are additional consequences to this approach. Critical thinking is a virtue that is applied to various aspects of life and is not constrained simply to one's theology. The lack of critical thinking is the precise reason why many pastors and their congregations struggle to understand how to engage a dynamic culture. Add additional challenges or abrupt changes, like a pandemic, drive those without critical thinking skills into tribal retreat.

No doubt, much of this is unintentional. The current seminary systems in place are meant to cycle through people as quickly as possible, making quantity their priority instead of quality. Although this may be a sound business practice, the consequences far outweigh the advantages if one's mission is compromised in the process.

Binary thinking is a product of indoctrination and is a direct result of Modern Hegelianism. The individual who thinks in binary categories looks at the world in black and white. They see everything as "either/or" instead of "both/and." They see the world with certainty instead of possibility. In other words, something is either true or false. There is no nuance in binary thinking. The problem with it is that every indication we have suggests this world is much more nuanced—much more complex. We don't live in a black-and-white world. We live in a world of light and shade and lots of uncertainty.

This raises a significant question: how can a binary thinker navigate a non-binary world? There is a substantial intellectual divide between the culture and the binary group. The sole means of preserving a binary perspective is by acquiring enough power to establish binary thinking as the primary epistemic element of the wider culture. This is currently observable in contemporary America. The culture is faced with two alternatives: either succumb to binary thinking or resist it. For a prolonged period, American culture passively accepted binary thinking alongside the Church. However, in today's era, American culture has progressed, while the Church has remained entrenched in a binary mindset.

There are several significant examples of binary thinking within evangelical culture. For example, as previously alluded to, evangelicals have been heavily influenced by anti-abortion ideology, which leaves little room for nuanced considerations. Consequently, there exists a political binary predicament, whereby evangelicals are compelled to endorse Republican candidates without any alternative options. This is referred to as the *political binary problem.*

The political binary predicament, in turn, also has a significant impact on Evangelicalism. This is because evangelicals are often influenced by more radical perspectives, particularly when people who hold those perspectives are in their tribe. It is widely recognized that the most vocal individuals are often extremists who attract media attention. Extremism inherently adopts an "us versus them" stance, leaving no room for alternative choices in one's political worldview. Consequently, adopting extreme views becomes almost inevitable, especially when tribalism is at play.

Ultimately, modern Hegelianism's insistence on binary thinking has far-reaching implications and can often have unintended consequences. One of those consequences is deceit.

Deceit

In Evangelicalism, the issues of tribalism as well as religious and political binary thinking have created an environment that is self-contained. It is not an environment that has the ability to re-evaluate without losing important aspects of its identity. Anyone leaving the group is subjected to ridicule and ostracization because they threaten the status quo and thus the well-being and cohesion of the remaining group.

As a result, we see a group of people incapable of handling critical evaluation from both external and internal sources. They resist broadening their worldview or considering new perspectives because they know that as soon as people begin to think for themselves, they will lose their power. Those in power create a sanitized narrative that is believed wholesale by their followers. Trust is initially produced through spiritual manipulation and subsequently passed on generationally. The narrative presented as truth is accepted, not questioned, and the group thrives. The revelation of deceit often occurs through the indiscretions of those in leadership. Indiscretion catalyzes individuals to confront the truth behind their beliefs. For instance, when men possess exclusive spiritual authority over women, some inevitably abuse this power, which challenges the notion that God meant for men to exclusively govern the Church. Nevertheless, years of ingrained resistance to challenging the status quo make it very difficult for problems to be acknowledged. Victims often resist reporting the abuse for this very reason. Similarly, certain theological perspectives require individuals to accept specific truths about the Bible. When they are confronted with instances of divinely sanctioned genocide, rape, or other indiscretions, they are forced to question the validity of their beliefs and seek a deeper understanding outside of their environment.

Oftentimes, it takes more than one theological discrepancy or moral indiscretion to bring change. Eventually, deceit rises to the surface when the discrepancies become too numerous. And when people develop the courage to question their leaders and are turned away, it becomes obvious that something lurches behind the scenes. Those willing to take the first step, often take subsequent steps of deconstruction that broaden their worldview and take them beyond the boundaries of their groups. Many, however, are not willing to take the first step because it risks their belonging to their tribal group and the only way of life they know.

Moreover, this is one of the reasons that many pastors discourage questioning. These pastors disguise their fear of being identified as charlatans by asserting theological authority. With that said, it is important to note that many evangelical leaders are not aware of this dynamic. Most of it has become a subconscious part of their religious experience.

Evangelicals & Truth

Evangelicalism has a long-standing reputation for valuing truth. This emphasis on truth has been a hallmark of Evangelicalism since its formation. Even many of Evangelicalism's predecessors had a similar interest in communicating truthfully. For example, in classical theology, renowned theologians and philosophers like Augustine, Anselm, Aquinas, and Leibniz relied heavily on logical reasoning to establish their conclusions. As a result, these esteemed scholars are widely regarded as philosophers of religion and are appreciated in secular settings as well as religious ones.

However, the significance of truth in Evangelicalism extends beyond apologetics and philosophy of religion, as it is also evident in the emphasis placed on biblical interpretation and their relentless pursuit of knowledge throughout history. Moreover, the relentless pursuit of truth has remained a fundamental tenet of Evangelicalism throughout its rich intellectual history.

Navigating the Paths of Truth?

There is an age-old question that philosophers have been debating since the dawn of time: what is truth? This is a much more complicated question than it seems at first. For many of us, truth is something axiomatic. That is, we know something is true when it is based on facts or experience. Truth is commonly understood as a statement or idea that is reflected in reality. Ironically, this definition does not entirely reflect the nature of truth. It is tempting to define truth as a fact (as science does), but even this definition falls short in reflecting reality. The reason for this is that facts can change over time. What might be considered a fact at a particular moment may not hold true forever because evidence can change. This creates a dilemma where a particular idea can be both true and not true at the same time, which is not an accurate reflection of reality, it's a reflection of perspective.

In the pursuit of truth, it is important to recognize that there are multiple paths that can lead us there. Despite the modernist worldview telling us that truth is binary—that is, something is either true or false—determining truth and its variants requires a dynamic understanding. For example, there is a difference between the truth of something in and of itself and a human's ability to know that truth.

Let's illustrate our issue with a thought experiment. Consider gravity. Gravity is something we all believe to be true. Both science and our experience of it confirm gravity's existence. We know that when we jump we will not float off into space—ever. We will always fall back to the ground—always. We refer to this as absolute truth. Science tells us that gravity is like a fabric or blanket that our planet sits on and it rotates on this fabric much like a bowling ball moving around on a blanket. Because of Earth's mass, it creates indents as it moves, warping the smooth surface of the blanket—or gravity. This is why the greater the mass of an object, the greater the pull of gravity on that object.

Now imagine that you die and when that happens you are invited by some divine being to ask any question about life. And suppose you ask about this mysterious thing called gravity by asking the question, how does gravity actually work? To your amazement, the divine being says there is no such thing as gravity. There is a magical gnome-like creature that pushes everything down to the ground with a magic spell.

The question this thought experiment requires us to ask is, even though everyone believed in this concept called gravity (even if they did not know how it worked or agree on its name) was it ever true?

There are two ways to consider this question. The first is in space and time. Assuming that everyone in history up to the point of one's existence believed in gravity, does that make gravity true? From the individual's perspective, yes. You may not be able to explain it but you know that every time you go up you come down. That is gravity. This is referred to as the *Pragmatic* or *Consensus Theory of Truth.*

The second consideration is when we are given the "divine perspective". Having the larger view outside of space and time you learn about the magical gnome and realize that it was not gravity causing things to fall. Was gravity true? No. This is referred to as the *Ontological Theory of Truth*. This theory is based on what actually is within the nature of the thing itself instead of what someone believes about the thing.

This illustrates the various ways that truth can be ascertained and is ultimately why truth is relative. Truth always requires a context for a proposition to be rendered within. However, that rendering is always relative based on one's perspective and position relative to that context. This is how a proposition can render two separate conclusions based on one's perspective. For the person who died, their truth was "gravity does not exist". For the person in time, their truth was "gravity exists." And both are justified in their reasoning.

The issue of truth must also consider its practical application to life. If one is going to have any hope of understanding anything properly, they are required to make compromises and certain assumptions. If truth has any hope of actually existing it must be able to operate in the gray.

Our assumptions are often influenced by our *sense* of truth. When an idea resonates with us it may have what is called the "ring of truth" to it, and we tend to accept it without further investigation. Although this can be useful, it can also lead to confirmation bias, where we only seek out information that supports our preconceived ideas. This occurs because experiencing something that has the ring of truth means that it is something that has appealed directly to our presuppositions, which could be wrong. Recognizing that distinction is important.

For critical thinkers, it is crucial to remain open-minded in their pursuit of truth, recognizing that there may be multiple perspectives and interpretations for the same information. By doing so, we can arrive at a more comprehensive understanding of the world around us. If we give in to binary thinking it becomes much easier to miss that truth.

I have included a chart below that concisely illustrates some of the major variations of truth.

THEORY NAME	DEFINITION	EXAMPLE
Correspondence	The view that truth corresponds to, or with, a fact.	"A dog is on a mat" is true if, and only if, there is in the world a dog and a mat and the dog is related to the mat by being on it.
Coherence	The truth of any (true) proposition consists in its coherence with some specified set of propositions.	Stating that an object is a certain color requires belief in a number of other things being true, such as perception, ability to see colors correctly, time of day, amount of light, etc.
Linguistic (Semantic)	Related tangentially to the correspondence theory, the linguistic theory says that something is true when the words someone utters correspond to the thing being described.	"Snow is white" is a true statement only if we agree as to what we mean by "snow" and "white" and that those definitions correspond to reality.
Pragmatic	Something is true based on its utility and general consensus.	The ocean is beautiful.
Ontological	Something is true in and of itself.	The Earth exists.

**All definitions are from the Stanford Encyclopedia of Philosophy*

In the realm of truth theories, the ontological dimension plays a critical role in ensuring that what is being uttered corresponds to the nature of the thing. It is important to note that this is distinct from the correspondence theory of truth, as ontological truth must always refer to the nature of the thing as it actually is, whereas correspondence theory is bound by the fact that something seems to correspond to reality. While the two may sound similar on the surface, the ontological dimension requires a deeper understanding of the nature of the object being referred to, which we may not have access to. People who are concerned with truth must recognize the importance of this distinction in order to accurately convey truth in discourse.

Relative & Absolute Truth

The question of relative or absolute truth goes to the question of knowability. Do humans have the ability to know something objectively or is every observation of truth done so subjectively? This was the crux of the debate between Hegel and Kierkegaard. Hegel's belief that nature had at its disposal its own way of rendering things objectively true, meant that one could understand absolute truth because that understanding was determined apart from one's subjective bias. Kierkegaard, on the other hand, believed that we can never escape our subjectivity as it always acts as the presupposition to objective understanding.

This also serves as an example of the crux of the debate between Christian Idealism and Realism. For the idealist, as long as one is able to construct a belief based on objectivity (which, for evangelicalism, is based on biblical inerrancy), then that belief is true regardless of its existence in reality. The mind and the certainty promised by objectivity is the only criteria for true religious belief.

In opposition to that is Christian Realism which forms beliefs based on their actual existence. Part of the reason that this does not appeal to the evangelical is because it might be the case that certain beliefs that are considered orthodox are, in fact, not true. Therefore, in order to maintain their orthodoxy, they must compromise the truth of reality for the truth of systematic consistency. That consistency is from God who is the lord of logic and order, not one of chaos and subjectivity. And that truth is justified through objectivity.

Christian Idealism

Germany was the central hub of intellectualism for most of the 18th and 19th centuries. Out of that rich intellectual environment came German Idealism. Specifically, between 1780 and 1840, philosophers Immanuel Kant, Johann Fichte, Friedrich Schelling, and G.W.H. Hegel were the minds who birthed, refined, and popularized idealism.

Religious idealism is an offshoot of German Idealism and has been mostly unsuccessful in providing a voice within German Idealism. In an attempt to distinguish our discussion from Religious Idealism and to increase its specificity to comprise only the Judeo-Christian God, I am using the term Christian Idealism.

I am defining Christian Idealism as: *beliefs one forms about God as a result of intellectual assent regardless of its manifestation in the real world.* In other words, Christian idealists construct their faith through their ability to understand and relate a belief to a logical system. Ultimately, this construct manifests itself in its most ideal form and it is that idealism that forms the basis for their faith. Consequently, the object of their faith and worship is not God *in se* but the idea of God.

There exists an incongruity between word and deed within Evangelicalism. This has both theological and philosophical elements. Theologically, evangelicals are often suspicious of the relationship between faith and works. This is largely due to their Reformed heritage which protested the works-based system of the Catholic Church.

However, the more significant reason for the incongruity is largely a specific philosophical posture that underlies the evangelical worldview. This disconnect is exhibited through their approach to education as well as their beliefs.

The first theological posture through which evangelicals demonstrate their idealism is their belief about salvation. The idea behind justification by faith alone is a throwback to the Reformation, which, in an attempt to thwart the Catholic Church's belief in works-based salvation, made this a prominent component of their theological campaign. The message of salvation is the foundation of not just Evangelicalism but all of Protestantism's mission. For evangelicals, salvation is an intellectual activity that is not contingent upon having any real-world application. This is illustrated through their "faith alone" posture that eliminates any works or real-world practices. All that is required is faith in a set of beliefs (as opposed to practices). Those beliefs are anchored in the fact that Jesus was who he said he was. It is that reality from which their other beliefs become idealized.[6]

For example, evangelicals in the Reformed tradition hold that salvation is an aspect of God's sovereignty. It's not the human who seeks and then acquires salvation because humans are incapable of doing so due to their inherent depravity. Instead, God is the one who grants it, and bestows it upon the human.[7] These evangelicals believe that intellectual assent is a specific moment that God determines and is completely devoid of human ambition, work, or practice.[8] This, despite passages like Philippians 2:12, which tells us that we must "work out" our "salvation with fear and trembling" and James 2:14-26, which tells us that faith must be a part of reality as illustrated through the believers' behaviors. Even the Apostle Paul recognized this as he states throughout many of his writings that the resurrection (an important moment in time) is the foundation of salvation because without it the Christian faith is absurd. Paul even goes further in stating that one simply believing in the Gospel message (that Jesus was who he said he was) means nothing apart from the *reality* of the resurrection.[9] Here Paul is making the distinction between intellectual assent and reality.

The idealism that exists within the theology of evangelicalism is reflected in their worldview. Their foundational beliefs about the Bible and its inerrancy, justification by faith alone, and even their dogmatic perspective on orthodoxy are all aspects of an intellectualism that is planted firmly in their minds but not necessarily rooted in real-world implementation.

As we have hinted at throughout but have yet to articulate, Christian idealism has dire consequences that undermine the Christian message of the Gospel and its relationship to building the Kingdom of God. Idealists fail to understand the consequences of their worldview. That is, their idealism—what they imagine the world should be like and the things they do or say to make that happen—impacts real people and real lives.

This is why the religious leaders of Jesus' day felt justified in stoning a woman caught in adultery. They had every right according to the law to do so. But Jesus understood her situation in light of her humanity and applied the law as it was intended instead of the idealism that the Law permitted.

Because Christian Idealism lacks a sense of reality, the only types of consequences evangelicals have to face are theoretical in nature. Evangelicals diverge from this only when judging non-Christians. There has been an example of this in the media recently with the investigation into rap mogul P. Diddy Combs. It was revealed that Bishop T.D. Jakes, prolific author and pastor of the megachurch, The Potter's House, recently responded to allegations of having a homosexual affair with many people at P. Diddy's home. Jakes' response was revealing as he stated in December of 2023 to his congregation that his accusers were "liars" and that "even if everything was true, all I got to do is repent sincerely from my heart."[10]

This is a prevalent attitude for many evangelicals as illustrated by the numerous scandals that have plagued them for the last 40 years. In the end, there are no real consequences because their faith has no basis or accountability in reality. Additionally, any consequences one might face from law enforcement is often obfuscated by the Church and as we have learned, some of these coverups go far up the chain to the denominational level.

The Ultimate Consequence

There is a reason that German Idealism is not compatible with any form of theism. Namely, it results in a God that is not real. Christian Idealism posits a God who exists only in an idealistic form. Idealism takes the humanity and Jewishness out of Jesus and makes him an idol of the mind—something for us to intellectually exploit. In doing this we strip the narratives of the Bible and make them pieces to intellectually ascend to; instead of understanding their reality.

Idealism takes the life-long struggle away from the blind man, or the woman caught in adultery, or the paraplegic, in exchange for simple healings that occur across a few verses. The humanity behind the miracles of Jesus is exchanged for works meant to prove he was God. However, *Jesus did not perform miracles to prove he was God, he healed to prove he was human.*

This idealistic image is what many worship and preach about across the world on Sunday mornings. It is this image that is prayed to in the quiet of the morning or during the darkness of the night. This is the image that is cried out to when the soul falls to the deepest point of despair. However, when people pray to an idealistic image, they are not praying to a living God but simply the idea of a living God.

When Scripture is read as a metaphysical treatise on truth its realism is sucked out of it—it possesses no humanity within it and offers no humility in its interpretation. Instead, it puts forth an idealistic picture of achieving a sense of nirvana—a sense of true enlightenment. Scripture becomes a book of intellectual assent over and above an exercise in the practical aspects of its wisdom.

In Evangelicalism's attempt at creating an American faith, its leaders have inevitably succumbed to the same temptation for power and prestige that their Catholic and Jewish ancestors fell into. Ironically, in their attempt at hastening the Kingdom of God on Earth, they have instead established a different kingdom. A kingdom not built upon the Will of

God but one made of human ambition. A kingdom not made for the poor and downtrodden, but built upon their backs. It is not a kingdom of humility but of pride. It is not The Kingdom of God but the Kingdom of man.

9

Concluding Unscientific Postscript to Christian Idealism

Christian Realism

In the last chapter, we discussed how Evangelicalism has capitulated to a form of German Idealism that we are calling Christian Idealism. Several examples were provided to demonstrate how this form of idealism explains their current situation. In this chapter, we will provide the antithesis to Christian Idealism - Christian Realism.

In order to understand what is meant by Christian Realism we must begin with some context. In 1846 Søren Kierkegaard published a book titled *Concluding Unscientific Postscript to Philosophical Fragments*.[1] No doubt such a convoluted, unappealing title would be a publisher's nightmare in today's world; and it certainly was not attractive to the layperson in Kierkegaard's day either. Despite this, its significance was important not only for his day but for ours as well.

Kierkegaard's title was meant to be ironic. It was written to be an attack on Hegelianism. Kierkegaard chose each word carefully for his title because each word was significant to his thesis. Kierkegaard wanted to be the antithesis of Hegel—also ironic. Since Hegel believed his philosophy was the end-all for philosophy, Kierkegaard titled his work "Concluding" which was meant to emphasize the fact that clearly Hegel's work was not final. Additionally, since Hegel considered his work a "Scientific" philosophy, then Kierkegaard wanted his to be "Unscientific." Finally, despite Kierkegaard's use of the word "Postscript' his publication was one of his largest works, spanning two volumes, and was not the end but just the beginning of his attack.

The similarities between Kierkegaard's day and our own are striking. In this chapter, I seek to present an alternative approach that is both rational and faithful to what we observe in Jesus and his ministry.

What is Realism?

Christian Realism naturally exists in opposition to Christian Idealism. But it is not as simple as just being its corresponding opposite. As in any perspective, there exists nuance that is important to understand.

The crux of realism lies in its pragmatism. The inability of evangelicals to be realists lies in their unwillingness to accept the pragmatic consequences of what they believe. Despite the fact that pragmatism leads a person to a more rational view of the world, evangelicals rely on their ability to perceive a truth that is far above what they could possibly understand. Ultimately, this leads them to have to defend some irrational ideas in order to save face.

The primary objective for a realist remains the pursuit of truth—a truth that transcends mere adherence to a closed ideological system and instead resonates as something inherent to oneself and the world that person experiences. In order to get to the point where one is able to understand what it means to be a Christian Realist we have to briefly wade through some philosophical context.

Traditional Realism is understood as the idea that truth exists independently of our ability to perceive it. This is an antithetical perspective to Hegel's German Idealism (discussed earlier). Realism, can in part, participate in an objective framework because at its core it's about truth in the physical world.

However, for Christian doctrine, the physical world alone is not sufficient since God transcends the physical. Therefore, Metaphysical Realism is more useful than Traditional Realism. Metaphysical Realism makes the same claims as traditional realism except it is applied to metaphysical properties such as God and belief which we will be calling Christian Realism.[2]

Additionally, there are various ways that Christian Realism takes form. It can participate in conversations surrounding ethics, physics, metaphysics, ontology, phenomenology, and epistemology. Much of our conversation about Christian Realism will focus on how the concept of nominalism (an aspect of the evangelical worldview) can be differentiated from realism within a Christian context.

Nominalism & Christian Realism

Nominalism is the notion that ideas have no (real) correspondence to reality. For example, say we have two breeds of dog, a Chihuahua, and a Great Dane. Despite their vast differences, we still know that both are dogs (we refer to this as "dogness"). But, how do we know that? How do we know that a chihuahua is not a large cat? We know this because we recognize that there is some universal property that is common to these animals that we call dogness. There is a form they take and based upon that form we know what they are—generally speaking. In Christian Realism, this concept can act as a connecting point between the physical and the metaphysical. This is how we can include ideas about a metaphysical God in the reality of the physical world.

In opposition, nominalism argues that there is no (real) connection between dogness and reality. In other words, there is no such thing as dogness. However, in stating this they are equally arguing that there are no universal properties to *being*—which would include God. As a result, there is no bridge connecting the metaphysical to the physical.

A realist on the other hand would argue that there *is* a correspondence between the form of something and its essence.[3] A connection that can also be understood through the function that the form performs. In the case of our dogs, it could be as simple as the universal attribute of barking. In Christianity, it could be the creation as a source of God's revelation.

At first, nominalism seems incompatible with the evangelical worldview. This is primarily because nominalism is used within a scientific context. Therefore, such a worldview would posit that God is unknowable because our language about God is meaningless and there is no real ontological connection between a human and the divine. This chapter in no way argues that evangelicals think God is unknowable. Instead, we are applying nominalism to their faith—or *how* they believe. In other words, we are not talking about *ontology* but *epistemology*.[4]

What Does All of this Mean?

Christian Idealism faces practical challenges, notably concerning the interplay between idealism and symbolism. This dilemma arises as idealism often fosters a faith predominantly rooted in symbolism, existing primarily in an abstract realm. Evangelicals, in their endeavors to reconcile this disparity, encounter insurmountable difficulties. Consequently, they resort to constructing a theological mosaic aimed at remedying the inconsistencies within their worldview and therefore rely solely on objective systems to maintain theological consistency.

Examples of this are littered throughout evangelical theology. A prime example is the theology of atonement. The evangelical model for atonement envisages the work of the cross as one that has paid a penalty for human transgressions. It holds that since Jesus was ethnically pure, his sacrifice was considered to be substitutionary for humanity's sin.

The problem with this level of reasoning is that it is an anachronistic interpretation based on the Apostle Paul's theology of sin. Paul's theology of sin, which was simply based on his perspective, not God's per se, is then read into the crucifixion narrative as a sacrifice for sin. However, if you understand the nature of the cross within its context (the Old Testament), then it is not about a sacrifice for sin but a reconciliation between God and humanity. About making right what went wrong in the Garden of Eden.

The evangelical perspective requires one to interpret not just atonement theory but much of scripture through ethical obligations. This was the same mistake that Jesus confronted the religious leaders about. Ultimately, Jesus argues that no one can maintain the law (ethical dimension) and that what the religious leaders believed was devotion to God, through the law, was instead religious puffery.

Ultimately, if the law was the primary means of atonement throughout the Hebrew Scriptures, then no one could be saved; no one could be considered God's chosen. The law is meant to reveal sin, yes, but only in the sense that it also reveals hypocrisy. Jesus calls out the Pharisees in particular about this very idea in Matthew 23 when he calls them hypocrites.

> Then Jesus said to the crowds and to his disciples: "The teachers of the law and the Pharisees sit in Moses' seat. So you must be careful to do everything they tell you. But do not do what they do, for they do not practice what they preach. They tie up heavy, cumbersome loads and put them on other people's shoulders, but they themselves are not willing to lift a finger to move them.
>
> "Everything they do is done for people to see: They make their phylacteries wide and the tassels on their garments long; they love the place of honor at banquets and the most important seats in the synagogues; they love to be greeted with respect in the marketplaces and to be called 'Rabbi' by others."

The problem with the anachronistic reading of Jesus' atonement is that, if read properly within its Jewish context, Paul's ideas surrounding atonement are radically different. This problem coupled with their view of inerrancy creates an idealist environment where consistent theory is paramount but not its application in the real world. For evangelicals, their primary goal is not truth, as we have been told for so long, but preserving God's authority through the scriptures.

This is not just true of atonement theory but can be observed throughout evangelical theology. So much of evangelical theology is built upon the foundation of inerrancy, that inerrancy itself has become the goal, not God's truth.[5] Ultimately, the result of this is a construct of God that is not *real*, but *ideal*. God becomes a metaphysical object in their minds that they can worship and they assign to these mental image attributes and ideas that become mixed in with their reality to the point where the two are indistinguishable.

The Gospels illustrate the same concept through how Jesus interacts with the religious leaders of his day. The religious leaders of Jesus' day were expecting the Messiah to be a certain way. They had been told by the prophets (their Word of God), that he would come as a military leader; one who would smite their enemies and restore their land to its former glory. They had this mental picture of what they believed he would be—their ideal. They assigned all of these attributes to him so that when he arrived they would be able to recognize him. However, when Jesus appeared, they did not recognize him because he did not fit their preconceived ideas. Because their worldview had become fused, they were unable to recognize the real thing through the filter of their idealism. This is what we see in Evangelicalism today. Just as the religious leaders of Jesus' time did not recognize God in the flesh during his time, so too will evangelicals have the same problem if Jesus returns.

There is a secondary problem with evangelical idealization. It results in a type of intellectualism that makes God unrecognizable. They worship the idea of God and who they believe he should be based on their modern thinking instead of how the Bible portrays him to be. Their theology is what draws the picture for their followers to think that what they are worshiping is real. This is none the more evident than in Dispensationalism end-times theology. From guessing dates to creating second-coming narratives, there is a picture and expectation that has been created. The belief has been established that in order for God to return certain things must be accomplished. My fear, however, is that their fate will be the same as that of the religious leaders. That one day when Jesus returns he will be completely unrecognizable to the "experts" who will have long awaited his arrival.

Schrodinger's Cat: Idealism Versus Realism

There is a famous thought experiment in physics called Schrodinger's Cat, which was meant to describe some of the paradoxes that exist between physics and quantum physics. However, the thought experiment has diverse applications due to its philosophical nature including our current conversation.

In the thought experiment, a cat is placed in a box with a vile of poison. The box is then closed. The question that is then asked: did the cat consume the poison and die or did he ignore the poison and remain alive? For scientists, when the box is closed the cat exists in a paradoxical state. That is, the cat is both alive and dead at the same time. Therefore, we cannot know the answer until the box is opened.

The *idealist* would argue that it's illogical for the cat to exist in this paradox; therefore, the cat must be *either* dead *or* alive but not both. This is necessary because as a modernist the idealist exists in an either/or world. The idealist is always consumed by the need to know whether the cat is alive or dead. It has been promised to them through Hegelianism that such things can be known. And, that this knowledge corresponds to reality. This requires the idealist to commit entirely to either one or the other, even if they are wrong in the end.

On the other hand, the *realist* would argue that the cat's fate cannot be known until its truth is revealed, which can only happen when the box is opened (in our discussion that would correspond to death or heaven). However, what the realist understands is that the rules of the thought experiment are not the only rules. They are just the rules that have been set for the experiment.

For example, what if one were to listen closely for the sound of purring? What if one were to touch the box to detect movement? What if one were to peek through the air holes to observe the cat?

The idealist would declare this cheating because the rules were not being followed. The realist would argue that the goal of the experiment was not to uphold rules but to determine if the cat was alive or not. In other words, the truth is more important than the things that govern how we arrive at that truth.

Furthermore, the example set by Christ himself as well as passages like James 2:14-26 clearly promote a faith that is rooted in the truth of reality and not objective reasoning. Faith is a subjective experience, not an objective one.

The Absolute Truth About Postmodernism

Modernists never really understood Postmodernism because they could not imagine a world where the objective reality of truth could not be ascertained, or where the rules for arriving at truth could not be agreed upon. This meant that any attempt at dialogue between the two movements always resulted in people talking past each other. Postmodernism was a movement rooted in the realism of its day and questioned one's ability to know objective reality, ultimately believing that such proclamations were philosophically arrogant.

In opposition to Postmodernism, modernists viewed postmodernists as superficial and incapable of understanding the convoluted and intellectually demanding role of obtaining objective knowledge. They believed their views on subjectivity were an ideological attempt to allow anyone to construct their own truth so that everyone could exist in harmony.

In reality, Postmodernism was much more complex than it was given credit for. And their concerns had nothing to do with existential harmony but with legitimate questions about the consequences that existed when one believed in absolutism. For example, despite stereotypes by modernists, postmodernists did not deny the existence of truth or even the existence of absolute truth. Instead, they denied one's ability to understand that truth in its absolute form. This did not sit well with Christian modernists because they fully believed that through Scripture they could know absolute truth. For them, the Bible was God's direct revelation of himself to humanity. Since God is absolute, then what he tells us must also be absolute.

What evangelicals did not understand was that there is a difference between having absolute truth and understanding it. Even the religious leaders of Jesus' day had the Torah and they still failed to understand its truth. What evangelicals also could not grasp was the level of arrogance one had to have to believe that they had insight into the mind of God. Having such insight would make them divine. Furthermore, did not the fact that Evangelicalism was laden with denominations prove that their presuppositions about absolutism could not possibly be true? Which denomination had the truth? Which biblical canon was God's revelation? Were those who decided on the canon also as inspired as the writers themselves; if not, how did they know which books were revelations from God and which were not? These were the practical questions that concerned Christian postmodernists. They were not trying to be lazy thinkers, they were trying to make sense out of a nonsensical paradigm.

Idealists believe that the truth of God should be black or white because God is the author of logic and order. To them, God in a postmodern worldview is chaotic and messy. But what they fail to recognize is that it is not God who is chaotic and messy, it is humanity. It is from our chaotic and messy perspective that we view God. That is because, for the most part, our lives are not ordered and logical; they are not black and white. They are messy lives that exist in a perpetual state of uncertainty.

As Kierkegaard points out, objective Christianity always leads to a cycle of indecision. He mockingly states that the objective Christian is always looking for the answers and in so doing forgets to ever get about the business of doing what Christ demands. The back and forth that is required for the either/or of Hegelianism comes at the cost of indecision. Kierkegaard's advice is that one must "dare to decide."[6] In this sense, objectivity is not the more rigorous of the two but results in a type of laziness where one never gets out of their head to do the work that Christianity requires. The idealist has to "figure it out" before they can "live it out" in the real world, otherwise, there is no way to know if what one is putting into practice is true.

The lack of humility that accompanies idealism is reminiscent of the story of Jesus after his resurrection on the road to Emmaus. In this story, Jesus encounters two men who had been speaking about what had happened to him. Not knowing it was Jesus who they were speaking to, they invited him to dinner. After dinner, Jesus vanished and they became aware of who they had been with and they said to each other: "Were not our hearts burning within us while he talked with us on the road and opened the Scriptures to us?" Like their forefathers before them, idealists exist in the presence of a *real* God but are unaware of it. Their hearts do not burn because their eyes are not open.

The Reality of Idealism's Shame

Throughout the Bible, we see individuals who encounter God and immediately fall to their faces. In Evangelicalism, the idea of God's presence creates shame within the individual because they believe their sinful nature cannot exist in the presence of a holy God. The only response a sinner can have is to fall on their face and hope that God will not smite them. The emphasis on wrath is a predominant theme in Evangelicalism and has been since its inception. Much of evangelical theology is based on the concept that the nature of humanity and the holiness of God stand in eternal opposition to one another. As a result, the only way reconciliation is possible is through Christ's redemptive work on the cross.

This could be characterized as a militant or violent perspective because it imagines Jesus as one who is meant to conquer sin and death like a general going off into battle. Or, like a superhero who defeats his arch nemesis, Satan, through his death and resurrection. Although this representation is a clear idealization of what actually happened in history, it nevertheless rings just as true within the evangelical imagination as though it actually happened. This is due to the inability to distinguish between their mental view of God and what God may actually be like.

Because of this, shame has often been used as a way to keep evangelicals in line. Shame is a tool that allows leaders to look down on those under their care in such a way that the individual feels just as responsible for the death of Jesus as those who actually killed him. The intended outcome is contrition and right action. In Part One we detailed many indiscretions that evangelical leaders have perpetrated against their people but an additional dimension exists within the idealist framework: people are not really people. Instead, they are characters in some grand narrative which God is directing and Evangelicalism is central to. This is next-level dehumanization.

Not only have many of these leaders participated in the same behaviors they shame others for, but they also use shame to protect their power and authority so that the abuse can continue. There is no need for real contrition because they are already saved—they are already forgiven.

There is a distinction between guilt and shame that many evangelicals have failed to make. As a result, evangelicals have preached a Gospel of shame for decades. During the purity culture years, shame was utilized to instill fear in young men and women. Violating one's purity resulted in young women being castigated and ridiculed as if they had committed an unforgivable sin. This same method is used to shame women who consider getting an abortion, even in cases of rape or incest. For the past century, millions of people have been convinced that their worth is based solely on their relationship with Jesus and that those that reject his "free gift of salvation" are not only damned to eternal hell but also to a life of worthlessness and depravity. However, God did not create shame, and the Bible tells us this in Romans 10:11: "As Scripture says, 'Anyone who believes in him will never be put to shame.'" Instead, evangelicals created it as part of their sales pitch for evangelism.[7]

In evangelical idealism one is constantly confronted with one's inadequacies, both from the pulpit and through relationships with other church members. It must be understood that encountering God does not mean one falls on their face in shame because there is no shame in God. Instead, one falls on their face *because* there is no shame when perhaps there should be.

One falls on their face out of sheer gratitude for undeserved grace. Out of an awe-filled recognition that God's love is large enough to forgive anyone and his arms wide enough to embrace all people. If only we could show the same love and compassion to others that Christ shows to us, instead of trying to sell people an idealism that has no roots in reality. Perhaps then more people could experience the life-transforming hope Jesus offers. This is the mission that Jesus gave to his disciples, this is the type of Kingdom he desired to establish. When understanding objective truth is up to the fallible human, one has no choice but to create idealism to house that truth. When communicating truth to people comes out of idealism there is no chance of ever establishing the Kingdom of God; we are only left with a kingdom built of human hands.

What Does It Mean to Be a Christian Realist?

All of this begs the question: what does it mean to be a Christian Realist? So far in this chapter we have seen what taking the wrong path looks like. This means that some sort of explanation is required on what we should do—what does the right path look like. Unfortunately, there is some bad news, there is no right path. Believing that there exists a right path is the type of certainty that got Evangelicalism into its current predicament.

With that said, there are ways that one can exist in the world and spread the hope of Christ without idealism. Sure, one might not be able to package Jesus up and sell him to the masses like many evangelicals have done. The realist may also not be able to guarantee certain things to those they lead. And, the realist may not be able to convert large stadiums of people desperate to belong to Christianity. However, the resulting depth of authenticity and quality will more than make up for superficial quantity.

It was never Jesus' intent for believers to pack stadiums full of people to hear a superficial theological message about him, but to walk alongside him as their Rabbi. Believers are to *live the Gospel and be the hope to our world that Jesus was in his.* This may result in only one life being transformed through deep relationships at a time, but that is the work of the Kingdom. Having large groups of people pray a prayer is not going to save them and it's not going to bring about God's Kingdom any faster. In fact, it does more damage than good and ultimately prevents God's Kingdom from unfolding (whatever that may look like).

It is through investing one's life in one's "neighbor" that one's investment will be fruitful. Despite all of the objective truth that evangelicals believe they can ascertain, there is one truth that can not be denied - the truth of living one's beliefs in the real world as an example of the transforming power of Jesus. That truth has no counter argument. Ultimately, real world truth is far more effective and convincing than one conjured up in the imagination through logical manipulation.

Is there Theological Truth in Realism?

One may wonder if there is any type of reliable truth in realism. Yes, and ironically, it results in a greater truth because it is based on reality and not logical consistency. It is a truth that is often discovered through common sense and not special systematic methods that require symmetry in order to be true. As we have stated, the idealist needs everything in their theological system to be true. Any deviation from that means the whole system is wrong or at least begins to break down. In fact, some even take it to the level where they say any deviation from absolute symmetry means that God himself is not true and as a result they become atheists.

However, if one can resist the urge to create an innumerable amount of presuppositions about what they read in the Bible and just allow the words to speak to them as the author intended, then the meaning is richer and more authentic. Truth does not manifest itself through the abstraction of certain principles or axioms, but only when the individual has an appreciation for what the author is saying within the context they are saying it in. In other words, one should adopt a view of the Bible that eliminates the abstraction of propositional truths and instead uses the real world of the Bible to inform their understanding of the real world they live in today.

Truth is not dependent upon correlating systems or even doctrinal symmetry but is found in understanding, and in the wisdom that is necessary to apply it in the real world. This may mean that one, at times, believes in two ideas that are seemingly paradoxical. It may also mean that it is not possible to understand something an author has said. These are important aspects that the realist must become comfortable with. Ultimately, Christians must become comfortable with the idea that there are other aspects of truth and other ways to discover it. Namely, those truths that are revealed by standing in the presence of mystery. Basking in that mystery is what informs us that we are in the presence of our God who is, above all, mysterious.

Taking the Path Least Traveled: Deconstructing Evangelicalism

Historian John M. Barry said, "...when you mix politics and science you get politics." The same could be said of mixing religion and politics. Politics has a way of subsuming one's worldview because of the dedication it requires. Moreover, in a fight between politics and an idealistic worldview, politics will always win because the idea of God lacks a pragmatism that politics fills. However, when God himself fills an individual's reality, their relationship with Christ transforms them so that they view everything through the eyes of hope and restoration. Everything gets filtered through the work of Christ to transform their community and society, which they themselves participate in. That is what the Kingdom of God means—to transform the world through the love of Christ with the hope of the Gospel. Jesus never forced people to follow him the way many try to do through political means. Instead, he declared the truth, and then demonstrated its veracity through how he lived.

In the 1980s and 1990s, it was common to hear evangelical leaders using intolerant rhetoric that made it sound like same-sex couples were the reason for America's perceived decline in economic power and global standing. This rhetoric was not limited to the '80s and '90s but is still an underlying belief of many within the evangelical world. The idea that God will bless those who follow him and curse those who do not is primarily found in the Old Testament.

Israel was commanded to follow the law given by Moses, and promised that if they did, God would bless them. However, failing to do so would result in a curse. This has become known in theology as the blessings and cursings of Israel. This theology was a part of the covenant God had established with Israel and was given to no other nation. Therefore, when contemporary evangelicals quote biblical passages about God's blessings and cursings upon America, they are putting forth fallacious theology argued out of context.

Furthermore, both the law and the blessings and cursings associated with it were dismantled, or perhaps more accurately clarified, by Jesus in his newly established covenant. In fact, this issue comes up during the ministry of Jesus and is addressed by him in John 9:1-5:

> As he went along, he saw a man blind from birth. His disciples asked him, "Rabbi, who sinned, this man or his parents, that he was born blind?" "Neither this man nor his parents sinned," said Jesus, "but this happened so that the works of God might be displayed in him. As long as it

> is day, we must do the works of him who sent me. Night is coming, when no one can work. While I am in the world, I am the light of the world."

The notion of an evangelical theocracy in America, aiming to facilitate the return of Jesus, is a belief held by many evangelical Americans—even if some of them deny it. Despite its popularity, this concept lacks any biblical foundation. The idea suggests that through adherence to God's law, America can become the pivotal nation for Jesus' return. This theological perspective persists within the discourse of conservative evangelical figures and is a cornerstone of dispensationalism, yet it is not supported by Scripture.

Unfortunately, many within Evangelicalism—particularly white evangelicals, often equate the communication God had with Israel in the Old Testament as relating to the United States. This faulty equivocation is responsible for much of the motivation behind this perspective. Despite this faulty equivocation, evangelicals can learn from Israel's relationship with God and their nationalism. Understanding this relationship will demonstrate the extent to which the nationalist worldview is both wrong and dangerous.

One lesson in particular is quite applicable. During the era of God's rule in Israel, the people consistently shifted blame for their hardships onto external entities rather than taking responsibility themselves. Despite prophetic warnings advising otherwise, Israel habitually accused other nations, the prophets, and occasionally even God for their adversities. When faced with the uncomfortable truth that their own actions were the root cause of their troubles, they opted to punish the messengers of God instead of acknowledging and acting upon the warnings provided to them.

The same could be said about Evangelicalism. Although evangelicals may not be treating widows poorly, they should be held accountable for how they have subjugated women. Evangelicals may not be directly creating hardships for the poor, but they have certainly contributed to legislation that does. Evangelicals may not punish the messengers of God (like the Prophets) for their warnings, but they do ostracize those who think differently from them and restrict participation in their community. Ultimately, like Israel, evangelicals have cut themselves off from any accountability.

Faith & Doubt

It has been an axiom for most of Evangelicalism's history that questioning one's faith is a sin. The logic behind this belief is that questioning one's faith quickly leads to doubt, and doubt to disbelief. For example, in Alissa Childer's best-selling book *Another Gospel*, she argues that doubt is antithetical to Jesus. That when someone doubts they are not relying on Jesus but on their own abilities to weather their intellectual storms.[8]

Dr. Richard Caldwell, teaching pastor of the megachurch Founders Baptist Church, is a product of John MacArthur's Masters Seminary. In the Straight Truth Podcast, Caldwell was clear that Jesus condemns doubt in Mark 9:17. Caldwell's rationale is, if Christianity is the ultimate truth, then to doubt is to doubt that truth as well as him who created that truth. For Caldwell, Childers, and people like them, doubt is synonymous with disbelief.[9]

It's not just Caldwell and Childers, but this has been an aspect of evangelical culture for as long as people have called themselves evangelical. In an article published by the evangelical group the Association of Certified Biblical Counselors, an association with counselors stationed all over the world, columnist Ruth Granlund equates doubt to temptation, citing "O, you of little faith, why did you doubt." This quote is from the Gospels where Peter takes a leap of faith and steps out of a boat onto the stormy waters, walking toward Jesus. However, once Peter realizes what he is actually doing, he begins to sink. The quote is Jesus' response to Peter. Granlund asserts that faith is given to us by God and therefore must always exist. However, in the story of Peter and Jesus, it is clear that faith is a product of the individual, otherwise, he would have never sunk. Granlund is saying that when faith fails to be present (in cases of doubt), then we are saying God is not present with us. Citing Genesis 3:1, she states that "doubt is something Satan uses and has used throughout history to dissuade God's people from the truth."[10]

It's no secret that the culture within Evangelicalism discourages questioning and elevates doubting to the level of one losing their faith. This fosters a reliance on leaders for guidance rather than critical thinking because critical thinking will almost always plant seeds of doubt. This dynamic leads individuals to accept information without scrutiny, particularly when provided by authoritative figures in the media or on religious platforms.[11] Consequently, many adherents fall prey to confirmation bias, a cognitive phenomenon where a person only pursues ideas that already confirm their beliefs instead of challenging them.

What Is the Kingdom of God?

Throughout this book, we discussed the many ways that Christians have misunderstood and distorted the Kingdom of God. However, we have yet to articulate what Jesus meant by the Kingdom of God—and to what extent that includes human participation.

The Kingdom of God is often conflated with the term "gospel," but it is not merely a New Testament concept. It is derived from the Hebrew Scriptures. Moreover, it is necessary to have an understanding of the larger narrative to see the development of this concept throughout those scriptures.

The idea of the Kingdom of God originated in Genesis as the dwelling place of Adam and Eve. In this idyllic setting, they lived harmoniously amidst lush vegetation and diverse wildlife. Their unity was exemplified through their obedience to the Will of their God and King. However, their decision to disobey God's command by eating the forbidden fruit created a barrier between humanity and their Creator. Consequently, they were exiled from the Kingdom of God, where humankind has remained ever since. This idea of exile will become a predominant theme in the story of Israel as it unfolds throughout the Hebrew Scriptures.

Since Genesis acts as the Preamble to the development of Israel, our understanding of this concept is vital to understanding not just the remainder of the Hebrew Scriptures but the overall purpose of Jesus. The remainder of the Old Testament, therefore, should be understood within the context of the various ways that God attempted to re-establish fellowship between humanity and himself; to re-establish some resemblance of what once was.

Despite God's various attempts at restoration, Israel failed to take advantage of the grace he bestowed upon them. Instead of rebuilding the Kingdom of God, they opted for building a kingdom made of human ambition and conceit—*a kingdom of man*. Israel never understood the extent to which God was attempting to re-establish himself as their God and King.

God desired to shape the Jews into better humans, enabling them to thrive in this life and the next. Israel's sole purpose was to reveal God to the world, which could only happen if they followed his Will. Unfortunately, they failed to comprehend this purpose by repeating the sin of their foreparents and exacerbating their disconnect with God. This ultimately necessitated that God use his one and only Son as his source of revelation and reconciliation.

The primary purpose of the incarnation was to disclose God's Will to humanity, enabling them to know and follow his plan for reconciliation. This revelation occurred not only through his re-articulation of Judaism but also through the example he set by how he lived his life. Jesus' life showcased the pinnacle of human potential, as well as the depths of human depravity. It highlighted the cavernous distance that existed between humans and God. The gap had become so wide between God and humanity that many could not even recognize his presence among them. This lack of understanding was evidenced by the arrogant rejection and subsequent murder of Jesus.

Jesus came to reveal God to the world by clarifying for the Jews what it meant to be residents in the Kingdom of God. As Jesus pointed out many times to the religious leaders of his day, the Law was not meant to be observed but embodied.[12] He taught that the Law centered around a single ethic - love. Jesus declared this when the religious leaders asked him what he thought the greatest commandment was. The simple elegance of his statement should be the one doctrine that unites all Christians. Jesus stated that the Torah and Prophets could be summed up in a single command: "*...Love the Lord your God with all your heart and with all your soul and with all your mind... And love your neighbor as yourself.*"[13]

Repeating the Cycle

We have discussed at length how Evangelicalism needs to learn from the mistakes of the past. As philosopher George Santayana rightly pointed out: "Those who cannot remember the past are condemned to repeat it."[14] Like Israel, evangelicals have failed to recognize their mistakes and learn from them; often demonstrating the same type of hubris that the ancient Israelite leaders exhibited. Ironically, Evangelicalism suffers from the same plight as the religious leaders of Jesus's time. Namely, they fail to understand what it means for one to participate in the Kingdom of God.

Evangelicalism's inability to recognize their error arises out of their distortion of the Gospel message. This distortion is a result of an anachronistic reading of Scripture. Instead of allowing the narrative of the Bible to inform the larger purpose of God, they often filter the larger biblical narrative through their Pauline theology. This means that for the evangelical theologian, much of the Bible is understood in the context of a particular belief about the atonement called, Penal Substitutionary Atonement (PSA). Instead of allowing the narrative to unfold naturally, it is reinterpreted within this presupposition.

The anachronistic interpretation in question presents a narrative that diverges from what was described in the previous section. In contrast to the Fall of humanity which is understood in terms of exile and separation from the Kingdom of God, evangelical theologians emphasize sin and death. Their perspective characterizes the Fall as an ontological problem, leading to the subsequent focus on how humans must overcome their corrupted nature.

Ultimately, the Fall is not as much about our human nature (though it does touch on it) as it is about our separation from God. It's not about our inability to choose God because of our depravity, it is about our unwillingness to do so. It's about the pride that accompanies our will and freedom to express our dominion. Humans love exercising their power too much to give it away for the humility that is required by Jesus. Just as was true in the garden, we will always choose that which we are told to avoid.

When one views the Fall primarily as the result of sin and the establishment of human depravity, then the remainder of the story of Israel is viewed as a group of people always in need of atonement. It views the Law and the subsequent sacrificial system as a means of redemption - though how that is accomplished in their theology remains unclear. This perspective fuels the evangelical theologian to reimagine Jesus as the representative lamb that acts as the one-time replacement for the sacrificial system. This makes the life of Jesus the way through which he became qualified to be that sacrifice; instead of the example for humanity to follow for reconciliation.

Moving Towards a Kingdom Theology

If it is true that the incarnation was meant to provide humanity with an example of what it means to live for the Kingdom of God, then it becomes imperative to understand *how* Jesus lived his life. This means that believing the "right" things about Jesus takes a back seat to our ability to observe his life. It is through these observations that our beliefs about him should be understood.

We might rightly ask then, what are some things we can observe in the life of Jesus that should inform our theology about him? First, and perhaps the most obvious, is that Jesus did not come in power but in humility. Paul's letter to the Philippians expresses this perfectly:

> In your relationships with one another, have the same mindset as Christ Jesus: Who, being in very nature God, did not consider equality with God something to be used to his own advantage; rather, he made himself nothing by taking the very nature of a servant, being made in human likeness. And being found in appearance as a man, he humbled himself by becoming obedient to death—even death on a cross!
>
> Therefore God exalted him to the highest place and gave him the name that is above every name, that at the name of Jesus every knee should bow, in heaven and on earth and under the earth, and every tongue acknowledge that Jesus Christ is Lord, to the glory of God the Father.[15]

This passage points out the important idea that power only comes as a result of humility. It's Jesus' humble rejection of power—despite being entitled to it—that ultimately gave him power. Jesus demonstrated that the chief attribute of the Christian should be humility.

This passage also demonstrates that power is not something that can be grabbed, but it must be bestowed. This concept may seem contradictory to how we experience power in the world. However, this is a power brought about by the kingdom of man and not the Kingdom of God. The kingdom of man murdered Jesus but the Kingdom of God resurrected him. In the end, only Jesus had true power, demonstrated by the fact that billions follow him even today.[16]

The fact that Jesus never forced anyone to follow him is a valuable lesson in a day and age where many Christians attempt to legislate their morality across the nation. Their own hypocritical actions often accompany this arrogance, as we have documented throughout this book. Instead of forcing people into their personal ethics, Christians should live in such a way that the benefits of Christianity are illuminated through their actions. Jesus demonstrated that kingdom living is not about coercion. Instead, he showed us that it is through the power of one's example that will convince others of the integrity of one's message. Unfortunately, in our present time, we have very few examples that demonstrate the benefits of following Jesus. It is difficult to show people hope when it is tied up in contempt. People do not want to follow Jesus if in doing so it requires them to show contempt towards others.

Being A Living Word

Actions alone should not be the sole focus of the Christian faith; beliefs are equally important. The term "works" can make evangelicals uncomfortable due to the Reformation's rejection of the Catholic Church's works-based theology. One of Protestantism's defining principles, Sola Gratia (Grace Alone), contributes to this theological aversion to the idea of works in the New Testament. Unfortunately, this negative connotation hinders Evangelicalism's equal treatment of acts as a part of faith. This has led to an overemphasis on beliefs as the single core principle of Evangelicalism's theology.

However, the same can be said for those on the other side of the debate. For more liberal Christians, an over-emphasis on action can also become problematic as it can lead to a superficial theology that lacks meaningful content. In either case, it is the balance of the two that becomes the core principle of the Kingdom of God. This is what Jesus is referring to in Matthew 23:1-4:

> Then Jesus said to the crowds and to his disciples: "The teachers of the law and the Pharisees sit in Moses' seat. So you must be careful to do everything they tell you. But do not do what they do, for they do not practice what they preach. They tie up heavy, cumbersome loads and put them on other people's shoulders, but they themselves are not willing to lift a finger to move them.

This is further bolstered by James in chapter 2, which in part says:

> What good is it, my brothers and sisters, if someone claims to have faith but has no deeds? Can such faith save them? Suppose a brother or a sister is without clothes and daily food. If one of you says to them, "Go in peace; keep warm and well fed," but does nothing about their physical needs, what good is it? In the same way, faith by itself, if it is not accompanied by action, is dead...

Beliefs and actions are concepts that have long existed in a dualistic state. One always battling the other for supremacy. Jesus obliterated this idea by showing that the two can exist in a unifying whole. This is why Jesus is the living Word—because he embodied belief. Beliefs and actions were so tied together in Jesus that they were inseparable. Word and deed should bolster one another, not compete. When tension is exhibited between the two, then they are incongruent.

The Kingdom of God must be understood within a two-tier framework. That is, the Kingdom of God is both already here and not yet present. On the one hand, it is already present in the actions of Christians worldwide. These actions serve as a practice for what the Kingdom of God will be like when Jesus returns and establishes an earthly kingdom. In other words, the collective Church must project kingdom character as they accomplish the Will of God in the world. Ultimately, this means that Christians are expected to live in a way that reflects the values and principles of the Kingdom of God. It is through their actions that they demonstrate the presence of the Kingdom in preparation for its future establishment.[17]

The Kingdom of Man & The Kingdom of God

The kingdom of man is mostly focused on oneself and what an individual can do to escape hell. This results in a belief system that is often more focused on the future than the present. It takes the focus off God and his Will in exchange for one's own ambitions.

Instead of learning from the mistakes that Israel exemplified, Evangelicalism, in many ways, has emulated Israel's practices and, in so doing, believes they have inherited the Jewish birthright through the new covenant. However, in following this example they are also inheriting the same consequences that Israel did—consequences that can be observed today. The kingdom of man is about power and control, instead of humility and influence. It's about waging war instead of waging peace.

The kingdom of man presents a Gospel message that is based on shame through its representation of sin and salvation. However, this emphasis on sin and salvation is an inadequate representation of what Jesus has required. The kingdom of man focuses mainly on a future state (heaven), while oftentimes neglecting the present. Salvation is oftentimes presented as simply a way of escaping hell which communicates fear as its primary motivating factor instead of hope. In many ways, the accusations Jesus made against the religious leaders of his day still ring true today. Just like the ancient Israelites, many evangelicals are missing the larger point.

The essential message of the Gospel should be the hope that the Kingdom of God provokes within us. A kingdom that is ruled by a loving God who longs to reestablish the relationship he had with humanity in the beginning. This kingdom is made up of people whose joy in serving God is infectious and whose example is also their witness. This hope demonstrates that one can live as a resident of God's Kingdom now. There is no war in this kingdom, only peace. There is no disdain or ostracization, only acceptance. There is no hierarchy of influence or power, only equality. There is no shame, only grace. There is no hate. There is only love.

The Future of Evangelicalism

Throughout this book we have looked at the evolution of Evangelicalism. We showed how various leaders manipulate followers through biblical exaltation and logic to convey subversive messages. We showed how this messaging was communicated through a larger subliminal framework that served as the mode for much of Evangelicalism's propaganda.

We also demonstrated and analyzed the philosophical and theological reasons why this trajectory occurred as we identified their Hegelian presuppositions and biases which inform their Christian Idealism; an idealism that makes God the center of their imagination instead of the center of their reality. The evangelical worldview once consisted of clear boundaries between the various aspects of its worldview but in recent years has become fused into a unified whole under the label of White Christian Nationalism.

In addition, we demonstrated how Evangelicalism's Christian Idealism is a worldview that is responsible for creating a dispensational theology that is utilized to energize its constituents. Christian Idealism is not only the environment that fosters the evangelical worldview but also serves as the reason for why evangelicals are unable to see the forest for the trees. Their idealism clouds their ability to engage in the real world because they are unable to separate themselves from their idealism. Essentially, their idealized world has fused with the real world, which makes them unable to differentiate the two. When God lacks reality for someone then this lack of reality means a person is never in a position to see God as he is - only how they imagine him to be. As we pointed out, this is not a new phenomenon but is part of a cycle that was defined by Israel and revisited by the Medieval Catholic Church.

In the end, it is important to understand that Christians believe in a living God as exemplified through Jesus Christ. If there is ever going to be any hope of accomplishing God's will in our generation God's people will have to stop imagining and striving for their ideal and start living for what is real. Moving forward, it will be important for evangelicals to become courageous. They will have to understand and accept the real consequences of their actions. They will need to deconstruct the mess they have been handed in order to find the truth they need to live rightly in this world. Once evangelicals take back their lives from their leaders and begin critically evaluating their faith, recognizing that what they have built thus far is merely a kingdom of man, they can finally participate in truly bringing forth the Kingdom of God.

Appendix A

The Chicago Statement on Biblical Inerrancy (1978)

Preface

The authority of Scripture is a key issue for the Christian Church in this and every age. Those who profess faith in Jesus Christ as Lord and Saviour are called to show the reality of their discipleship by humbly and faithfully obeying God's written Word. To stray from Scripture in faith or conduct is disloyalty to our Master. Recognition of the total truth and trustworthiness of Holy Scripture is essential to a full grasp and adequate confession of its authority.

The following Statement affirms this inerrancy of Scripture afresh, making clear our understanding of it and warning against its denial. We are persuaded that to deny it is to set aside the witness of Jesus Christ and of the Holy Spirit and to refuse that submission to the claims of God's own Word which marks true Christian faith. We see it as our timely duty to make this affirmation in the face of current lapses from the truth of inerrancy among our fellow Christians and misunderstanding of this doctrine in the world at large.

This Statement consists of three parts: a Summary Statement, Articles of Affirmation and Denial, and an accompanying Exposition. It has been prepared in the course of a three-day consultation in Chicago. Those who have signed the Summary Statement and the Articles wish to affirm their own conviction as to the inerrancy of Scripture and to encourage and challenge one another and all Christians to growing appreciation and understanding of this doctrine. We acknowledge the limitations of a document prepared in a brief, intensive conference and do not propose that the Statement be given credal weight. Yet we rejoice in the deepening of our own convictions through our discussions together, and we pray that the Statement we have signed may be used to the glory of our God toward a new reformation of the Church in its faith, life and mission.

We offer this Statement in a spirit, not of contention, but of humility and love, which we by God's grace to maintain in any future dialogue arising out of what we have said. We gladly acknowledge that many who deny the inerrancy of Scripture do not display the consequences of this denial in the rest of their belief and behavior, and we are conscious that we who confess this doctrine often deny it in life by failing to bring our thoughts and deeds, our traditions and habits, into true subjection to the divine Word.

We invite response to this statement from those who see reason to amend its affirmations about Scripture by the light of Scripture itself, under whose infallible authority we stand as we speak. We claim no personal infallibility for the witness we bear, and for any help which enables us to strengthen this testimony to God's Word we shall be grateful.

A Short Statement

God, who is Himself Truth and speaks truth only, has inspired Holy Scripture in order thereby to reveal Himself to lost mankind through Jesus Christ as Creator and Lord, Redeemer and Judge. Holy Scripture is God's witness to Himself.

Holy Scripture, being God's own Word, written by men prepared and superintended by His Spirit, is of infallible divine authority in all matters upon which it touches: it is to be believed, as God's instruction, in all that it affirms; obeyed, as God's command, in all that it requires; embraced, as God's pledge, in all that it promises.

The Holy Spirit, Scripture's divine Author, both authenticates it to us by His inward witness and opens our minds to understand its meaning.

Being wholly and verbally God-given, Scripture is without error or fault in all its teaching, no less in what it states about God's acts in creation, about the events of world history, and about its own literary origins under God, than in its witness to God's saving grace in individual lives.

The authority of Scripture is inescapably impaired if this total divine inerrancy is in any way limited or disregarded, or made relative to a view of truth contrary to the Bible's own; and such lapses bring serious loss to both the individual and the Church.

Articles of Affirmation and Denial

Article I

We affirm that the Holy Scriptures are to be received as the authoritative Word of God. We deny that the Scriptures receive their authority from the Church, tradition, or any other human service.

Article II

We affirm that the Scriptures are the supreme written norm by which God binds the conscience, and that the authority of the Church is subordinate to that of Scripture.

We deny that Church creeds, councils, or declarations have authority greater than or equal to the authority of the Bible.

Article III

We affirm that the written Word in its entirety is revelation given by God.

We deny that the Bible is merely a witness to revelation, or only becomes revelation in encounter, or depends on the responses of men for its validity.

Article IV

We affirm that God who made mankind in His image has used language as a means of revelation. We deny that human language is so limited by our creatureliness that it is rendered inadequate as a vehicle for divine revelation. We further deny that the corruption of human culture and language through sin has thwarted God's work of inspiration.

Article V

We affirm that God's revelation within the Holy Scriptures was progressive.

We deny that later revelation, which may fulfill earlier revelation, ever corrects or contradicts it. We further deny that any normative revelation has been given since the completion of the New Testament writings.

Article VI

We affirm that the whole of Scripture and all its parts, down to the very words of the original, were given by divine inspiration. We deny that the inspiration of Scripture can rightly be affirmed of the whole without the parts, or of some parts but not the whole.

Article VII

We affirm that inspiration was the work in which God by His Spirit, through human writers, gave us His Word. The origin of Scripture is divine. The mode of divine inspiration remains largely a mystery to us.

We deny that inspiration can be reduced to human insight, or to heightened states of consciousness of any kind.

Article VIII

We affirm that God in His work of inspiration utilized the distinctive personalities and literary styles of the writers whom He had chosen and prepared.

We deny that God, in causing these writers to use the very words that He chose, overrode their personalities.

Article IX

We affirm that inspiration, though not conferring omniscience, guaranteed true and trustworthy utterance on all matters of which the Biblical authors were moved to speak and write.

We deny that the finitude of fallenness of these writers, by necessity or otherwise, introduced distortion or falsehood into God's Word.

Article X

We affirm that inspiration, strictly speaking, applies only to the autographic text of Scripture, which in the providence of God can be ascertained from available manuscripts with great accuracy. We further affirm that copies and translations of Scripture are the Word of God to the extent that they faithfully represent the original.

We deny that any essential element of the Christian faith is affected by the absence of the autographs. We further deny that this absence renders the assertion of Biblical inerrancy invalid or irrelevant.

Article XI

We affirm that Scripture, having been given by divine inspiration, is infallible, so that, far from misleading us, it is true and reliable in all the matters it addresses.

We deny that it is possible for the Bible to be at the same time infallible and errant in its assertions. Infallibility and inerrancy may be distinguished, but not separated.

Article XII

We affirm that Scripture in its entirety is inerrant, being free from all falsehood, fraud, or deceit.

We deny that Biblical infallibility and inerrancy are limited to spiritual, religious, or redemptive themes, exclusive of assertions in the fields of history and science. We further deny that scientific hypotheses about earth history may properly be used to overturn the teaching of Scripture on creation and the flood.

Article XIII

We affirm the propriety of using inerrancy as a theological term with reference to the complete truthfulness of Scripture.

We deny that it is proper to evaluate Scripture according to standards of truth and error that are alien to its usage or purpose. We further deny that inerrancy is negated by Biblical phenomena such as a lack of modern technical precision, irregularities of grammar or spelling, observational descriptions of nature, the reporting of falsehoods, the use of hyperbole and round numbers, the topical arrangement of material, variant selections of material in parallel accounts, or the use of free citations.

Article XIV

We affirm the unity and internal consistency of Scripture.

We deny that alleged errors and discrepancies that have not yet been resolved vitiate the truth claims of the Bible.

Article XV

We affirm that the doctrine of inerrancy is ground in the teaching of the Bible about inspiration.

We deny that Jesus' teaching about Scripture may be dismissed by appeals to accommodation or to any natural limitation of His humanity.

Article XVI

We affirm that the doctrine of inerrancy has been integral to the Church's faith throughout its history.

We deny that inerrancy is a doctrine invented by scholastic Protestantism, or is a reactionary position postulated in response to negative higher criticism.

Article XVII

We affirm that the Holy Spirit bears witness to the Scriptures, assuring believers of the truthfulness of God's written Word.

We deny that this witness of the Holy Spirit operates in isolation from or against Scripture.

Article XVIII

We affirm that the text of Scripture is to be interpreted by grammatico-historical exegesis, taking account of its literary forms and devices, and that Scripture is to interpret Scripture.

We deny the legitimacy of any treatment of the text or quest for sources lying behind it that leads to relativizing, dehistoricizing, or discounting its teaching, or rejecting its claims to authorship.

Article XIX

We affirm that a confession of the full authority, infallibility, and inerrancy of Scripture is vital to a sound understanding of the whole of the Christian faith. We further affirm that such confession should lead to increasing conformity to the image of Christ.

We deny that such confession is necessary for salvation. However, we further deny that inerrancy can be rejected without grave consequences, both to the individual and to the Church.

Appendix B

Evangelicalism & Emerging Church Comparison Chart

BELIEFS/PRACTICES	EVANGELICALISM	EMERGING CHURCH
Philosophical Context	Modernism	Postmodernism
Theological Methods	Systematic	Contextual
Evangelism	Informational	Communal
Church Form	Institutional	Missional
Main Focus	Bible and Salvation	Community/Incarnation
Hermeneutics	Inductive	Narrative
Worship	Traditional/Contemporary	Ancient Orthodox/Meditative
Inclusion	Selective	Egalitarian
Spiritual Gifts	Individualized	Communal
Spirituality	Prayer and Education	Interspiritual
Salvation	Grace through Faith	Mercy through Action
The Gospel	Salvation from Sin	Social Justice (Missio Dei)
Authority of Scripture	Inerrant	Sufficient for Faith
Ethics	Absolute	Subjective

APPENDIX C

THE THREE SPHERES OF THE EVANGELICAL WORLDVIEW

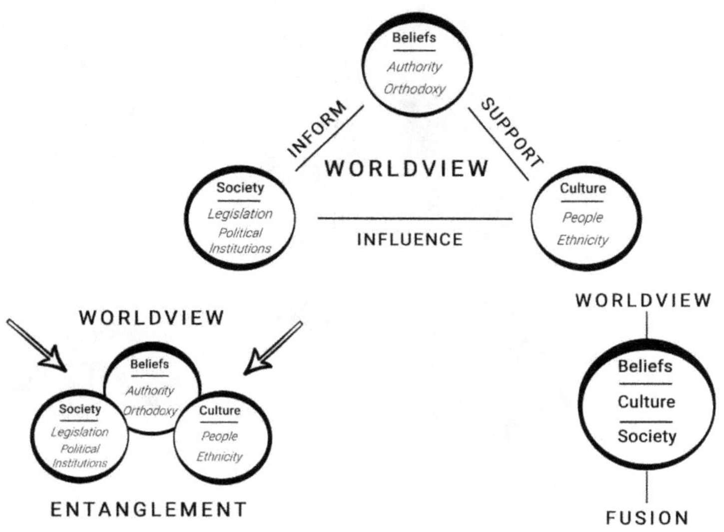

END NOTES

Fundamentalism & Conservative Evangelicalism

1. Hillerbrand, Hans J. 2004. *The Encyclopedia of Protestantism*. Routledge. p. 390.

2. Hodge, Charles. (1891) 2003. *Systematic Theology*. 3rd ed. Vol. 2. New York: Charles Scribner's Sons. pp. 1-12.

3. The Bible Institute of Los Angeles (Biola). 1921. "Wanted - More Mothers." *The King's Business*, February 1921.

4. The Bible Institute of Los Angeles (Biola). 1919. "Woman Suffrage and the Bible." *The King's Men*, April 1919. pp. 700-702.

5. Ellis, William T. 1914. *Billy Sunday: The Man and His Message, with His Own Words Which Have Won Thousands for Christ*. The Thomas Manufacturing Co. pp. 22, 229.

6. Talmage Dewitt, T. 1887. *"The Queens of the Home", Christian Herald and Signs of Our Times 10*. p. 565.

7. Talmage Dewitt, T. 1887. "The Queens of the Home", Christian Herald and Signs of Our Times 10. pp. 156-163.

8. Smith, Michael. 2010. "Christian Fundamentalism: Militancy and the Scopes Trial." Thesis, Clemson. p.114.

9. English, Eric. 2021. "A Conversation with Frank Schaeffer." Www.youtube.com. November 2, 2021.

10. After Frank left Evangelicalism he would apologize about his role in creating the pro-life movement.

11. Fitzgerald, Frances. 2018. *The Evangelicals: The Struggle to Shape America*. New York: Simon & Schuster Paperbacks. p. 25.

12. Matthew Avery Sutton. 2014. *American Apocalypse: A History of Modern Evangelicalism*. Cambridge, Massachusetts: Belknap Press Of Harvard University Press.

13. Peirce, Christine Kerr. 1935. "Pentecostal Evangel." *Pentecostal Evangel*, September 1935.

14. Timothée, BALBONÉ. 2019. "The Great Depression and the Expansion of the Assemblies of God." Flower Pentecostal Heritage Center. September 12, 2019.

15. Rosenberg, Joel. n.d. "Evangelical Attitudes toward Israel Research Study Evangelical Attitudes towards Israel and the Peace Process Sponsored by Chosen People Ministries and Author."

16. Gregory, Sheryl. 2012. "Can the Date of Jesus' Return Be Known?" *Bibliotheca Sacra* 169: 27.

17. Colorado Springs Gazette Telegraph. 1988. "Book Predicts End of World: Some Quit Jobs." *Colorado Springs Gazette Telegraph*, September 31, 1988.

18. Much could also be said about how this time, especially with Government oversight, affected minorities. Although this would certainly be a worthy task, it is not part of the scope of this book.

19. The Billy Graham Library. 2017. "Billy Graham's First Crusade - the Billy Graham Library Blog." The Billy Graham Library. September 1, 2017.

20. West, T.C. 2018. *Shards of Identit: The Origins of the Evangelical Movement during the Cold War, 1945-1981*. Washington: Academica Press.

21. Wendy Murray Zoba. 2007. *The Beliefnet Guide to Evangelical Christianity*. Harmony.

22. "Billy Graham." 2018. Billy Graham Memorial. February 26, 2018.

23. Newport, Frank. 2018. "In the News: Billy Graham on 'Most Admired' List 61 Times." Gallup.com. February 21, 2018.

24. Christianity Today. 2024. "ChristianityToday.org." ChristianityToday.org. 2024.

25. Billy Graham's speech given on the steps of the U.S. Capitol during his Washington D.C. revival held from Jan. 13 to Feb. 7, 1952.

26. This philosophy was popularized by H. Richard Niebuhr in his book *Christ and Culture*.

27. "Billy Graham." 2018. Billy Graham Memorial. February 26, 2018.

28. As quoted in: M.G. Long's *The Legacy of Billy Graham: Critical reflections on America's Greatest evangelist (2008)* Westminster John Knox Press. P. 100.

29. Lord, Debbie. 2018. "Billy Graham-Richard Nixon Tapes: The One Time Graham's Image Was Tarnished." AJC. 2018.

30. Conversation No. 662-4 (Nixon, Haldeman, Graham).

31. Meyer, Holly. 2018. "Billy Graham Was 'Most Important Evangelist since the Apostle Paul,' Russell Moore Says." The Tennessean. The Tennessean. February 21, 2018.

1. Hyer, Marjorie. 1981. "Evangelical Christians Meet to Develop Strategy for 1980s." *Washington Post*, January 30, 1981.

2. Falwell, Jerry. 1980. "Moral Majority Report." Presented at the Sermon, March 14, 1980, 2. https://liberty.contentdm.oclc.org/digital/collection/p17184coll4/id/4090/.

3. Dowland, Seth. 2009. "'Family Values' and the Formation of a Christian Right Agenda." *Church History* 78 (3): 606–31.

4. See TheKingdomOfMan.com for my compiled list of abusers.

5. As reported by the Lynchburg News in 1966.

6. Falwell, Jerry. 1965. "Ministers and Marches." Presented at the Sermon, March 21. pp. 7-8.

7. Liberty University. 2019. "Journal |» New Financial Report Shows Liberty's Business Model Adds up to More Resources and Aid for Students." Liberty Journal. October 25, 2019.

8. Being keenly aware of the heterosexual bias in the term "homosexual" I have chosen to use the term that best fits the context. Moreover, as time progresses and the issues change I will evolve the language along with the context.

9. Falwell, Jerry. 1981. "Newsletter," August 13, 1981.

10. McGrory, Mary. 1985. "The Spread of Fear." *Washington Post*, September 17, 1985.

11. Ridgely, Susan B. 2017. "Tuning in to Focus on the Family." *Oxford University Press EBooks*, January, 20–51.

12. Falwell, Jerry. 1988. *Strength for the Journey: An Autobiography*. New York: Pocket Books.

13. Greenhouse, Linda, Reva B Siegel, and George G. 2010. *Before Roe v. Wade: Voices That Shaped the Abortion Debate before the Supreme Court's Ruling*. New York: Kaplan Pub. pp. 334-335.

14. Stripe, C., R.H. Bube, E.J. Reeves, and R.L. Mixter. 1970. "Science in Christian Perspective." *Science in Christian Perspective*, June.

15. Garrett, W.B. 1973. "High Court Holds Abortion to Be a 'Right of Privacy." Edited by Baptist Press News Services. *SBC Annuals*, January 31, 1973.

16. Turner, Daniel L. 1997. *Standing without Apology*. BJU Press. pp. 225, 369.

17. Balmer, Randall. 2017. "The Historian's Pickaxe Uncovering the Racist Origins of the Religious Right."

18. Green, Lisa. 2015. "Women Distrust Church on Abortion - Lifeway Research." Researc h.lifeway.com. Lifeway Research. November 23, 2015.

19. I cover this issue in my book *UNenlightenment*.

20. Acts 18:24-26; Romans 8:1-3; Romans 16.

21. Mohler, Albert. 2018. "Report on Slavery and Racism in the History of the Southern Baptist Theological Seminary." Southern Baptist Theological Seminary. December 13, 2018.

22. Despite Mohler's good intentions he mischaracterizes the idea that the founders were simply products of their time. This is both untrue and a complete misunderstanding of the role that evangelicals played in the proliferation of slavery. I address this issue more fully in Part Two.

23. Blakemore, Erin. 2021. "Interstate Highways Were Touted as Modern Marvels. Racial Injustice Was Part of the Plan." *Washington Post*, August 17, 2021.

24. J Russell Hawkins. 2021. *The Bible Told Them So: How Southern Evangelicals Fought to Preserve White Supremacy*. New York, NY: Oxford University Press.

25. Cordes, Helen. 2000. "Battling for the Heart and Soul of Home-Schoolers." Salon. October 2, 2000.

26. Clarkson, Frederick. 1994. "Christian Reconstructionism." *Political Research Associates*, March.

The Hearts & Minds of the Evangelical Youth

1. Natarajan, Madison, Kerrie G. Wilkins-Yel, Anushka Sista, Aashika Anantharaman, and Natalie Seils. 2022. "Decolonizing Purity Culture: Gendered Racism and White Idealization in Evangelical Christianity." *Psychology of Women Quarterly* 46 (3): 036168432210911.

2. Kobes Du Mez, Kristin. 2020. *Jesus and John Wayne: How White Evangelicals Corrupted a Faith and Fractured a Nation*. New York, NY: Liveright Publishing Corporation, A Division of W.W. Norton & Company, Inc. pp. 243-244.

3. Aristotle. (1952) 1992. *[Great Books of the Western World]*. Edited by Mortimore Adler. Vol. 8. Chicago: Encyclopedia Britannica.

4. Saller, R.P. 1999. "Pater Familias, Mater Familias, and the Gendered Semantics of the Roman Household." *Classic Philology* 94 (2).

5. Seneca, and John W Basore. 1935. *Seneca. [T.] III, Moral Essays, Vol. III*. Cambridge, Massachusetts: Harvard University Press.

6. Le Juif, Philon. 2022. *The Works of Philo*. Translated by C.D. Yong. Hendrickson Publishers. pp. 518-533.

7. Shaddy, D. 2012. "A Christ-Centered Marriage." Web.archive.org. May 12, 2012.

8. Fowler, James. 1999. "WOMEN in the CHURCH. An Outline Study of What the Bible Has to Say about Women in Church." Www.christinyou.net. 1999.

9. Any environment that promotes disparities between men and women by not allowing women the same opportunities and privileges that men have.

10. Homan, Patricia, and Amy Burdette. 2021. "When Religion Hurts: Structural Sexism and Health in Religious Congregations." *American Sociological Review* 86 (2): 234–255.

11. Ibid., 4-5.

12. "Pat Robertson Tells Man to Become Muslim so He Can Beat His Wife." 2012. HuffPost.

13. Ibid.

14. Taylor, Annabel, and Vicki Lowik. 2019. "Evangelical Churches Believe Men Should Control Women. That's Why They Breed Domestic Violence." The Conversation. December 8, 2019.

15. Baird, Julia, and Hayley Gleeson. 2017. "'Submit to Your Husbands': Women Told to Endure Domestic Violence in the Name of God." *ABC News*, July 17, 2017.

16. Berkowitz, Bill. 2021. "Domestic Violence: The Dirty Little Secret of Conservative Christian Evangelicals." Daily Kos. October 26, 2021.

17. PonTell, Michelle Louise. 2009. "Sacred Silence: Domestic Abuse in Conservative Christian Communities." Thesis, California State University, San Bernardino.

18. Knickmeyer, Nicole, Heidi Levitt, and Sharon G. Horne. 2010. "Putting on Sunday Best: The Silencing of Battered Women within Christian Faith Communities." *Feminism & Psychology* 20 (1): 94–113.

19. Jones, Tony. 2019. *The New Christians: Dispatches from the Emergent Frontier*. Minneapolis, Minnesota: Fortress Press. pp. 44-45.

20. Ibid., 42.

21. One could argue that quantum mechanics proves this hypothesis. There are numerous times in quantum theory where this is the case. For example, in some cases, effects precede their causes. That is fundamentally illogical and yet it is true. Quantum entanglement also seems illogical because it should be ontologically impossible and yet we know that it happens.

22. I want to be clear that not all megachurches behave this way. And, not all megachurches are evangelical. There were and still are certainly churches that this does not apply to. However, many of these principles identify general trends that can be observed within evangelical megachurches. It is also important to note that megachurches were not Formed in the 90s. The term megachurch has a couple of different meanings. There is the organic kind where the establishment of a megachurch is based on growth. In this context megachurch just means a large church. The other type of megachurch is one that is formed with the specific purpose of being a megachurch. These inorganic churches are those that much of this section is referencing.

23. Some megachurches like Willow Creek Church in Barrington, Illinois who boast around 25,000 people, saw this as a problem and began developing ways for large churches to create smaller communities within their church. This approach aimed to help foster relationships in a place where people could easily get lost and help them try to find their place in smaller gatherings.

For God & Country

1. Stephen Mansfield, *The faith of George W. Bush* (Tarcher, 2003), pp. 10-11.

2. Walsh Andrew. Returning to Normalcy. *Religion in the News.* 2002 Spring.

3. Jimmy Swaggart Ministries, Nov. 10, 2002.

4. Green, T. (2021, May 24). *Confronting Christian Islamophobia*. Berkleycenter.georgetown.edu. https://berkleycenter.georgetown.edu/responses/confronting-christian-islamophobia.

5. Nadeem, R. (2022, November 17). *How Religion Intersects With Americans' Views on the Environment*. Pew Research Center's Religion & Public Life Project. https://www.pewresearch.org/religion/2022/11/17/how-religion-intersects-with-americans-views-on-the-environment/.

6. Pew Research Report. (2001, December 6). *Post September 11 Attitudes*. Pew Research Center - U.S. Politics & Policy. https://www.pewresearch.org/politics/2001/12/06/post-september-11-attitudes/.

7. Time. (2005, January 30). *The 25 Most Influential EVANGELICALS in America*. Time Magazine Archives. https://content.time.com/time/press_releases/article/0,8599,1022576,00.html.

8. Shimron, Y. (2022, July 26). *Disgraced pastor Ted Haggard faces new allegations*. Religion News Service. https://religionnews.com/2022/07/26/disgraced-pastor-ted-haggard-faces-new-allegations/.

9. Driscoll, M. (2000, December 5). *Pussified Nation.pdf*. Mars Hill Blog. https://docs.google.com/file/d/0By0MyUeolZbgU2FMOEVUYTRuTmc/preview.

10. It should be understood that if postmodernism posited what Carson and others have suggested, then it could not make any substantive claim since doing so would require them to assert a statement of belief that was absolute and thus negate their premise. Moreover, their argument is not with one's ability to know true things but in one's ability to know the nature of truth in its purest form. Postmodernism does not reject truth, it rejects Modernsim's lack of nuance.

11. J Russell Hawkins. (2021). *The Bible told them so: how Southern Evangelicals fought to preserve white supremacy*. Oxford University Press.

12. Cline, S. (2000). Competition and Fluidity in Latin American Christianity. *Latin American Research Review, 35*(2), 244–251. https://www.jstor.org/stable/2692143.

13. Brouwer, S., Gifford, P., & Rose, S. D. (2013). *Exporting the American Gospel*. Routledge.

14. Earls, A. (2020, March 2). *3 in 5 Evangelicals Live in Asia or Africa - Lifeway Research*. Research.lifeway.com. https://research.lifeway.com/2020/03/02/3-in-5-evangelicals-live-in-asia-or-africa/.

15. Namubiru, L., & Wepukhulu, K. S. (2020, October 29). *Exclusive: US Christian Right pours more than $50m into Africa*. OpenDemocracy. https://www.opendemocracy.net/en/5050/africa-us-christian-right-50m/.

16. Zoll, R. (2008, December 26). *Rick Warren's biggest critics: other evangelicals*. Chron. https://www.chron.com/lifestyle/houston-belief/article/rick-warren-s-biggest-critics-other-1584578.php.

17. Kirkpatrick, D. D. (2007, October 28). The Evangelical Crackup. *The New York Times*. https://www.nytimes.com/2007/10/28/magazine/28Evangelicals-t.html

18. Ibid.

19. Ibid.

20. Ibid.

21. Center, P. R. (2008, February 8). *Does McCain Need Evangelical Voters?* Pew Research Center's Religion & Public Life Project. https://www.pewresearch.org/religion/2008/02/08/does-mccain-need-evangelical-voters/.

22. Mansfield, S. (2011). *The faith of Barack Obama*. Thomas Nelson. p.130.

23. Barna Research Group. (2009, January 28). *How People of Faith Voted in the 2008 Presidential Race*. Barna Group. https://www.barna.com/research/how-people-of-faith-voted-in-the-2008-presidential-race/.

24. Inc, G. (2012, January 5). *Obama Begins 2012 at 46% Job Approval*. Gallup.com. https://news.gallup.com/poll/151907/Obama-Begins-2012-Job-Approval.aspx.

25. *Evangelical Voters Strongly Support Romney Despite Religious Differences | PRRI.* (2012, May 10). PRRI | at the Intersection of Religion, Values, and Public Life. https://www.prri.org/press-release/may-rns-2012-news-release/.

26. Dobson, J. (2008). Letter from 2012 in Obama's America. *SCRIBD.* https://www.scribd.com/document/109290045/Focus-On-The-Family-Propaganda-Letter-From-Obama-s-America-2012.

Donald Trump & White Christian Nationalism

1. Cillizza, Chris. 2022. "A Very Revealing Donald Trump Quote about Why He Ran for President | CNN Politics." CNN. September 26, 2022.

2. At least 30 had been elected by 2024.

3. Coster, Helen. 2024. "Christian TV Evangelicals Fire up Trump Support with Messianic Message." Reuters. March 22, 2024.

4. The bakery owner argued that creating a cake was an artistic expression because every cake is unique. From there he stated that by creating these works of art for the celebration meant at the very least a perceived endorsement of their union. Because this was the argument that was made, the courts had to determine whether or not decorating Good, even though it was to be consumed, could be considered art. He Greely admitted that the couple could have chosen one of the standard cakes but because they wanted it custom made he had the right to refuse.

5. Mooney, Michael J. 2019. "Trump's Apostle." Texas Monthly. July 23, 2019.

6. Nathan, Rich. 2021. "Clinging to Truth." National Association of Evangelicals. June 15, 2021.

7. "White House Spiritual Adviser Prays for 'Angels from Africa' to Cement Trump's Re-Election." 2020. The Independent. November 5, 2020.

8. Jaffe-Hoffman, Maayan. 2023. "Trump's Faith Advisor: Christians Must Learn from Jews, Not Convert Them." The Jerusalem Post - Christian World. June 15, 2023.

9. Glenza, Jessica. 2019. "Paula White: The Pastor Who Helps Trump Hear 'What God Has to Say.'" *The Guardian*, March 27, 2019, sec. US news.

10. Duin, Julia. 2023. "She Led Trump to Christ: The Rise of the Televangelist Who Advises the White House." *Washington Post*, April 9, 2023.

11. Worldometer. n.d. "United States Coronavirus." Www.worldometers.info.

12. Guidry, Jeanine P. D., Carrie A. Miller, Paul B. Perrin, Linnea I. Laestadius, Gina Zurlo, Matthew W. Savage, Michael Stevens, et al. 2022. "Between Healthcare Practitioners and Clergy: Evangelicals and COVID-19 Vaccine Hesitancy." *International Journal of Environmental Research and Public Health* 19 (17): 11120.

13. Corcoran, Katie E., Christopher P. Scheitle, and Bernard D. DiGregorio. 2021. "Christian Nationalism and COVID-19 Vaccine Hesitancy and Uptake." *Vaccine* 39 (45).

14. Nortey, Justin. 2021a. "Most White Americans Who Regularly Attend Worship Services Voted for Trump in 2020." Pew Research Center. August 30, 2021.

15. Jenkins, Jack. 2021a. "As 'Jericho Marchers' Descend on Washington, Local Faith Leaders Brace for Attacks." Religion News Service. January 6, 2021.

16. Jenkins, Jack. 2021b. "For Insurrectionists, a Violent Faith Brewed from Nationalism, Conspiracies and Jesus." Religion News Service. January 12, 2021.

17. Whitehead, Andrew L, and Samuel L Perry. 2020. *Taking America Back for God: Christian Nationalism in the United States.* Oxford University Press.

18. Ibid.

19. Brown, Joela. 2017. "The Klan, White Christianity, and the Past and Present | A Response to Kelly J. Baker by Randall J. Stephens | Religion & Culture Forum." Voices.uchicago.edu. June 26, 2017.

20. Whitehead and Perry, *Taking America Back*. P.30.

21. Ibid., 34.

22. Ibid., 30.

23. PRRI. 2024. "After Three Years and Many Indictments, the 'Big Lie' That Led to the January 6th Insurrection Is Still Believed by Most Republicans | PRRI." PRRI | at the Intersection of Religion, Values, and Public Life. January 5, 2024.

24. Jenkins, J. 2022. "New Report Details the Influence of Christian Nationalism on the Insurrection." Religion News Service. February 9, 2022.

The American Precipice

1. Abrams, Abigail. 2017. "Evangelical Women Just Joined #MeToo." Time. December 21, 2017.

2. Smietana, Bob. 2017. "Good Intentions, Lack of Plans Mark Church Response to Domestic Violence." Lifeway Newsroom. February 20, 2017.

3. Crone, Billy. 2022. *The Great Covid Deception*. Get a Life Ministries.

4. Downen, Robert, Lisa Olsen, and John Tedesco. 2019. "20 Years, 700 Victims: Southern Baptist Sexual Abuse Spreads as Leaders Resist Reforms." Houston Chronicle. February 10, 2019.

5. United States Attorney of New York Southern District. 2024. "Former Professor Charged with Obstructing Justice by Falsifying Records." Justice.gov. May 21, 2024.

6. There are many examples of large-scale systemic abuses by conservative evangelical churches that could fill an entire book. To demonstrate the extent of the abuse, I have attempted to document many of those evangelical leaders from the last 40 years who have been involved in some sort of sexual misconduct and/or abuse which can be viewed on TheKingdomOfMa n.com. However, even that documentation falls drastically short of recording all major cases and I do not include abuses in medium or small churches and organizations. Additionally, I limited my research to just the United States and Protestantism.

7. The conference was put on hold indefinitely in 2018.

8. It is important to note that being homosexual is not misconduct in and of itself (although their denomination would argue that). Instead, the misconduct refers to the multiple affairs that Cain had.

9. Religion News Blog. 1991. "Minister Bob Jones Removed after Confession of Sexual Misconduct." Religion News Blog. November 13, 1991.

10. Bailey, Sarah Pulliam. 2020. "Ravi Zacharias, Popular Evangelical Defender of the Christian Faith, Dies at 74." *Washington Post*, May 20, 2020.

11. Silliman, Daniel, and Kate Shellnutt. 2021. "Ravi Zacharias Hid Hundreds of Pictures of Women, Abuse during Massages, and a Rape Allegation." News & Reporting. February 11, 2021.

12. Ibid.

13. PBS. 2020. "Not All Women Gained the Vote in 1920 | American Experience | PBS." Www.pbs.org. July 6, 2020.

14. *Let America be America Again* by Langston Hughes (In Part).

15. Tarman, Christopher, and David O. Sears. 2005. "The Conceptualization and Measurement of Symbolic Racism." *The Journal of Politics* 67 (3): 731–61.

16. Sears, David, and P.J. Henry. 2008. "Symbolic and Modern Racism." In *Encyclopedia of Race and Racism*, edited by J.H. Moore, 3:111–12. Macmillan.

17. Smedley, Audrey, Peter Wade, and Yasuko Takezawa. 2019. "Race | Human." In *Encyclopedia Britannica*.

18. Jemar Tisby. 2020. *Color of Compromise: The Truth about the American Church's Complicity in Racism.* S.L.: Zondervan. p. 92.

19. Matthew 11:28-30.

20. Isaiah 52:13-53:3.

21. Luke 4:18.

22. J. Tisby, p. 97.

23. Baker, Kelly. 2017. *Gospel according to the Klan: The KKK's Appeal to Protestant America, 1915-1930.* Lawrence, Kan.: University Press of Kansas.

24. Benbow, Mark E. 2010. "Birth of a Quotation: Woodrow Wilson and 'Like Writing History with Lightning.'" *The Journal of the Gilded Age and Progressive Era* 9 (4): 509–33.

25. Vischer, Robert K. 2001. "Racial Segregation in American Churches and Its Implications for School Vouchers." *Florida Law Review* 53 (2): 193.

26. Cox, Daniel, and Robert Jones. 2016. "America's Changing Religious Identity." PRRI. October 14, 2016.

Theology & Politics in the Fundamentalist-Evangelical Imagination

1. This is an application of the philosopher Ludwig Wittgenstein's idea of Language Games. Each aspect is better understood, articulated, and ultimately meaningful if maintained separately. But, through time if one is not careful, these different areas can become intertwined and eventually entangled to such an extent that they begin to create contradictions. Finally, if they are never confronted they become fused together making them completely indistinguishable from one another.

2. See Appendix C for a diagram illustrating the three spheres and how they break down through lack of introspection.

3. Matthew 20:28, Mark 10:45, John 13:1-17.

4. There is an irony here in that evangelicals embrace dispensationalism and yet ardently argue against the process that led Darby to develop dispensationalism. Moreover, the whole Darby experience is not all that different from what the Emerging Church went through.

5. Fuller, D.P. 1957. "The Hermeneutics of Dispensationalism." Dissertation, Northern Baptist Theological Seminary.

6. Gaebelein, Arno C. 2017. *The History of the Scofield Reference Bible.* CrossReach.

7. "Editorially Speaking", The Kings Business (January 1946) p.8.

8. Matthew Avery Sutton. 2014. *American Apocalypse: A History of Modern Evangelicalism*. Cambridge, Massachusetts: Belknap Press of Harvard University Press.

9. Michaelson, Jay. 2024. "The Head of the Largest Christian Zionist Organization Is No Friend to Israel — He Wants an Apocalypse There." The Forward. April 16, 2024.

10. According to Van Impe's website he has worked with: W. A. Criswell, Dr. Robert Ketchem, Dr. Oswald J. Smith, Dr. Carl Baugh, Lance Latham, Dr. John Walvood, Dr. Billy Graham, Dr. Bob Jones II, Dr. Jerry Falwell, Dr. Torrey Johnson, M. R. DeHaan, Dr. Joseph Stowell, Sr., Charles Stanley, George Sweeting, Peter Marshall, Dr. J. Vernon McGee, Dr. Lee Roberson, Dr. Robert Cook, Jack Wyrsen, Dr. David Otis Fuller, Dr. Hyman Appleman.

11. The Chicago Statement on Biblical Inerrancy – etsjets.org. The Chicago Statement on Biblical Inerrancy. (n.d.). Also, see Appendix A for the full statement.

12. Evangelical theologians are the exception to this. For the most part they understand the intricacies of this doctrine. However, theologians do not create public policy, lay people do. Moreover, if lay people are not privy to the nuances they are stuck with the generic version, which is why that version is so prevalent within evangelical churches.

13. Propositionalism is a way of looking at the Bible that allows the reader to extract simple propositions to represent larger metaphysical truths they were never intended to represent.

14. Circular reasoning is a defect in an argument where the premise of one's argument is just as much in need of proof as the conclusion that is drawn from it. It's circular because both are in need of each other to be true and neither can be true apart from one another.

15. The question of authorship is important here because of the logic that is used. Paul uses a logic that is fairly consistent and his thinking is rigorous. The logic displayed for arguments in First Timothy are significantly flawed and lack Paul's argumentative standards. Additionally, the style of writing and word usage indicate a different author. There are around 300 words used in First Timothy that cannot be found anywhere in Paul's authentic writings.

16. It is important to remember that the addition of chapters and verses was meant to help delineate within the text and were not included until the mid 1500s. That means that these texts were not meant to be read as separate sections but as a single whole.

17. Conversely, it also means that there is nothing wrong with women choosing to take on a more traditional role within the home. But, they must be free to make that choice themselves.

18. This statement is included in the document called the Danvers Statement, which is their official belief statement.

19. Danvers Statement, section 6:1.

20. Kinnaman, David, and Gabe Lyons. 2007. *Unchristian: What a New Generation Really Thinks about Christianity—and Why It Matters*. Grand Rapids, Mich.: Baker Books.

21. Wokeism is a movement within the African American community meant to put a spotlight on racial injustice, prejudice and other forms of racial discrimination. Since its formation it has expanded to include discrimination against women and within the LGBTQ+ community.

22. Grace to You. 2012. "Slavery and True Liberty (John MacArthur)." www.youtube.com. 2012.

23. Wilson, Douglas, and Steve Wilkins. 1996. *Southern Slavery, as It Was*. Moscow, Id.: Canon Press.

24. Lykins, Liz. 2024. "Woman Claims John MacArthur's Grace Community Church Wrongly Disciplined and Shamed Her." The Roys Report. September 10, 2024.

25. Gryboski, Michael. 2024. "Woman Says Grace Community Church Wrongfully Disciplined Her over Marital Separation." Christianpost.com. The Christian Post. September 9, 2024.

Christian Idealism

1. Dwoskin, Elizabeth. 2021. "On Social Media, Vaccine Misinformation Mixes with Extreme Faith." *Washington Post*, February 16, 2021.

2. It is worth noting that this same attitude was infused into early American culture as many immigrants came from these environments and integrated these practices into the new societies they were forming.

3. Søren Kierkegaard, Howard V Hong, and Edna H Hong. (1846) 1992. *Kierkegaard's Writings, XII, Volume I: Concluding Unscientific Postscript to Philosophical Fragments Concluding Unscientific Postscript to Philosophical Fragments*. New Jersey: Princeton University Press.

4. Newsome, M.A.C. 2019. "Tyndale's Heresy." Catholic Answers. February 19, 2019.

5. It is noteworthy that the majority of seminaries are affiliated with a particular denomination, as this is the primary source of their funding.

6. Another reason for opposition towards practice over belief is that it is a slippery slope that leads to the possibility that someone who has never "confessed Jesus" is just as much a Christian, or even more so, than the individual who has confessed. However, this is yet another example of how binary thinking limits options. It is not an either/or but a both/and situation where only the confessing believer who also practices those beliefs is the only one able to call themselves Christian.

7. Frame, John M. 2002. *The Doctrine of God*. Phillipsburg, N.J.: P & R Pub. pp. 70-71.

8. Ibid. p. 70.

9. 1 Corinthians 15.

10. Lykins, Liz. 2023. "Megachurch Pastor Bishop T.D. Jakes Denies Sexual Misconduct at Diddy's Parties." The Roys Report. December 28, 2023.

Concluding Unscientific Postscript to Christian Idealism

1. Philosophical Fragments had been written two years prior and is also ironic since it is postscript and it was written first.

2. Christian Realism exists in its more colloquial form as Theological Realism and is also related to Religious Realism. I am using Christian Realism to stay consistent with Christian Idealism as well as to have the ability to borrow from both religious and theological realism. Additionally, both Theological and Philosophical Realism are problematic in certain respects. Utilizing Christian Realism allows us to tease out some of those problems in order to reframe them for our context.

3. Although the idea for the relationship between the form of something and reality oftentimes gets linked to Plato, this particular view is not platonic in the sense that these forms do not have their own ontological status that exists apart from the physical world. Instead these forms are simply shapes that exist in minds that have been culturally conditioned to accept those forms as ontologically and linguistically true. Additionally, the idea of function added to the formula helps to further distinguish the form from its platonic counterpart. Oftentimes function and form are contradictory perspectives; however, in this case they help to further define what is real.

4. Ontology studies the nature of being, whereas epistemology studies how people justify their beliefs to acquire knowledge. In other words there exists an incongruity within evangelical philosophy which oftentimes means that they have a realist view of God using a nominalist approach to knowing him.

5. To be fair, evangelicals would argue that God's truth and the truth of inerrancy are one and the same.

6. Søren Kierkegaard. (2003) 2014. *Provocations: Spiritual Writings of Kierkegaard.* Plough Publishing House. Pp.191-203.

7. This is very similar to how technology companies innovate. The idea is that before you invent, you must first create the need for the product you want to introduce. That means that the product will be purchased not based on appearance or the compulsiveness of the consumer but out of the need the customer has for it. Evangelicals introduced Americans to salvation as a product. They created the need through their crusades and missions, then introduced the product of salvation through their churches.

8. Childers, Alisa. (2024) 2020. *Another Gospel?: A Lifelong Christian Seeks Truth in Response to Progressive Christianity*. Carol Stream, Illinois: Tyndale Momentum, The Tyndale Non-fiction Imprint. p.234.

9. "Should Christians Doubt Their Faith?" 2022. www.youtube.com. 2022.

10. Granlund, Ruth. 2021. "Doubt: A Common Temptation among Believers - Association of Certified Biblical Counselors." Https://Biblicalcounseling.com/. The Association of Certified Biblical Counselors. November 17, 2021.

11. I refer you back to "The Box" in the introduction as an illustration for why this happens.

12. Matthew 5:17.

13. Matthew 22:37-39 and Mark 12:28-31. Jesus was referencing Deuteronomy 6:5 and Leviticus 19:18.

14. Santayana, George. 1905. *The Life of Reason: The Phases of Human Progress*. Vol. 1. United States: Echo Library.

15. Philippians 2:5-11.

16. There are interesting leadership principles that can be observed here too. Principles that could help Church leaders better understand their role in the lives of believers. For example, one's authority in the life of another cannot happen by force - but through the care of one's humility. In exchange for one's humble leading, others give part of their freedom to the one who they have come to trust. People did not follow Jesus because they had to. They followed him because they were compelled by what they saw.

17. Towards the beginning of Matthew and Mark's gospel the authors quote John the Baptist as saying: "Repent for the Kingdom of God is near". Some translations say "at hand". They also quoted Jesus using the same terminology. (The word "near" is not a designation of time but of location. In other words "near" does not mean almost but not yet. Instead, it refers to the proximity of the Kingdom. Jesus embodied the Kingdom and he is proximal to humanity (or near to them). This is why some translations say "at hand".) Regardless, the idea is that the Kingdom is both present and not present which reflects Jesus's life and future actions.

BIBLIOGRAPHY

Abrams, Abigail . 2017. "Evangelical Women Just Joined #MeToo." Time. December 21, 2017. https://time.com/5076537/evangelical-women-church-speak-out-metoo/.

Aristotle. 1952. *Great Books of the Western World*. Edited by M. Adler. Vol. 8. Encyclopedia Britannica.

———. (1952) 1992. *[Great Books of the Western World]*. Edited by Mortimore Adler. Vol. 8. Chicago: Encyclopaedia Britannica.

Bailey, Sarah Pulliam. 2020. "Ravi Zacharias, Popular Evangelical Defender of the Christian Faith, Dies at 74." *Washington Post*, May 20, 2020. https://www.washingtonpost.com/local/obituaries/ravi-zacharias-popular-evangelical-defender-of-the-christian-faith-dies-at-74/2020/05/19/e1e094c6-96a0-11ea-9f5e-56d8239bf9ad_story.html.

Baird, Julia, and Hayley Gleeson. 2017. "'Submit to Your Husbands': Women Told to Endure Domestic Violence in the Name of God." *ABC News*, July 17, 2017. https://www.abc.net.au/news/2017-07-18/domestic-violence-church-submit-to-husbands/8652028.

Baker, Kelly. 2017. *Gospel according to the Klan: The KKK's Appeal to Protestant America, 1915-1930*. Lawrence, Kan.: University Press Of Kansas.

Balmer, Randall. 2017. "The Historian's Pickaxe Uncovering the Racist Origins of the Religious Right." https://amc.sas.upenn.edu/sites/default/files/Balmer%20-%20Historian%27s%20Pickaxe.pdf.

Barna Research Group. 2009. "How People of Faith Voted in the 2008 Presidential Race." Barna Group. January 28, 2009. https://www.barna.com/research/how-people-of-faith-voted-in-the-2008-presidential-race/.

Benbow, Mark E. 2010. "Birth of a Quotation: Woodrow Wilson and 'like Writing History with Lightning.'" *The Journal of the Gilded Age and Progressive Era* 9 (4): 509–33. https://doi.org/10.1017/s1537781400004242.

Berkowitz, Bill. 2021. "Domestic Violence: The Dirty Little Secret of Conservative Christian Evangelicals." Daily Kos. October 26, 2021. https://www.dailykos.com/stories/2021/10/26/2060334/-Domestic-Violence-The-Dirty-Little-Secret-of-Conservative-Christian-Evangelicals.

"Billy Graham." 2018. Billy Graham Memorial. February 26, 2018. https://memorial.billygraham.org/official-obituary/.

Blakemore, Erin. 2021. "Interstate Highways Were Touted as Modern Marvels. Racial Injustice Was Part of the Plan." *Washington Post*, August 17, 2021.
https://www.washingtonpost.com/history/2021/08/16/interstate-highways-were-touted-modern-marvels-racial-injustice-was-part-plan/.

Brouwer, Steve, Paul Gifford, and Susan D Rose. 2013. *Exporting the American Gospel*. Routledge.

Brown, Joela. 2017. "The Klan, White Christianity, and the Past and Present | a Response to Kelly J. Baker by Randall J. Stephens | Religion & Culture Forum." Voices.uchicago.edu. June 26, 2017. https://voices.uchicago.edu/religionculture/2017/06/26/the-klan-white-christianity-and-the-past-and-present-a-response-to-kelly-j-baker-by-randall-j-stephens/.

CBMW. 2009. "CBMW about Us." web.archive.org. January 30, 2009. https://web.archive.org/web/20090130045824/http://www.cbmw.org/About-Us.

———. 2021. "Our History." CBMW. April 6, 2021. https://cbmw.org/about/history/.

Center, P.R. 2007. "Thompson Demonstrates Broad Potential Appeal." Pew Research Center - U.S. Politics & Policy. June 4, 2007. https://www.pewresearch.org/politics/2007/06/04/thompson-demonstrates-broad-potential-appeal/.

Center, Pew Research. 2008. "Does McCain Need Evangelical Voters?" Pew Research Center's Religion & Public Life Project. February 8, 2008. https://www.pewresearch.org/religion/2008/02/08/does-mccain-need-evangelical-voters/.

Childers, Alisa. (2024) 2020. *Another Gospel?: A Lifelong Christian Seeks Truth in Response to Progressive Christianity*. Carol Stream, Illinois: Tyndale Momentum, The Tyndale Nonfiction Imprint.

Christianity Today. 2024. "ChristianityToday.org." ChristianityToday .org. 2024. https://christianitytoday.org/what-we-do/.

Cillizza, Chris. 2022. "A Very Revealing Donald Trump Quote about Why He Ran for President | CNN Politics." CNN. September 26, 2022. https://www.cnn.com/2022/09/26/politics/donald-trump-president-quote-maggie-haberman-book/index.html.

Cimino, Richard. 2005. "'No God in Common:' American Evangelical Discourse on Islam after 9/11." Review of Religious Research 47 (2): 162–74. https://doi.org/10.2307/3512048.

Clarkson, Frederick. 1994. "Christian Reconstructionism." *Political Research Associates*, March. https://politicalresearch.org/1994/03/01/christian-reconstructionismtheocratic-dominionism-gains-influence.

Cline, Sarah. 2000. "Competition and Fluidity in Latin American Christianity." Edited by Kurt Bowen, Steve Brouwer, Paul Gifford, Susan D. Rose, Elizabeth Brusco, Anthony Gill, Gary H. Gossen, et al. *Latin American Research Review* 35 (2): 244–51. https://www.jstor.org/stable/2692143.

Colorado Springs Gazette Telegraph. 1988. "Book Predicts End of World: Some Quit Jobs." *Colorado Springs Gazette Telegraph*, September 31, 1988.

Corcoran, Katie E., Christopher P. Scheitle, and Bernard D. DiGregorio. 2021. "Christian Nationalism and COVID-19 Vaccine Hesitancy and Uptake." Vaccine 39 (45). https://doi.org/10.1016/j.vaccine.2021.09.074.

Cordes, Helen. 2000. "Battling for the Heart and Soul of Home-Schoolers." Salon. October 2, 2000. https://www.salon.com/2000/10/02/homeschooling_battle/.

Coster, Helen. 2024. "Christian TV Evangelicals Fire up Trump Support with Messianic Message." Reuters. March 22, 2024. https://www.reuters.com/world/us/god-gave-us-trump-christian-media-evangelicals-preach-messianic-message-2024-03-22/.

Cox, Daniel, and Robert Jones. 2016. "America's Changing Religious Identity." PRRI. October 14, 2016. https://www.prri.org/research/american-religious-landscape-christian-religiously-unaffiliated/.

Crone, Billy. 2022. *The Great Covid Deception*. Get a Life Ministries.

Dobson, James. 2008. "Letter from 2012 in Obama's America." SCRIBD, October.
https://www.scribd.com/document/109290045/Focus-On-The-Family-Propaganda-Letter-From-Obama-s-America-2012.

Door Søren Kierkegaard, Howard V Hong, and Edna H Hong. (1846) 1992. *Kierkegaard's Writings, XII, Volume I: Concluding Unscientific Postscript to Philosophical Fragments Concluding Unscientific Postscript to Philosophical Fragments*. New Jersey: Princeton University Press.

Dowland, Seth. 2009. "'Family Values' and the Formation of a Christian Right Agenda." *Church History* 78 (3): 606–31. https://doi.org/10.1017/s0009640709990448.

Downen, Robert, Lisa Olsen, and John Tedesco. 2019. "20 Years, 700 Victims: Southern Baptist Sexual Abuse Spreads as Leaders Resist Reforms." Houston Chronicle. February 10, 2019.

https://www.houstonchronicle.com/news/investigations/article/Southern-Baptist-sexual-abuse-spreads-as-leaders-13588038.php.

Driscoll, Mark. 2000. "Pussified Nation.pdf." Mars Hill Blog. December 5, 2000. https://docs.google.com/file/d/0By0MyUeolZbgU2FMOEVUYTRuTmc/.

Duin, Julia. 2023. "She Led Trump to Christ: The Rise of the Televangelist Who Advises the White House." Washington Post, April 9, 2023. https://www.washingtonpost.com/lifestyle/magazine/she-led-trump-to-christ-the-rise-of-the-televangelist-who-advises-the-white-house/2017/11/13/1dc3a830-bb1a-11e7-be94-fabb0f1e9ffb_story.html.

Dwoskin, Elizabeth. 2021. "On Social Media, Vaccine Misinformation Mixes with Extreme Faith." *Washington Post*, February 16, 2021. https://www.washingtonpost.com/technology/2021/02/16/covid-vaccine-misinformation-evangelical-mark-beast/.

Earls, Aaron. 2020. "3 in 5 Evangelicals Live in Asia or Africa - Lifeway Research." Research.lifeway.com. March 2, 2020. https://research.lifeway.com/2020/03/02/3-in-5-evangelicals-live-in-asia-or-africa/.

Ellis, William T. 1914. *Billy Sunday: The Man and His Message, with His Own Words Which Have Won Thousands for Christ*. The Thomas Manufacturing Co.

English, Eric. 2021. "A Conversation with Frank Schaeffer." www.youtube.com. November 2, 2021. https://www.youtube.com/watch?v=_QNqOkp75Nw.

"Evangelical Voters Strongly Support Romney despite Religious Differences | PRRI." 2012. PRRI | at the Intersection of Religion, Values, and Public Life. May 10, 2012. https://www.prri.org/press-release/may-rns-2012-news-release/.

Falwell, Jerry. 1965. "Ministers and Marches." Presented at the Sermon, March 21. https://liberty.contentdm.oclc.org/digital/collection/p17184coll4/id/4090/.

———. 1980. "Moral Majority Report."

———. 1988. *Strength for the Journey: An Autobiography*. New York: Pocket Books.

Falwell, Jerry . 1981. "Newsletter," August 13, 1981.

Fitzgerald, Frances. 2018. *The Evangelicals: The Struggle to Shape America*. New York: Simon & Schuster Paperbacks.

Fowler, James. 1999. "WOMEN in the CHURCH. An Outline Study of What the Bible Has to Say about Women in Church." www.christinyou.net. 1999. https://www.christinyou.net/pages/womeninchurch.html.

Frame, John M. 2002. *The Doctrine of God*. Phillipsburg, N.J.: P & R Pub.

Fuller, D.P. 1957. "The Hermeneutics of Dispensationalism." Dissertation, Northern Baptist Theological Seminary.

Gaebelein, Arno C. 2017. *The History of the Scofield Reference Bible*. CrossReach.

Garrett, W.B. 1973. "High Court Holds Abortion to Be a 'Right of Privacy." Edited by Baptist Press News Services. SBC Annuals, January

31, 1973. http://media.sbhla.org.s3.amazonaws.com/3521,31-Jan-1973.pdf.

Glenza, Jessica. 2019. "Paula White: The Pastor Who Helps Trump Hear 'What God Has to Say.'" The Guardian, March 27, 2019, sec. US news. https://www.theguardian.com/us-news/2019/mar/27/paula-white-donald-trump-pastor-evangelicals.

Grace to You. 2012. "Slavery and True Liberty (John MacArthur)." Www.youtube.com. 2012. https://www.youtube.com/watch?v=HSKj3LQilcI.

Granlund, Ruth. 2021. "Doubt: A Common Temptation among Believers - Association of Certified Biblical Counselors." Https://Biblicalcounseling.com/. The Association of Certified Biblical Counselors. November 17, 2021. https://biblicalcounseling.com/resource-library/articles/doubt-a-common-temptation-among-believers/.

Green, Lisa. 2015. "Women Distrust Church on Abortion - Lifeway Research." Research.lifeway.com. Lifeway Research. November 23, 2015. https://research.lifeway.com/2015/11/23/women-distrust-church-on-abortion/.

Green, Todd. 2021. "Confronting Christian Islamophobia." Berkleycenter.georgetown.edu. May 24, 2021. https://berkleycenter.georgetown.edu/responses/confronting-christian-islamophobia.

Greenhouse, Linda, Reva B Siegel, and George G. 2010. *Before Roe v. Wade: Voices That Shaped the Abortion Debate before the Supreme Court's Ruling*. New York: Kaplan Pub.

Gregory, Sheryl. 2012. "Can the Date of Jesus' Return Be Known?" Bibliotheca Sacra 169: 27.

Gryboski, Michael. 2024. "Woman Says Grace Community Church Wrongfully Disciplined Her over Marital Separation." Christianpost.com. *The Christian Post*. September 9, 2024. https://www.christianpost.com/news/woman-says-grace-community-church-wrongfully-disciplined-her.html.

Guidry, Jeanine P. D., Carrie A. Miller, Paul B. Perrin, Linnea I. Laestadius, Gina Zurlo, Matthew W. Savage, Michael Stevens, et al. 2022. "Between Healthcare Practitioners and Clergy: Evangelicals and COVID-19 Vaccine Hesitancy." *International Journal of Environmental Research and Public Health* 19 (17): 11120. https://doi.org/10.3390/ijerph191711120.

Hillerbrand, Hans J. 2004. The Encyclopedia of Protestantism. Routledge.

Hodge, Charles. (1891) 2003. *Systematic Theology*. 3rd ed. Vol. 2. New York: Charles Scribner's Sons.

Homan, Patricia, and Amy Burdette. 2021. "When Religion Hurts: Structural Sexism and Health in Religious Congregations." *American Sociological Review* 86 (2): 234–55. https://doi.org/10.1177/0003122421996686.

Howard Clark Kee, and Et Al. 1998. *Christianity: A Social and Cultural History*. Upper Saddle River, Nj: Prentice Hall, Cop.

Hyer, Marjorie. 1981. "Evangelical Christians Meet to Develop Strategy for 1980s." Washington Post, January 30, 1981. https://www.washingtonpost.com/archive/local/1981/01/30/evangelical-christians-meet-to-develop-strategy-for-1980s/3ee92602-35a7-413a-ae2a-bb786fb3b396/.

Inc, Gallup. 2012. "Obama Begins 2012 at 46% Job Approval." Gallup.com. January 5, 2012. https://news.gallup.com/poll/151907/Obama-Begins-2012-Job-Approval.aspx.

Israel, Charles A. 2004. *Before Scopes: Evangelicalism, Education, and Evolution in Tennessee, 1870-1925*. Athens: University Of Georgia Press.

J Russell Hawkins. 2021. *The Bible Told Them so: How Southern Evangelicals Fought to Preserve White Supremacy*. New York, NY: Oxford University Press.

Jaffe-Hoffman, Maayan. 2023. "Trump's Faith Advisor: Christians Must Learn from Jews, Not Convert Them." The Jerusalem Post - Christian World. June 15, 2023. https://www.jpost.com/christianworld/article-746372.

Jemar Tisby. 2020. *COLOR of COMPROMISE: The Truth about the American Church's Complicity in Racism*. S.L.: Zondervan.

Jenkins, Jack. 2021a. "As 'Jericho Marchers' Descend on Washington, Local Faith Leaders Brace for Attacks." Religion News Service. January 6, 2021. https://religionnews.com/2021/01/05/as-jericho-marchers-descend-on-washington-local-faith-leaders-brace-for-attacks/.

———. 2021b. "For Insurrectionists, a Violent Faith Brewed from Nationalism, Conspiracies and Jesus." Religion News Service. January 12, 2021. https://religionnews.com/2021/01/12/the-faith-of-the-insurrectionists/.

———. 2022. "New Report Details the Influence of Christian Nationalism on the Insurrection." Religion News Service. February 9,

2022. https://religionnews.com/2022/02/09/new-report-details-the-influence-of-christian-nationalism-on-the-insurrection/.

Jones, Tony. 2019. *The New Christians: Dispatches from the Emergent Frontier*. Minneapolis, Minnesota: Fortress Press.

Kinnaman, D. 2021. "One in Three Practicing Christians Has Stopped Attending Church during COVID-19." Barna Group. 2021. https://www.barna.com/research/new-sunday-morning-part-2/.

Kinnaman, David, and Gabe Lyons. 2007. *Unchristian: What a New Generation Really Thinks about Christianity—and Why It Matters*. Grand Rapids, Mich.: Baker Books.

Kirkpatrick, David D. 2007. "The Evangelical Crackup." *The New York Times*, October 28, 2007, sec. Magazine. https://www.nytimes.com/2007/10/28/magazine/28Evangelicals-t.html.

Knickmeyer, Nicole, Heidi Levitt, and Sharon G. Horne. 2010. "Putting on Sunday Best: The Silencing of Battered Women within Christian Faith Communities." *Feminism & Psychology* 20 (1): 94–113. https://doi.org/10.1177/0959353509347470.

Kobes Du Mez, Kristin. 2020. *Jesus and John Wayne: How White Evangelicals Corrupted a Faith and Fractured a Nation*. New York, Ny: Liveright Publishing Corporation, A Division Of W.W. Norton & Company, Inc.

Le Juif, Philon. 2022. *The Works of Philo*. Translated by C.D. Yong. Hendrickson Publishers.

Liberty University. 2019. "Journal | New Financial Report Shows Liberty's Business Model Adds up to More Resources and Aid for

Students." Liberty Journal. October 25, 2019. https://www.liberty.edu/journal/article/new-financial-report-shows-libertys-business-model-adds-up-to-more-resources-and-aid-for-students/.

Long, Michael G. 2008. *The Legacy of Billy Graham: Critical Reflections on America's Greatest Evangelist*. Westminster John Knox Press.

Lord, Debbie. 2018. "Billy Graham-Richard Nixon Tapes: The One Time Graham's Image Was Tarnished." AJC. 2018. https://www.ajc.com/news/national/billy-graham-richard-nixon-tapes-the-one-time-graham-image-was-tarnished/DCj06gfORZJLYa30cLawWL/.

Lykins, Liz. 2023. "Megachurch Pastor Bishop T.D. Jakes Denies Sexual Misconduct at Diddy's Parties." The Roys Report. December 28, 2023. https://julieroys.com/bishop-t-d-jakes-denies-sexual-misconduct-diddys-parties/.

———. 2024. "Woman Claims John MacArthur's Grace Community Church Wrongly Disciplined and Shamed Her." The Roys Report. September 10, 2024. https://julieroys.com/woman-claims-john-macarthurs-grace-community-church-wrongly-disciplined-and-shamed-her/.

Mansfield, Stephen. 2003. *The Faith of George W. Bush*. Penguin.

———. 2011. *The Faith of Barack Obama*. Nashville: Thomas Nelson.

Martínez, Jessica, and Gregory A. Smith. 2016. "How the Faithful Voted: A Preliminary 2016 Analysis." Pew Research Center. November 9, 2016. https://www.pewresearch.org/short-reads/2016/11/09/how-the-faithful-voted-a-preliminary-2016-analysis/.

Matthew Avery Sutton. 2014. *American Apocalypse: A History of Modern Evangelicalism.* Cambridge, Massachusetts: Belknap Press Of Harvard University Press.

McGrory, Mary. 1985. "The Spread of Fear." *Washington Post*, September 17, 1985. https://www.washingtonpost.com/archive/politics/1985/09/17/the-spread-of-fear/ee19427b-3894-4eaf-9082-cb3823920e96/.

McRay, J. 2015. In *Leadership Glossary Essential Terms for the 21st Century*.

Meyer, Holly. 2018. "Billy Graham Was 'Most Important Evangelist since the Apostle Paul,' Russell Moore Says." *The Tennessean*. February 21, 2018. https://www.tennessean.com/story/news/religion/2018/02/21/billy-graham-dead-99-tennessee-reaction/358116002/.

Michaelson, Jay. 2024. "The Head of the Largest Christian Zionist Organization Is No Friend to Israel — He Wants an Apocalypse There." *The Forward*. April 16, 2024. https://forward.com/opinion/603310/john-hagee-christian-zionist-iran-israel/.

Mohler, Albert. 2018. "Report on Slavery and Racism in the History of the Southern Baptist Theological Seminary." Southern Baptist Theological Seminary. December 13, 2018. https://www.sbts.edu/southern-project/.

Mooney, Michael J. 2019. "Trump's Apostle." Texas Monthly. July 23, 2019. https://www.texasmonthly.com/news-politics/donald-trump-defender-dallas-pastor-robert-jeffress/.

Nadeem, Reem. 2022. "How Religion Intersects with Americans' Views on the Environment." Pew Research Center's Religion & Public Life Project. November 17, 2022. https://www.pewresearch.org/religion/2022/11/17/how-religion-intersects-with-americans-views-on-the-environment/.

Namubiru, Lydia, and Khatondi Soita Wepukhulu. 2020. "Exclusive: US Christian Right Pours More than $50m into Africa." OpenDemocracy. October 29, 2020. https://www.opendemocracy.net/en/5050/africa-us-christian-right-50m/.

Natarajan, Madison, Kerrie G. Wilkins-Yel, Anushka Sista, Aashika Anantharaman, and Natalie Seils. 2022. "Decolonizing Purity Culture: Gendered Racism and White Idealization in Evangelical Christianity." *Psychology of Women Quarterly* 46 (3): 036168432210911. https://doi.org/10.1177/03616843221091116.

Nathan, Rich. 2021. "Clinging to Truth." National Association of Evangelicals. June 15, 2021. https://www.nae.org/clinging-to-truth/.

Newport, Frank. 2018. "In the News: Billy Graham on 'Most Admired' List 61 Times." Gallup.com. February 21, 2018. https://news.gallup.com/poll/228089/news-billy-graham-admired-list-times.aspx.

Newsome, M.A.C. 2019. "Tyndale's Heresy." Catholic Answers. February 19, 2019. https://www.catholic.com/magazine/print-edition/tyndales-heresy.

Nortey, Justin. 2021a. "Most White Americans Who Regularly Attend Worship Services Voted for Trump in 2020." Pew Research Center. August 30, 2021. https://www.pewresearch.org/short-reads/2021/08/30/most-white

-americans-who-regularly-attend-worship-services-voted-for-trump-in-2020/.

———. 2021b. "Most White Americans Who Regularly Attend Worship Services Voted for Trump in 2020." Pew Research Center. August 30, 2021. https://www.pewresearch.org/short-read/2021/08/30/most-white-americans-who-regularly-attend-worship-services-voted-for-trump-in-2020/.

Novak, Kat. 2023. "Why Some People Are Willing to Believe Conspiracy Theories." Apa.org. June 26, 2023. https://www.apa.org/news/press/releases/2023/06/why-people-believe-conspiracy-theories.

"Pat Robertson Tells Man to Become Muslim so He Can Beat His Wife." 2012. *HuffPost*. September 11, 2012. https://www.huffpost.com/entry/pat-robertson-become-muslim-to-beat-your-wife_n_1873142.

PBS. 2020. "Not All Women Gained the Vote in 1920 | American Experience | PBS." Www.pbs.org. July 6, 2020. https://www.pbs.org/wgbh/americanexperience/features/vote-not-all-women-gained-right-to-vote-in-1920/.

Peirce, Christine Kerr. 1935. "Pentecostal Evangel." *Pentecostal Evangel*, September 1935. https://archives.ifphc.org/DigitalPublications/USA/Assemblies%20of%20God%20USA/Pentecostal%20Evangel/Unregistered/1935/FPHC/1935_09_14.pdf.

Pew Report. 2012. "Little Voter Discomfort with Romney's Mormon Religion." Pew Research Center's Religion & Public Life Project. July 26, 2012. https://www.pewresearch.org/religion/2012/07/26/2012-romney-mormonism-obamas-religion/.

Pew Research Center. 2018. "An Examination of the 2016 Electorate, Based on Validated Voters." Pew Research Center - U.S. Politics & Policy. Pew Research Center. August 9, 2018. https://www.pewresearch.org/politics/2018/08/09/an-examination-of-the-2016-electorate-based-on-validated-voters/.

Pew Research Report. 2001. "Post September 11 Attitudes." Pew Research Center - U.S. Politics & Policy. December 6, 2001. https://www.pewresearch.org/politics/2001/12/06/post-september-11-attitudes/.

PonTell, Michelle Louise. 2009. "Sacred Silence: Domestic Abuse in Conservative Christian Communities." Thesis, California State University, San Bernardino. https://scholarworks.lib.csusb.edu/etd-project/3936.

PRRI. 2023. "Religion and Congregations in a Time of Social and Political Upheaval." PRRI. May 16, 2023. https://www.prri.org/research/religion-and-congregations-in-a-time-of-social-and-political-upheaval/.

———. 2024. "After Three Years and Many Indictments, the 'Big Lie' That Led to the January 6th Insurrection Is Still Believed by Most Republicans | PRRI." PRRI | at the Intersection of Religion, Values, and Public Life. January 5, 2024.
https://www.prri.org/spotlight/after-three-years-and-many-indictments-the-big-lie-that-led-to-the-january-6th-insurrection-is-still-believed-by-most-republicans/.

Religion News Blog. 1991. "Minister Bob Jones Removed after Confession of Sexual Misconduct." Religion News Blog. November

13, 1991. https://www.religionnewsblog.com/16929/minister-removed-after-confession-of-sexual-misconduct.

Ridgely, Susan B. 2017. "Tuning in to Focus on the Family." *Oxford University Press EBooks*, January, 20–51. https://doi.org/10.1093/acprof:oso/9780199755073.003.0002.

Rosenberg, Joel. n.d. "Evangelical Attitudes toward Israel Research Study Evangelical Attitudes towards Israel and the Peace Process Sponsored by Chosen People Ministries and Author." https://research.lifeway.com/wp-content/uploads/2017/12/Evangelical-Attitudes-Toward-Israel-Research-Study-Report.pdf.

Saller, R.P. 1999. " Pater Familias, Mater Familias, and the Gendered Semantics of the Roman Household." *Classic Philology* 94 (2). https://www.jstor.org/stable/270558.

Santayana, George. 1905. *The Life of Reason: The Phases of Human Progress*. Vol. 1. United States: Echo Library.

Sears, David, and P.J. Henry. 2008. "Symbolic and Modern Racism." In Encyclopedia of Race and Racism, edited by J.H. Moore, 3:111–12. Macmillan.

Seneca, and John W Basore. 1935. Seneca. *[T.] III, Moral Essays, Vol. III.* Cambridge, Massachusetts: Harvard University Press.

Shaddy, D. 2012. "A Christ Centered Marriage." web.archive.org. May 12, 2012. https://web.archive.org/web/20120512065547/http://www.lcms.org/Document.fdoc?src=lcm&id=492.

Sherman, Gabriel, and G.L. 2022. "Inside Jerry Falwell Jr.'S Unlikely Rise and Precipitous Fall at Liberty University." Vanity Fair. January

24, 2022. https://www.vanityfair.com/news/2022/01/inside-jerry-falwell-jr-unlikely-rise-and-precipitous-fall.

Shimron, Yonat. 2022. "Disgraced Pastor Ted Haggard Faces New Allegations." Religion News Service. July 26, 2022. https://religionnews.com/2022/07/26/disgraced-pastor-ted-haggard-faces-new-allegations/.

"Should Christians Doubt Their Faith?" 2022. www.youtube.com. 2022. https://www.youtube.com/watch?v=DSP9nQwjrTI.

Silliman, Daniel, and Kate Shellnutt. 2021. "Ravi Zacharias Hid Hundreds of Pictures of Women, Abuse during Massages, and a Rape Allegation." News & Reporting. February 11, 2021. https://www.christianitytoday.com/news/2021/february/ravi-zacharias-rzim-investigation-sexual-abuse-sexting-rape.html.

Smedley, Audrey, Peter Wade, and Yasuko Takezawa. 2019. "Race | Human." In Encyclopædia Britannica. https://www.britannica.com/topic/race-human.

Smietana, Bob. 2017. "Good Intentions, Lack of Plans Mark Church Response to Domestic Violence." Lifeway Newsroom. February 20, 2017. https://news.lifeway.com/2017/02/20/good-intentions-lack-of-plans-mark-church-response-to-domestic-violence/.

Smith, Michael. 2010. " Christian Fundamentalism: Militancy and the Scopes Trial." Thesis, Clemson. https://tigerprints.clemson.edu/cgi/viewcontent.cgi?article=1962&context=all_theses.

Søren Kierkegaard. (2003) 2014. *Provocations: Spiritual Writings of Kierkegaard*. Plough Publishing House.

Stripe, C., R.H. Bube, E.J. Reeves, and R.L. Mixter. 1970. "Science in Christian Perspective." *Science in Christian Perspective*, June. https://www.asa3.org/ASA/PSCF/1970/JASA6-70Christian.html.

Talmage Dewitt, T. 1887. "The Queens of the Home", *Christian Herald and Signs of Our Times* 10.

Tarman, Christopher, and David O. Sears. 2005. "The Conceptualization and Measurement of Symbolic Racism." *The Journal of Politics* 67 (3): 731–61. https://doi.org/10.1111/j.1468-2508.2005.00337.x.

Taylor, Annabel, and Vicki Lowik. 2019. "Evangelical Churches Believe Men Should Control Women. That's Why They Breed Domestic Violence." The Conversation. December 8, 2019. https://theconversation.com/evangelical-churches-believe-men-should-control-women-thats-why-they-breed-domestic-violence-127437.

The Bible Institute of Los Angeles (Biola). 1919. "Woman Suffrage and the Bible." The King's Men, April 1919. https://digitalcommons.biola.edu/kings-business-all/147.

———. 1921. "Wanted - More Mothers." *The King's Business*, February 1921. https://digitalcommons.biola.edu/kings-business-all/129.

———. 1946. "Editorially Speaking." *The Kings Business*, 1946. https://digitalcommons.biola.edu/kings-business-all/430.

The Billy Graham Library. 2017. "Billy Graham's First Crusade - the Billy Graham Library Blog." The Billy Graham Library. September 1, 2017. https://billygrahamlibrary.org/billy-graham-grand-rapids/.

The Master's Seminary. 2023. "John MacArthur | TMS Chapel | Q&A." Www.youtube.com. 2023. https://www.youtube.com/watch?v=42HoYT7hNd4.

Time. 2005. "The 25 Most Influential EVANGELICALS in America." Time Magazine Archives. January 30, 2005. https://content.time.com/time/press_releases/article/0,8599,1022576,00.html.

Timothée, Balone. 2019. "The Great Depression and the Expansion of the Assemblies of God." Flower Pentecostal Heritage Center. September 12, 2019. https://ifphc.wordpress.com/2019/09/12/the-great-depression-and-the-expansion-of-the-assemblies-of-god-2/.

Turner, Daniel L. 1997. *Standing without Apology*. BJU Press.

Turner, Matthew Paul. 2014. "Mark Driscoll's Pussified Nation..." Matthew Paul Turner. July 29, 2014. https://matthewpaulturner.com/2014/07/29/mark-driscolls-pussified-nation/.

United States Attorney of New York Southern District. 2024. "Former Professor Charged with Obstructing Justice by Falsifying Records." Justice.gov. May 21, 2024. https://www.justice.gov/usao-sdny/pr/former-professor-charged-obstructing-justice-falsifying-records.

University of Texas. 2022. "Groupthink - Ethics Unwrapped." Ethics Unwrapped. May 25, 2022. https://ethicsunwrapped.utexas.edu/glossary/groupthink.

Vischer, Robert K. 2001. "Racial Segregation in American Churches and Its Implications for School Vouchers." *Florida Law Review* 53 (2): 193.

Walsh, Andrew. 2002. "Returning to Normalcy." ChristianityToday.org. 2002. https://www.christianitytoday.org/what-we-do/.

Wendy Murray Zoba. 2007. *The Beliefnet Guide to Evangelical Christianity*. Harmony.

West, T.C. 2018. *Shards of Identity: The Origins of the Evangelical Movement during the Cold War, 1945-1981*. Washington: Academica Press.

"White House Spiritual Adviser Prays for 'Angels from Africa' to Cement Trump's Re-Election." 2020. The Independent. November 5, 2020. https://www.independent.co.uk/news/world/americas/us-election-2020/us-election-trump-paula-white-house-prayer-b1616014.html.

Whitehead, Andrew L, and Samuel L Perry. 2020. *Taking America Back for God: Christian Nationalism in the United States*. Oxford University Press.

Williams, John Milton. 1893. "Woman Suffrage." *Bibliotheca Sacra*, 1893.

Wilson, Douglas, and Steve Wilkins. 1996. *Southern Slavery, as It Was*. Moscow, Id.: Canon Press.

Worldometer. n.d. "United States Coronavirus." www.worldometers.info. https://www.worldometers.info/coronavirus/country/us/.

Zoll, Rachel. 2008. "Rick Warren's Biggest Critics: Other Evangelicals." Chron. December 26, 2008. https://www.chron.com/lifestyle/houston-belief/article/rick-warren-s-biggest-critics-other-1584578.php.

To contact Eric Scot English for speaking engagements, please visit www.ericsenglish.com.

Many Voices. One Message.

quoir.com

www.ingramcontent.com/pod-product-compliance
Lightning Source LLC
Chambersburg PA
CBHW062115020426
42335CB00013B/969

* 9 7 8 1 9 6 4 2 5 2 3 1 5 *